THE DEMOCRACY COOKBOOK

The DEMOCRACY COOKBOOK

RECIPES TO RENEW GOVERNANCE IN NEWFOUNDLAND AND LABRADOR

★

EDITED BY
ALEX MARLAND
& LISA MOORE

Library and Archives Canada Cataloguing in Publication

The democracy cookbook : recipes to renew governance in Newfoundland and Labrador / edited by Alex Marland & Lisa Moore.

(Social and economic papers ; no. 34)
Includes bibliographical references and index.
Issued in print and electronic formats.
ISBN 978-1-894725-44-6 (softcover).--ISBN 978-1-894725-43-9 (Open Access PDF)

1. Public administration--Newfoundland and Labrador. 2. Civil service reform--Newfoundland and Labrador. 3. Administrative agencies--Newfoundland and Labrador--Management. 4. Newfoundland and Labrador--Politics and government--2003- I. Moore, Lisa Lynne, 1964-, editor II. Marland, Alexander J., 1973-, editor

JL205.D46 2017 320.9718 C2017-906306-5
C2017-906307-3

Cover design: Alison Carr and Kimberley Devlin
Design and typesetting: Kimberley Devlin
Copy editing: Richard Tallman

Published by ISER Books — Faculty of Humanities and Social Sciences Publications
Institute of Social and Economic Research
Memorial University of Newfoundland
297 Mount Scio Road
St. John's, NL A1C 5S7
www.arts.mun.ca/iserbooks ★

FIGURES & TABLES

Figures

Tables

FOREWORD

Politics and governance around the world are changing. Public expectations of politicians and government are increasing faster than the public sector is able to keep pace. Calls for democratic reform take on added importance in such circumstances.

Like so many others, we love Newfoundland and Labrador. And like others, we are concerned about the political challenges facing this wonderful place. No matter what one's political leanings may be, everyone should recognize the value of Newfoundland and Labrador having a strong and vibrant democratic system of government.

We are pleased to see so many people coming together to express informed opinions and to share creative talents in *The Democracy Cookbook: Recipes to Renew Governance in Newfoundland and Labrador*. Such an array of voices and perspectives constitutes a microcosm of a free democracy in action, as embodied in the Canadian Charter of Rights and Freedoms (1982), particularly section 2(b), which legally protects a citizen's "freedom of thought, belief, opinion and expression, including freedom of the press and other media of communication."

We encourage readers to keep an open mind as they explore the diverse points of view expressed by such a variety of citizens who, like us, share an interest in good government.

Kathy Dunderdale 10th Premier of NL; Former Leader, Progressive Conservative Party of NL; Former MHA, Virginia Waters

Roger Grimes 8th Premier of NL; Former Leader, Liberal Party of NL; Former MHA, Exploits

Jack Harris Former Leader, New Democratic Party of NL; Former Member of the House of Assembly, Signal Hill-Quidi Vidi; Former MP, St. John's East

ACKNOWLEDGEMENTS

A broad, innovative undertaking such as this represents a significant team effort. The editors appreciate the work of the many people who provided help and assistance along the way, including in regard to project conceptualization, contributor recruitment, reviewing of drafts, revisions, publicity, and general support.

We wish to thank all of the authors for their contributions and for responding to editorial suggestions. Ramona Dearing, Simon Lono, Ross Reid and Jenny Wright offered valuable suggestions for recruiting contributors. Comments from Derek Butler and David Vardy on Chapter 3, which discusses how government works, and from Christopher Dunn and Robin Whitaker on Table 5.1 were quite helpful. Sincere appreciation is extended to the two anonymous external peer reviewers. Their detailed feedback, combined with suggestions offered independently from Sharon Roseman, on earlier drafts of the manuscript informed changes that improved its quality.

This project is possible in part because of a Public Engagement Accelerator Fund grant that was awarded by the Office of Public Engagement, Memorial University of Newfoundland (MUN) and a Publications Subvention Program grant from the Office of Research Services, MUN. Project partners include the Institute of Social and Economic Research (ISER), ISER Books, the Leslie Harris Centre of Regional Policy and Development, Apathy is Boring, and *The Telegram*. Promotional support and general enthusiasm were provided by Janet Harron in the Faculty of Humanities and Social Sciences at MUN; Steve Bartlett and *The Telegram*; Randy Drover at ISER Books; Mike Clair and the Harris Centre; Peggy Chafe at Print and Mail Services, MUN; and many others, including some of the authors.

In order for any book to be as clear and articulate as possible, writers rely on the formidable talents of the book's publication team. We are grateful to Elizabeth Hicks, an English student at Memorial University who performed a light copy-edit on draft submissions, and to Richard Tallman for his professional copy-editing and attention to detail. Above all, we are indebted to the multitasking excellence by ISER Books managing editors Alison Carr and Kim Devlin, whose ability to steer a manuscript through all phases of production impressed us considerably. Their mastery of graphic design — from the book cover through to obscurities such as pagination — and their general attention to timely workflow are an ideal combination of ingredients for a successful publication.

The Telegram

Special thanks to *The Telegram* for featuring content from *The Democracy Cookbook* in their newspaper and on their website: www.thetelegram.com

PREFACE

The last major review of governance in Newfoundland and Labrador was the Royal Commission on Renewing and Strengthening Our Place in Canada (2003).[1] The Commission focused on Newfoundland and Labrador's place in Confederation and its relationship with Ottawa. Many of its research reports are impressive and illuminating. Sadly, it was largely a political initiative. The Commission accomplished little insofar as tangible reform is concerned.

By comparison, *The Democracy Cookbook: Recipes to Renew Governance in Newfoundland and Labrador* is a grassroots project prepared on a shoestring budget. It is an arm's-length effort to kick-start the All-Party Committee on Democratic Reform that was mandated in letters from the Premier of Newfoundland and Labrador addressed to the government House Leader and the Minister Responsible for the Office of Public Engagement in 2015. More broadly, it is hoped that the collection will be of interest to all observers of the province's politics and government. The various contributors offer stand-alone suggestions for democratic reform, either in a scholarly format or through creative expression, expressed in under 1,000 words (see the Appendix for submission parameters). Many do so with a tone that is generally optimistic, as though they believe in the art of the possible. Some offer concrete and pragmatic suggestions for reform. Others belie an academic's or idealist's penchant to delve into socio-economic concerns that are of a global nature and beyond the control of local political actors. Whatever their practical application, all contributions are thought-provoking and add to a much-needed public conversation about changing the way Newfoundlanders and Labradorians are governed.

It is possible to improve the democratic system in Newfoundland and Labrador. This optimism must confront considerable pessimism, sometimes quite deserved, about the state of politics and government in this wonderful place.

The Democracy Cookbook is not presented as a typical study of public administration or politics. Contributors are from an array of backgrounds, blending a variety of academic disciplines with perspectives drawn from the broader community. For anyone counting, there are 87 contributions, comprised of 76 short essays and 11 food recipes. Including the editors, there are 89 contributors (some as co-authors), of which 46 are women, 42 are men, and one is transgender. The 89 participants could fill two NL Houses of Assembly – and there would still be some left to form a legislative committee or two. Authors of nearly two-thirds of the essays are affiliated with Memorial University of Newfoundland (MUN). There are 49 participants from the St. John's campus, most of them professors, along with five students and some staff. They represent over 17 disciplines. Within the Faculty of Humanities and Social Sciences, 37 contributors are from Political Science (nine), English (six), Sociology (six), Economics (four), Gender Studies (four), History (two), Anthropology (one), Archaeology (one, based at the Labrador Institute), Classics (one), French (one), German (one) and Philosophy (one). Others are from the Faculties of Business (three), Education (three) and Engineering (one), and from the School of Music (two). As well there are participants from the Harris Centre (one) and, at the MUN Grenfell Campus, with the Environmental Policy Institute (one) and the Office of Engagement (one). A number of participants are MUN alumni. Many others have no affiliation with MUN whatsoever, including some contributors who are based elsewhere in Canada. No matter their affiliation or political views, all of them care about a vibrant democracy in Newfoundland and Labrador.

A literary feel purposely runs throughout. Contributions can be read in any order: a reader is encouraged to hop between topics of interest, or may choose to read chronologically, whatever suits one's particular tastes. While the opinions expressed by any given author are not necessarily held by the editors, by other contributors, by the authors of the Foreword, or by this project's partners, all participants support the free expression of varied perspectives.

The book is notionally divided into 12 sections, followed by appendices. Sections are playfully named and are introduced with creative summaries. Poetry and other creative works are woven among essays that analyze more specific and technical issues of governance. Part 1, "Introduction" (essays 1 to 8), introduces readers to the project, the province's system of government, and its political culture. Part 2, "All Politics Is Local, B'y" (essays 9 to 15), deals with regionalism and localism. Part 3, "Captain Newfoundland & Labrador" (essays 16 to 22), explores different concepts of leadership. Part 4, "Communication" (essays 23 to 28), addresses changing dynamics brought about by a shifting media landscape. Part 5, "Engagement" (essays 29 to 37), argues for civic literacy and meaningful consultation processes. Part 6, "Power to the People(s)" (essays 38 to 46), identifies some of the many voices that deserve to be heard in an inclusive democracy. Part 7, "Oh Me Nerves, the Opposition Got Me Drove" (essays 47 to 53), discusses representation in the House of Assembly, and Part 8, "Scrutiny" (essays 54 to 62), explores increased accountability measures. Part 9, "Spend and Spend and Spend and Never Get Back Change" (essays 63 to 68), concerns the flow of money in political circles and beyond. In Part 10, "Orders of the Day" (essays 69 to 75), contributors write about natural resource development, public engagement, and the environment, several with a focus on the Muskrat Falls hydroelectric megaproject. Part 11, "Conclusion" (essay 76), paves a way forward for the All-Party Committee on Democratic Reform. This is followed by some recipes for meals and desserts with a Newfoundland and Labrador political theme. The recruitment document originally provided to contributors is provided in the Appendix.

Readers are not expected to agree with all of the arguments presented by the various contributors. Indeed, the editors themselves hold diverging opinions about which contributions are appropriate and viable. Regardless of a reader's impression of the arguments presented, and irrespective of the extent to which this project contributes to democratic renewal, it is an innovative mechanism to compile an array of voices and perspectives. To our knowledge, nothing like it has been attempted in Canada before. The exercise was guided by some principles that might be repeated in other forums: multi-partisanship, trying to avoid a demand for new financial resources, moving away from polemics that lack tangible action items, and being open to considering different perspectives. The editors are optimistic that *The Democracy Cookbook* will spur conversation towards improved processes for democratic governance and will inspire others to build upon this model of public engagement. Whether in the corridors of power, in public coffeehouses, at Memorial University, in the news media, in private settings, or online, we hope that ideas presented here will help advance a conversation about ways to meaningfully improve politics and governance in Newfoundland and Labrador.

Note

1. Government of Newfoundland and Labrador, *Our Place in Canada*. Main Report of the Royal Commission on Renewing and Strengthening Our Place in Canada (St. John's, 2003), at: http://www.exec.gov.nl.ca/royalcomm/finalreport/pdf/Final.pdf.

EDITORS' TIP

In a hurry? Look for tweets at the top of chapters to help you navigate the book quickly.

PART 1: INTRODUCTION

House of Parliament, Nfld. [Colonial Building], 1920s. Two children sitting on lawn beside Colonial Building, Military Road, St. John's. (Source: Provincial Archives)

Exposing the blemishes of politics and government is essential if we are to recognize that improvements are warranted. Papering over problems won't do. Rather, politicians and citizens should consider what controversial British leader Oliver Cromwell is reputed to have instructed while having his portrait painted: "Use all your skill to paint my picture truly like me, and not flatter me at all; but remark all these roughnesses, pimples, warts and everything as you see me, otherwise I will never pay a farthing for it." Governance in Newfoundland and Labrador needs to be examined warts and all, too.

In this opening section, the editors explain the scope of this project and its objective of providing a starting point for the province's All-Party Committee on Democratic Reform. Readers are taken on a journey of understanding the genesis of the idea and how this book came together. A "Politics and Government 101" primer is offered to those who have cursory awareness of the sausage-making of democratic governance or who could otherwise benefit from a refresher. Jared Wesley proceeds to make a case for studying provincial politics. Contributors David Cochrane, Robin Whitaker, and Drew Brown then touch on a sometimes inhospitable political culture in Newfoundland and Labrador where social pressure can demand group cohesion and rebuff innovation. Vicki Hallett introduces us to questions surrounding the special place of Indigenous peoples in our society. All told, this section paints a picture of a society whose pervasive nationalism makes it difficult to have a thorough discussion about provincial politics.

1 How *The Democracy Cookbook* Came Together

The Editors

It's here! Read how The Democracy Cookbook for Newfoundland & Labrador came together. #cdnpoli #NLpoli #DemocraticReformNL

In the following pages we provide information about the process, rationale, and chronology that we employed as we assembled contributions. The reason for documenting this is twofold. First, in the spirit of transparency, it is important that readers consider how we ended up with an eclectic collection of topics and authors. Thus, we err on the side of providing extensive information. Second, we hope that academics, community leaders, and other citizens throughout Newfoundland and Labrador and indeed across Canada will consider copying this model. They can benefit from awareness of the editors' experiences.

Project Preparation

The idea for this project originated at a public discussion about political crisis in Newfoundland and Labrador. The Leslie Harris Centre of Regional Policy and Development held a "Memorial Presents" session in June 2016 at Memorial University of Newfoundland (MUN). The gathering was predicated on more than the province's ominous financial situation, a consequence of short-term thinking, poor financial planning, and lower revenues than projected from offshore oil royalties. In addition to an unwieldy deficit and ballooning public debt, there was a revolving door in the Premier's office. There was considerable civil unrest even after the election of a new government. The discussion was billed by the Harris Centre as follows:

> Newfoundland and Labrador is going through a period of dramatic change. Some commentators are even drawing comparisons with the crisis of 1932, when the government of the time declared bankruptcy. It is too easy to point fingers at politicians, or the price of oil. The problems confronting Newfoundland and Labrador society are very much a reflection of the province's political culture and its institutions. As a modern democracy, we depend upon our institutions to ensure that we avoid crises. Our institutions include government departments and agencies, but also non-governmental organizations and media outlets who influence governments and hold them to account. These institutions directly reflect our society: its values, aspirations, fears and needs. So how did our institutional structure let us down? Did our current institutions not perform their function, or are we missing some key institutions? How can we make sure that those organizations to whom we, as a society, have entrusted our well-being do their work and avoid crises such as the one we are facing today? How can we avoid history repeating itself?[1]

The audience was eager to blame politicians for the province's political and economic instability. The idea that the public bears any responsibility was anathema to their views. Comments that criticized politicians were cheered on; anyone running up against that mood risked being the target of an angry mob. It was obvious that to get past blaming others someone would need to do something. Academics are granted tenure and hold dear the principle of academic freedom precisely so that they can safely challenge conventional wisdom. Unfortunately, few of them study local governance, and in recent years Memorial University has not even offered Newfoundland and Labrador politics courses. This is consistent with a so-called "comparative turn" whereby growing numbers of scholars and students are drawn to studying global phenomena.[2] As a public institution in a cash-strapped province, MUN could and should play a leadership role in helping to resolve the local political turmoil, provided that thinkers and writers could be encouraged to do so.

Our initial vision was loosely modelled on the University of British Columbia Press open-access compilation *Canadian Election Analysis 2015: Communication, Strategy and Democracy.*[3] That project published short, snappy pieces from over 60 political scientists and journalists from across Canada. We decided that a similar number of contributors could be mobilized to write about ways to improve democratic governance in Newfoundland and Labrador. This would provide a strong support resource and an energetic foray into exploring new ideas that might aid in the work of the province's All-Party Committee on Democratic Reform. It would become a reference tool for local journalists and a reminder of the range of issues and subject matter confronting political thinkers and the public. The compilation would generate awareness among contributors and others about the opportunities and challenges associated with democratic reform. It could be freely used in classroom settings and spur public conversation. Finally, it would connect the academic community with broader society on a matter of public concern.

A democratic project should convey diversity of authorship in terms of both demographics and political world views. Jacques Parizeau, Quebec's Premier during the 1995 referendum on sovereignty-association, once said that province's Quiet Revolution in the 1960s "consisted of three or four ministers, twenty civil servants and consultants, and fifty chansonniers."[4] The implication was that political elites were not responsible for political change: it was the broader populace, led by musicians who inspired the public through song. In Newfoundland and Labrador, the artistic and cultural community is strong and vibrant, but generally speaking this community is disconnected from the policy wonks involved with government administration. A democratic project would need to act as a bridge between these two solitudes.

After meeting each other for the first time in June 2016, we agreed to submit an application for a Public Engagement Accelerator Fund grant through the MUN Office of Public Engagement. Part of our application stated: "Bringing together a wide variety of voices will constitute grassroots mobilization on the matter of 'fixing' democratic governance in Newfoundland and Labrador after a period of acute political turmoil. . . . This is timely as it has the potential to inform a society and government that is preoccupied with other priorities in a period of fiscal restraint, and will constitute information for the All-Party Committee on Democratic Reform promised by the current administration." We recruited a number of external partners and collaborators: Apathy is Boring, a Montreal-based national advocacy group that urges citizen participation in democratic governance; *The Telegram*, the St. John's-based newspaper; the Harris Centre; and the Institute of Social and Economic Research (ISER Books). In mid-August 2016 we were awarded $9,575 towards author honorariums for community contributors,[5] to hire a copy editor, for photography, and to co-ordinate a public exhibit to raise awareness of the project. In-kind contributions were pledged by ISER for book publication processes and by the Harris Centre for publicity support.

How We Recruited Authors

We followed a two-step approach to recruiting authors. We began with academics, followed by members of the community at large. Potential contributors were provided with a background document to outline the nature of the project, establish contribution parameters, and identify some examples of topics that they might write about. Some members of Memorial University's Department of Political Science provided opinions on a draft list of suggested topics. The final version is reproduced in the Appendix and can serve to inform further research.

We determined that the compilation should be subject to external peer review, which would be co-ordinated by ISER Books. The feedback provided by two anonymous professors based elsewhere in Canada would provide an opportunity to consider arm's-length expert opinion. It would also provide young scholars with an opportunity to add a peer-reviewed entry on their academic résumés.

We decided early on that we would strive for gender equality among authors. We also sought to include people of different ethnicities (particularly Aboriginal people), ages, and geographic location. Moreover, diversity of subject matter, political ideology, and opinion were important editorial values. We would avoid recruiting contributions from office-holders, public servants, and others whose involvement might inhibit objectivity. This invokes a trade-off of sacrificing important insider perspectives. Our recruitment experience led to the following general pattern:

- Academics were more likely to acknowledge receipt of an e-mail invitation compared with members of the broader community.
- People who we personally know or to whom we were referred were more likely to agree than those we approached who did not know us.
- More people were willing to comment on a high-profile current event, to advance a pet issue involving a demand for more resources, and/or to propose a policy solution without engaging the broader populace than there were people interested in writing about issues that do not attract news coverage, who are aware of viable cost-efficient solutions to systemic problems, and/or who inherently recognize ways to engage the public in decision-making.

- Men were easier to identify as having previously written about and publicly commented on Newfoundland and Labrador politics.
- Our efforts in approaching Aboriginal individuals were not as successful as we would have liked.
- We theorize that partisans and interest group leaders were concerned with being publicly off-message with their political party or the special interests they represent.
- Self-identified social activists were far more likely to accept our invitation than were members of the business community, union leadership, or pollsters.

Recruitment of academics began with the MUN Department of Political Science, which, as it turns out, was an early signal of pending challenges. Some members gushed enthusiasm and readily agreed to participate. A couple of others initially agreed but later withdrew. More than half declined outright, for reasons that ranged from a lack of time to limited familiarity with the politics of Newfoundland and Labrador. The erosion of expertise about local politics is consistent with the aforementioned comparative turn hypothesis.

We proceeded to invite the participation of all members of the editorial board of the journal *Newfoundland and Labrador Studies*. We put out an open call to all academics in the Faculty of Humanities and Social Sciences at the St. John's campus of Memorial University. We asked associate deans in other faculties and schools to spread the word among their colleagues. We contacted a number of academics at the MUN Grenfell Campus in Corner Brook. Referrals were sought from political scientists to identify scholars based outside of the province with known expertise in the study of Newfoundland and Labrador politics. As a measure of independence, a Google search was performed to identify any other academics who had relevant expertise, which turned up a handful of Ph.D. students. They were also approached.

We are thrilled with the broad participation of so many scholars from diverse disciplines and institutions. Even so, we hoped for stronger uptake. Generally speaking, the reasons for declining centred on scholars prioritizing other commitments and lacking sufficient familiarity with the politics and governance of Newfoundland and Labrador. One MUN professor's reply summarizes this nicely: "Thanks for the invitation, but I am unable to accept. To be frank, while I complain about NL politics as much as the next person, it is not anything I feel capable of writing about in a professional way."[6] A number of Memorial academics thus share similarities with the cultural community and society at large. Citizens of Newfoundland and Labrador are all affected by local political decisions, but many do not pay sufficient attention to the technical intricacies of governance, and might not want to offer public comment. Some of those who closely follow political happenings offered other reasons for not participating. The regrets from one academic were sufficiently pointed that his remarks bear presenting here:

> I must say, firstly, that I am off put by the proposed title . . . [which] may be defended as a hook to lure a readership for whom "democratic governance" is simplistically equated with "good governance." I am increasingly with Plato on that, as opposed to Churchill, and see a second coming of Commission of Government as the best alternative to the current morass. We have a "governance deficit," not a "democratic deficit." And so on, with the rant. To be fair, in your proposal you have assembled a comprehensive list of provocative topics, many going to governance (not necessarily democratic) issues. Any solid treatment of even a fraction of these would yield an impressive volume. Most of them, I think, demand the expertise of political science or historical scholars, and some serious research. . . . So, while I appreciate the invitation, I think it is prudent for me to decline.

It bears considering that pessimism and malaise do not characterize the contributions in the volume — and yet, as this individual's concern indicates, the depth of problems associated with the province's political culture and institutions should not be understated.

Recruitment of community contributors was more challenging because, unlike academics, most private citizens do not have a public webpage with readily available contact information. We sought suggestions and referrals from various project contributors and from some of those who otherwise declined to participate. We followed up on each and every lead. We performed online searches for women involved with chambers of commerce across the province and arranged for an open invitation to be sent to women's centres. Editors of similar projects might experience more success using social media when recruiting members of the broader community.

We estimate the refusal to acceptance ratio at approximately 2:1 among academics. That is, for every academic who submitted work, roughly two others declined our invitation or initially agreed but did not come through.[7] It was roughly twice that among members of the community. Advice was sought from a faculty member in the Department of Gender Studies and from a representative of the St. John's Status of Women Council for guidance about recruiting women. They advised that the approach being taken was appropriate in light of the extra responsibilities that women face and potential discomfort in the political arena. Editors seeking gender balance should plan to ask more women than men. They should respond to withdrawals by remarking on the person's expertise, by commenting on the importance of hearing from women, and by extending a supportive offer to help with the delivery of the work. When Shannie Duff, a veteran of municipal and provincial politics in Newfoundland and Labrador, declined she made time to offer the following opinions:

> My personal number one suggestion for renewing democracy in our province and improving provincial governance would be to create a robust and functioning Standing Committee system in the House of Assembly. We could be making so much better use of the talent pool we have in the House of Assembly and creating a much more collegial and transparent working environment. I believe that the system in place currently in our House of Assembly is the least effective in the country. My number two suggestion would be to give serious consideration to some form of proportional representation in our election process. There are many variations on this . . . the end result would be to have a fairer representation of opinions of the public without making the process of governing ineffective. My third suggestion is to find more creative ways to inform and engage our youth in the democratic process. Our present decision makers are creating the world our young people will inherit and it is so important that they become more aware of how the world is being shaped. . . . In my view we need to step up our education of our young people while they are in high school on the principles of democracy and the responsibility of all citizens to be informed and active participants in the democratic process. We need to teach them discernment. And we need to find better ways to make their participation in the democratic process easier and more accessible. I know that there are pros and cons about how we do this but electronic voting and lowering the voting age to 16 might be worth considering. . . . I am very glad that you are taking this timely and constructive approach to addressing the

> urgent need to renew and strengthen the democratic process in Newfoundland and Labrador.

When another high-profile citizen declined he pointed to the need for political will among politicians rather than reforms to the democratic system:

> I can offer the view that what we need most of all in Newfoundland and Labrador — both in the House of Assembly (and in the Commons) and in public life in the broader sense — are men and women who are prepared to accept the fiscal realities of our era and then first to advocate for and subsequently to adopt and to implement programmes that would address our needs substantively and realistically. This requires courage, not reforms.

Here, we are struck by the forcefulness of those with experience in the political game. It is all well and good to assemble writers to pitch suggestions for reform. But we must be mindful that it will take pragmatism and political resolve among elected officials, led by the Premier, for change to happen.

As our foremost objective is to connect with the 40 Members of the House of Assembly and with the broader public, we determined that submissions should balance a variety of writing styles and approaches. This included extending an opportunity to submit poetry or other forms of creative works, thereby engaging the artistic and cultural community. This would offer some fresh perspectives amid a density of policy suggestions to the All-Party Committee on Democratic Reform and others.

How We Reviewed Submissions

Our editorial approach was to ensure that submissions were of a reasonably high standard and generally followed our contributor guidelines (see Appendix). Draft submissions were reviewed independently by each of us. Our comments were merged into a feedback file that included a checklist of common parameters, such as word count limits. Sometimes alternate sources were suggested for the author to consult, as we did not want an editor's own publications to be unduly emphasized.

Authors then resubmitted their work. All resubmissions from academics were ultimately accepted for inclusion in the draft manuscript. One academic did not resubmit and thus that work is not included. Community contributors needed a bit more guidance given that we were following academic conventions in order to ready the work for external peer review. One contributor remarked that the feedback was communicated in a manner that "very much embodied that balance between rigour and support." A common frustration for some members of the community was citing obscure information. As one put it when resubmitting, "I've been out of university for a long time, so I'm not sure if I got the citation format exactly right." Submissions from eight community contributors were rejected because the work was deemed to be unsuitable for this project or else the author was unwilling to act on our suggested changes. In some cases there was a distinct similarity of subject matter, which rendered a few well-written pieces nevertheless redundant.

The draft manuscript was sent out by ISER Books for external review to two anonymous academics located elsewhere in Canada. They provided detailed feedback on the work as a whole and comments on individual contributions. All authors were given the opportunity to revise their work and, if applicable, to make changes in response to the external reviewers' suggestions. The revised manuscript is considerably stronger as a result. The peer review process meant that the time from submission to publication was much longer than with the *Canadian Election Analysis 2015* project. In any event, political life in the province was preoccupied with an ominous budgetary situation. Few people were publicly discussing democratic reform. One exception was changing the rules surrounding political financing, a matter that the government House leader said would get underway in 2018.[8]

As we were readying the manuscript for publication, a staff member at MUN saw the book's cover, and wondered what kind of food recipes it contained. We decided to recruit some recipes for meals and desserts with a Newfoundland and Labrador political theme. We contacted a number of former premiers, ministers and MHAs by drawing on our own networks, suggestions from contributors and by performing an online search. We then contacted a variety of restaurants around the province drawn from a tourism contact list. Recruitment challenges persisted, particularly among those affiliated with political parties.

As with any edited collection, the content of this book is somewhat different from what we imagined. Some ideas and approaches pleasantly surprised us. Conversely, many of our initial questions surrounding ways to improve governance in Newfoundland and Labrador (again, see Appendix) went unaddressed and warrant attention in another forum. Some authors were captivated by topical issues, such as the Muskrat Falls hydroelectric project on the Lower Churchill River in Labrador, which will generate renewable energy but is billions of dollars over budget and has been the source of heated protests.[9] Much should also be read into what is *not* presented in these pages. Nobody we contacted was willing to put their name to an indictment of a society that historically pushes for public funding and protests government cutbacks, for example. We lack a deep appreciation for some voices that are under-represented in political circles, such as recent immigrants. What we compiled is indicative of a diversity of opinion, but also of the limited number of public commentators who are intimately familiar with the inner workings of governance, who have training in the study of public administration, or who are willing to push the boundaries of what can be publicly expressed in a small place — for more on this dynamic, see the contributions by David Cochrane (Part 1, #5) and Robin Whitaker (Part 1, #6). Conversely, new perspectives and ideas are raised that represent a meaningful addition to the conversation. All told, as editors we share the opinion expressed by one contributor and echoed by many others: that no matter its strengths and shortcomings, this represents a "very worthwhile project." ★

Notes

1. "History Repeating: How Do We Make Sure Newfoundland and Labrador Doesn't End Up in Crisis Again?" Harris Centre, Memorial University of Newfoundland (2016), at: http://www.mun.ca/harriscentre/policy/memorialpresents/2016d/index.php.
2. Linda A. White, Richard Simeon, Robert Vipond, and Jennifer Wallner, eds., *The Comparative Turn in Canadian Political Science* (Vancouver: University of British Columbia Press, 2008).
3. See www.ubcpress.ca/CanadianElectionAnalysis2015.
4. Graham Fraser, *PQ: René Lévesque and the Parti Québécois in Power*, 2nd ed. (Montreal and Kingston: McGill-Queen's University Press, 2002), 161.
5. We offered $75 honorariums to community contributors and recipe authors as an ethical recognition for their work, given that, unlike full-time professors, they do not always have salaried jobs that include funded research opportunities. Alternatively, they could ask that the funds be put back into the project or direct us to donate to the Susan McCorquodale Memorial Scholarship for study in Newfoundland and Labrador politics, public policy, or public administration. A total of $1,575 was donated to the McCorquodale Scholarship on their behalf.
6. All quotes in this section are reprinted with permission of those who offered them.
7. By comparison, there was a low refusal rate for the *Canadian Election*

Analysis 2015 project, which speaks in part to the relationship between academic interests and media coverage of a topical issue, as well as the narrow specialized study of Newfoundland and Labrador politics.

8. James McLeod, "Parsons Too Busy Now to Reform Political Financing," *The Telegram*, 19 Apr. 2017, at: http://www.thetelegram.com/news/local/2017/4/19/parsons-waiting-until-2018-to-take-on-political-financing-reform.html.
9. Lukas Wall, "Muskrat Falls protesters 'fighting for land and food,'" CBC News, 23 Oct. 2016, at: http://www.cbc.ca/news/canada/newfoundland-labrador/want-to-keep-culture-safe-says-protester-1.3817864.

2 Reflections on the Governance in Newfoundland and Labrador Project

Lisa Moore

Lisa Moore reflects on the ingredients for a Democracy Boil-up. #NLpoli #DemocraticReformNL

When Alex Marland invited me to co-edit a book on governance in Newfoundland and Labrador, I immediately said yes. I recognized it as a unique opportunity to learn a tremendous amount about the inner workings of governance from a wide variety of voices. These voices would be drawn from across the province and across the country, both from within the university and from community contributors.

Democracy, as it has manifested in my life, has meant the ability to speak without censorship and to be able to listen to the voices of others, to have access to multi-voiced and complex debate in order to create equality throughout society, both locally and globally.

I already knew that democracy is open-ended and evolving, in a constant state of disruption and realignment; an amorphous state, subject to shape-shifting, acted upon by a variety of disparate forces, of which governance is only one.

But I also knew that voting is not just a right but a privilege. I wanted to learn what a vote could do. I wanted to learn how the machinery of governance works here in Newfoundland and Labrador and if it might be improved.

I am a fiction writer and most of my reading consists of literary fiction. Though I read fiction for pleasure, as most people do, I also read fiction in order to "keep up with" or to discover new stories, those stories from voices frequently overlooked, or outright silenced; those voices that articulate experiences very different from my own.

I try to read outside the literary canon to find the wildest innovation in form. New voices forge new modes of expression and narrative and result in new ways of thinking about the world. Hence, much of what I know about how the political touches down in our lives has been informed by this reading.

Consider the distinctive voice found in local literature — which, not so very long ago, belonged decidedly outside the canon — and how it reflects the political.

I've learned from Bernice Morgan's *Random Passage* about the compromised and vulnerable position of women who came from outport Newfoundland to work in the grand houses of the merchant class in St. John's in the mid-1800s. Michael Crummey's *Sweetland* reflects the pain caused by contemporary resettlement programs, the mobilization of Newfoundland populations to Fort Mac for work, and the instability inherent in those jobs. Michael Winter's *The Death of Donna Whalen* takes into account the trauma of poverty in St. John's and the cracks in our justice system. Ramona Dearing's short story, "An Apology," from her story collection, *So Beautiful*, explores the trauma inflicted through the child sexual abuse perpetrated by Catholic priests and the Christian Brothers in this province, and the incredible political power those institutions welded to create a systemic silence and denial throughout many sectors of Newfoundland and Labrador society.

The voices of fiction show us the way in which the political is *felt* in our lives; how we are shaped by, among other things, the social and political forces at work in society, how those forces infiltrate our most intimate moments and alter our notions of identity. Art is always political because it transforms us by awakening our imaginations and giving us access to the other's voice or point of view.

Alex and I began working together on this project at a moment when the American presidential election campaign was heating up and political storms in Germany and France were being fuelled by racist rhetoric, when the reverberating shock of Brexit was rippling through Europe and manifesting in unexpected ways in North America, and when the protests surrounding Muskrat Falls were reaching a fever pitch. While I was reading the incoming essays from academics and community contributors, Donald Trump was elected President of the United States, an event that surprised everyone, including, many surmised, Trump himself. How could such a historical and monumental shift in global politics not have been foreseen? Had democracy morphed so dramatically, overnight, that few political pundits could predict this shift? It seemed that governance, perhaps everywhere, was due for an overhaul.

Alex and I agreed that essays in the collection needed to offer "fixes" to local problems of governance that would be actionable no matter which party was in power. We agreed to encourage authors to identify fixes that would not require extra expenditures.

And as the essays rolled in, the breadth and depth of the subjects they addressed inspired excited discussions between us: the positive and negative repercussions of Newfoundland nationalism, the obfuscating lens of charisma in leadership, the under-representation of minorities in governance, the ethics of party fundraising, breastfeeding in the House of Assembly, and what role inadequate governance had played in the province's financial crisis — to name a just few of the topics.

We discussed the role of social media in the branding of political parties and, as one essay inspired, the history of democracy going back to the Byzantines, and the notion of real-time virtual democracy, as suggested by another author, who playfully described a sort of fit-bit bracelet or "democracy app" into which individuals might input political choices, to be aggregated to provide real-time democratic opinions.

Early in the development of this project I embarked on a cruise from Newfoundland, up the coast of Labrador to Greenland. On the way I visited the resettled communities of Hebron and Ramah. Inuit were resettled from Hebron in the 1950s and were torn away from their land and their way of life, and they had withered in the face of everything they lost. There is a plaque in Hebron with the text of an apology from then-Premier Danny Williams to the Inuit of Labrador and another plaque of the Inuit response, which accepts the apology graciously but does not deny the irreparable damage the government knowingly inflicted.

It was on this trip in the Arctic that I met the Inuk artist Billy Gauthier. I'd had the opportunity to listen to a lecture he gave on the ship about his art. Gauthier uses traditional Inuit carving materials, such as bone, antler, tusk, and stone. His iconography is an exploration of traditional and contemporary Inuit life on the land. There are touches of humour, but this work is also charged with a pride about Inuit history, about the knowledge required to hunt and fish, and the desire to protect that knowledge and way of life.

On the way back to the ship from the town of Hebron, Gauthier fished an Arctic char from the water and deftly cut the fish into pieces for everybody on the Zodiac. We ate it raw with the wind in our faces. I was deeply moved by Billy's generosity and his knowledge about the land and the ease with which he pulled several fish from the sea and shared with us. Later I would learn that he was one of the three hunger strikers protesting the development of the Muskrat Falls hydroelectric project who brought the voice of the people of Labrador to the attention of the country.

The social and political climate unfolding in this province as this publication came together was heating up, becoming increasing tumultuous, charged with political tension. As I read through these submissions, I was keenly aware that we are facing a critical and dire moment in the history of the province. Millions of dollars in spending are being cut in the name of budget austerity. The public sector faces substantial job losses, cuts to health care, and the outsourcing of public services, along with cuts to services in rural areas.

If ever there were a time for the citizens of Newfoundland and Labrador to ask what kind of life we want in this province, it is now. What is important to us? Why do we live here? What do we need? How do we ensure those needs are met by local governance?

Throughout the many discussions that occurred in the gathering of these essays, with colleagues, community contributors, friends, and fellow writers, many people voiced the opinion that Newfoundland and Labrador is most definitely not an easy place to govern. The province covers a large land mass and a very large number of small and aging communities in need of expensive services — snow clearing, road maintenance, ferry services, and access to health care, education, and clean drinking water — just to name a few services the government must deliver.

I entered into the project of working on this collection of essays in this moment of provincial crisis because the project offered an opportunity to explore democracy and its workings, just when this province most requires a healthy democracy.

These essays capture governance in Newfoundland and Labrador at a particular historical moment and they advocate for necessary improvements. Taken as a whole they illuminate the cogs and wheels of a complex machine, as well as the fractures and broken parts. This collection asks whose voices are represented and, more specifically, how can we eliminate the gaps and silences in these voices; how can they be amplified?

I read the essays hungrily, sometimes well into the night, and looked forward to meeting with Alex to discuss the ideas presented here. The more I read and the more we spoke, the more urgent the project began to feel.

Each of these essays — whether examining the atrophying organ of the press, addressing the unequal gender balance in governance, proclaiming the need for representation for those with disabilities, exploring the lack of Indigenous representation in government, or discussing how the education system might prepare youth for political debate — felt like a hammer, and made of governance the nail. There are essays concerned with questions about when to employ direct democracy, and how individual citizens can develop democracy in our daily lives. These essays call for a provincial democracy that allows for a variety of voices and the co-operation of all parties to work together within all levels of government to successfully navigate these difficult economic times.

By the time we had read the essays and discussed them thoroughly, knowing about how governance works began to matter to me very much, and I came to understand more than ever what a resource we have in the rich diversity of voices in the province. The issues these essays illuminate are urgent, the solutions imaginative. I sincerely hope the House of Assembly's All-Party Committee on Democratic Reform gives these complex and articulate arguments the scrutiny they deserve and implements the suggestions offered here. ★

3 How Democratic Government Works in Newfoundland and Labrador

Alex Marland

Here's a primer on how government works in Newfoundland and Labrador. #NLpoli #DemocraticReformNL

Some people have a greater awareness of how government works, or of what democracy entails. The following primer about the nuts and bolts of politics and public administration is offered to assist readers with their comprehension of democratic government in Newfoundland and Labrador.

Context

In many ways, Newfoundland and Labrador's democracy is outstanding, given the relative accessibility of the political elite and the government's general responsiveness to public demands. It has come a long way from the political corruption and dire financial circumstances that led to protestors storming the Colonial Building in 1932 and ultimately the Commission of Government era, a period from 1934 to 1949 that entailed a ruling council comprised of a governor, three British commissioners, and three Newfoundland commissioners. Elections were put on hold throughout that period — an unusual case of the people's elected representatives voluntarily relinquishing democratic government. It would be misguided to assume that the prospects of bankruptcy, or the reasons for it, were all that was wrong. The Commission observed many embedded problems with governance, such as the expectation of religious discrimination in the setting of electoral districts, in making appointments to cabinet, and during hiring in the public service.[1] In the ensuing decades, power was concentrated in Premier Joey Smallwood and the provincial Liberal Party, and it is widely understood that he operated a "one-man government."[2] Other charismatic men — principally Brian Peckford, Clyde Wells, Brian Tobin, and Danny Williams — followed suit. The influence of religious institutions persisted well into the 1990s, with churches administering the denominational school system, a matter that was settled after two divisive referendums. Government is now a large, professional organization compared with its former self, and yet chronic challenges persist.

In other ways, Newfoundland and Labrador's system of government is sorely in need of repair. In recent years considerable political and financial instability has constituted problems with the system itself, rather than with any given individual(s). It is a vicious circle: electors reward leaders who respond to public demands, yet short-term thinking results in inefficiencies and inequity, leading to crisis and civil unrest. The upheaval undermines public confidence in government institutions and political leaders. And these are only the big-picture issues that the public knows about!

Warning: Democracy Is Messy

Reformers should bear in mind that everyone seems to love democracy and despise politics. A large gap exists between expectations for democracy and the realities of what it delivers. A sizable number of citizens are disengaged, with many Canadians seeing themselves as outsiders.[3] As much as people might like the idealism of democracy, the struggle for power and influence inevitably results in a clash of opposing interests and frustration with systems and processes.

At the simplest level, a democratic system of government involves little more than the following: non-violent elections, a legitimate choice of options, citizens having the ability to determine who should be in power, and voters electing people to represent them in a legislature.[4] Since Newfoundland and Labrador joined Canada in 1949, provincial elections have been held every four years or so as citizens elect people to represent them in the House of Assembly, from which an executive is formed. The province's election campaigns may get heated, but they are bloodless affairs, and when a change of government occurs it is a peaceful transition. This does not necessarily mean that smooth governing will result, as captured by the brilliant title of *Telegram* reporter James McLeod's book, *Turmoil as Usual*, within which he summarizes absurd situations that contributed to the latest bout of political instability.[5]

Is democracy as we experience it really the best that Newfoundland and Labrador can do? Are our democratic expectations practical and grounded? The truth is that democracy is highly problematic wherever it is practised. While few citizens are familiar with the theories of democracy in the writings of Plato, Aristotle, and Hobbes, among others, much can be learned from them, as well as comparatively newer material and ways of thinking. Readers of classical and more recent theorists quickly learn democracy can be messy. The problems are nicely captured by Winston Churchill's famous quip that democracy is the worst form of government — except for all the others.[6] It is better than the alternative of authoritarianism or totalitarianism, but again, it is messy, as American political scientist John Mueller emphasizes:

> . . . democracy has characteristically produced societies that have been humane, flexible, productive, and vigorous, and under this system leaders have somehow emerged who — at least in comparison with your average string of kings or czars or dictators — have generally been responsive, responsible, able, and dedicated. On the other hand, democracy didn't come out looking the way many theorists and idealists imagined it could or should. It has been characterized by a great deal of unsightly and factionalized squabbling by self-interested, short-sighted people and groups, and its policy outcomes have often been the result of a notably unequal contest over who could most adroitly pressure and manipulate the system. Even more distressingly, the citizenry seems disinclined to display anything remotely resembling the deliberative qualities many theorists have been inclined to see as a central requirement for the system to work properly. Indeed, far from becoming the attentive, if unpolished, public policy wonks espoused in many of the theories and images, real people in real democracies often display an almost monumental lack of political interest and knowledge. . . . But it must be acknowledged that democracy is, and always will be, distressingly messy, clumsy and disorderly, and that in it people are permitted loudly and irritatingly to voice opinions that are clearly erroneous and even dangerous. Moreover, decision making in democracies is often muddled, incoherent, and slow, and the results are sometimes exasperatingly foolish, short-sighted, irrational, and incoherent.[7]

There is also widespread disagreement among scholars and citizens about the determinants and forms of democracy, as well as the many variables involved with good governance. For example, some of the contributors in this volume point to the importance of increased education and decolonization in providing the foundation for a better democracy. However, international research finds statistical evidence that a more vibrant democratic ethos is most strongly correlated with a higher standard of living, as measured through economic indicators such as per capita GDP.[8] On this basis, the idealism of *The Democracy Cookbook* must be weighed against pragmatism and the need for strong leadership to achieve the art of the possible.

Who Are the Main Public Officials in Newfoundland and Labrador?

Descriptions of a democratic system typically emphasize institutions, namely the executive, legislative, and judicial branches of government. Instead, let us begin by identifying who the key political actors are, and situate where they fit within the government system.[9] The provincial system's key actors are identified in Figure 3.1 and are described below.

Figure 3.1: The Three Branches of Provincial Government in Newfoundland and Labrador

Executive Branch	Legislative Branch	Judicial Branch
Lieutenant Governor Premier Cabinet ministers	Members of the House of Assembly	Judiciary and the courts, including the provincial chief justice

Newfoundland and Labrador's system of parliamentary government revolves around the ability of citizens to elect representatives. A *Member of the House of Assembly (MHA)* is one of 40 people elected to the provincial legislature, which is located in the Confederation Building in St. John's. Each MHA represents the residents who live in one of the 40 constituencies drawn on an electoral map of the province. There are 36 ridings on the Island of Newfoundland and four in Labrador.

All systems for electing representatives are problematic. The single-member plurality method of electing MHAs is routinely criticized. The candidate with the highest number of votes wins the seat, in a method commonly known as first-past-the-post — similar to how a racehorse who crosses the finish line first is the winner, except that in this electoral system there is no reward for placing second. To some, this creates a problem when a number of close races are won by the same party and weaker parties are shut out. As a result, the governing party tends to be over-represented in the House of Assembly and opposition parties are under-represented, particularly small parties whose support is spread across many electoral districts. Supporters count stability and simplicity among the strengths of the first-past-the-post system. A further issue is that the composition of the legislature, as elsewhere in Canada, is not sufficiently representative of the socio-demographic characteristics of those being governed. Though things have been improving, most obviously women have been under-represented in the House of Assembly, as well as in the executive branch and the judiciary.[10]

Another important aspect of elections is party finance. The rules for donating monies to political parties or candidates, and how money is spent by them and by others (e.g., interest groups, businesses, labour unions, private individuals), have been changing in other provinces. In Newfoundland and Labrador the political parties have displayed little interest in discussing reform, which is exactly why it must be discussed.

Most candidates and MHAs are affiliated with one of three provincial political parties: the Liberal Party, the New Democratic Party (NDP), or the Progressive Conservative (PC) Party. Since 1949, provincial governance has alternated between the Liberals and PCs, with the NDP perpetually the third party. An outsider might think that the PCs are right-wing (i.e., supporters of small government and traditional values), the NDP left-wing (i.e., advocates of big government and progressive values), with the Liberals straddling the political centre. In fact, by national standards, all three parties are more likely to huddle to the centre/centre-left on the ideological spectrum. The politics of Newfoundland and Labrador is a mix of traditional and socially progressive values, and above all resistance to free market forces in favour of big government, particularly if that involves securing funding from Ottawa. In many ways, the province's politics are a homogeneous monolith, such that "it is often difficult to distinguish Newfoundland parties in policy space."[11] Where the parties differ is their relationship with their federal cousins. The Liberals and NDP are deeply connected to the national parties that bear the same name, which means they share resources and often copy federal party policies, to the point that the provincial party is almost an arm of the national counterpart. Conversely, the Conservative Party of Canada, as constituted in 2004, has no formalized link with any provincial political party and some of its libertarian policies are shunned in Canada's easternmost province. Certainly there are connections between it and the provincial PC Party, but these are not as strong as federal–provincial connections among the other parties.[12]

Whatever their party, members who are elected to represent an urbanized area such as St. John's are likely to represent the highest number of constituents. MHAs in rural areas, particularly Labrador, have fewer constituents spread across a large land mass. On the floor of the House of Assembly, members are seated together by political party. Those with additional responsibilities, such as party leaders and ministers, are seated at the front of their respective groupings. Those with the least responsibility are seated behind them and are thus known as backbenchers. The role of an MHA is varied but typically involves helping constituents get access to government services, attending local events, listening to concerns, delivering statements in the House of Assembly, voting on bills, and communicating through the media. A constituency assistant helps each MHA with electoral district issues and sometimes works out of a constituency office in the riding.

Electing people to the House of Assembly is designed to ensure that the delegates of the King or Queen of Canada do not make government decisions without considering the views of the people. The *Lieutenant Governor of Newfoundland and Labrador* is the person appointed at the recommendation of the Prime Minister of Canada to represent the Crown's interests in the province. At a glance, the position hearkens to the British governor who oversaw the earlier Commission of Government. A lieutenant governor holds formal powers of appointing a premier to recommend a cabinet, granting royal assent so that a bill may become law, assenting to the decisions of the cabinet to create Orders of the Lieutenant Governor in Council, proroguing a session of the legislature, and signing a writ of election. The Canadian custom is that lieutenant governors rubber-stamp what is asked, and rise above political debate by concentrating on ceremonial duties. This includes reading the Speech from the Throne, handing out awards and medals, and hosting an annual tea party that is open to the public at Government House in St. John's.

The *Premier of Newfoundland and Labrador* is appointed by the lieutenant governor to head up the government, based on which party controls the most seats in the legislature. This occurs after a general election, unless a premier leaves the office before then, prompting the appointment of a successor. The premier is also the leader of the political party that controls the House of Assembly, and he or she, therefore, is expected to be an MHA. This individual alone recommends who to appoint to cabinet, who to demote, and who to shuffle out. Thus, it is foremost the premier who steers the shape and direction of government, with the support of political staff in the Premier's Office, who are partisan appointments.

Political power is primarily concentrated in this single individual, both a strength and weakness of parliamentary models of democracy.

The Premier's Office also has access to astute non-partisans in the Cabinet Secretariat and Communications Branch, among others. The most senior public servant is the *Clerk of the Executive Council*, who serves at the pleasure of the premier and is in constant contact with senior officials throughout government. The clerk navigates implementation of the premier's political agenda as well as requests emanating from departments.

A *cabinet minister* is a person appointed to be a member of the Executive Council of government. All ministers are members of the party that controls the legislature and almost always are MHAs. Ministers are assigned responsibility for portfolios, including a government department and/or government agencies. This means that they spend time overseeing their department while also having a presence in the legislature and dealing with constituent concerns. Their oversight of a department is much more hands-on than is the case with an arm's-length agency such as a Crown corporation, which faces competitive pressures in a private-sector marketplace.

Collectively, as a cabinet, ministers make broad decisions, whether in cabinet committees or in full cabinet meetings. Individually, as ministers, they are responsible for their own portfolios. As a group they are faced with balancing the needs of the province as a whole with the needs of their political party. By convention ministers must publicly support each other and vote with the government or else they must resign from cabinet. An outcome of the cabinet being embedded in the legislature is that this instills strict party discipline on backbenchers in the governing party, who are expected to vote with the government.[13] Each minister is supported by political staff and by non-partisan public servants in the department. Just as the premier works with the clerk of the Executive Council, a minister works with a *deputy minister*, who is the deputy head of the respective department. The clerk and deputy ministers (DMs) carry out their duties in a non-partisan manner, though to what extent they are apolitical depends on the individual. Both the clerk and DMs are accountable ultimately to the premier rather than to a minister.

A *parliamentary secretary* is an MHA with the governing party who is appointed to assist a cabinet minister with select duties. Serving in this role is often perceived as training ground for a future cabinet appointment. On the opposite side of the House is the *Leader of the Official Opposition*. This is the leader of the political party that has the second-most seats in the House of Assembly. The position, while significant, does not hold much legislative power because the party is not in charge of the government. However, as the premier's main critic including during Question Period, the opposition leader and the official opposition as a whole can complicate the ability of the governing party to advance an agenda.

Business in the House is moderated by the *Speaker*, an MHA who is usually a member of the governing party. The speaker does not vote except in the event of a tie. To manage daily activities, each party designates an MHA as their *House Leader* to negotiate proceedings, which tend to be directed by the government House Leader. Opposition MHAs assume critic portfolios to counter or shadow government ministers. Members on both sides of the House participate in various legislative committees to closely examine government business. Far too often the Committee of the Whole is used, a form of committee that includes all MHAs except the speaker, who simply exits the chamber so that it may be chaired by the deputy speaker.

An important principle of democratic governance is the rule of law. This means that power cannot be used in an arbitrary fashion. The highest law of the land in Newfoundland and Labrador is the Constitution of Canada, which outlines the division of powers between the federal and provincial governments, and which includes the Charter of Rights and Freedoms. The Supreme Court of Canada, which is located in Ottawa, is the top court in the country and is entrusted to be the final judge or arbiter on legal disputes and interpretations of national significance. In St. John's, the Supreme Court of Newfoundland and Labrador considers civil cases and criminal matters, and listens to appeals. Judges have considerable power, yet the province's process for appointing lawyers to the bench is somewhat opaque.[14] As well, the mechanisms to hold them to account do not involve public input even when there is public outcry over decisions.

The power of politicians and the public service in Newfoundland and Labrador is structured and constrained by the federal Constitution. For instance, if a bill is passed by a majority in the House of Assembly, and then signed into law by the lieutenant governor, the courts may nevertheless strike down the legislation if it is deemed to be unconstitutional. Reforming the Constitution is a topic that prime ministers have been unwilling to tackle since the failure of two divisive constitutional accords and two Quebec separation referendums in the late twentieth century.[15]

How the Government of Newfoundland and Labrador Is Organized

The main actors in each of the executive, legislative, and judicial branches of government contribute to making and interpreting decisions about public policies. In various ways this includes laws, practices, regulations, standards, and other legal instruments. A key difference between the federal and provincial levels of government is that there is only one legislative chamber in Newfoundland and Labrador, whereas the Parliament of Canada in Ottawa is comprised of the House of Commons and the Senate. Legislation moves comparatively swiftly through the House of Assembly due to the underutilized nature of review committees, under-resourced opposition parties, limited journalistic scrutiny, and a slew of other factors. Legislative business can nevertheless take quite some time to move through cabinet, then through the House, and then potentially on to the lieutenant governor for signature.

When trying to determine how much power a governing party has, the first thing to identify is not the party's standing in public opinion polls, but rather whether the party has a majority of seats in the House of Assembly. If so, the premier and cabinet can advance an agenda with confidence that it will be supported by enough MHAs to win a vote. Majority governments are prevalent in Newfoundland and Labrador, adding to the power that is concentrated in the Premier's Office. The main alternatives are a coalition government (the formal working union of two or more political parties that control the legislature, which then have a role within cabinet) or a minority government (whereby the premier's party does not control the legislature and has to negotiate with other parties in order to remain in office). Coalition governments are rare in Canada, in part a function of the electoral system and political culture. Minority governments are reasonably common across the country. They are unusual in Newfoundland and Labrador, which had a single brief experience with minority government in the early 1970s as the era of Joey Smallwood government came to an end.

The House of Assembly precinct is also a bit odd in that it is nestled within a government building that employs public servants. More significantly, the Premier's Office and a number of ministers' offices are in that same edifice. Thus, while the legislative branch is meant to hold the executive branch to account, there is symbolism in the fusion of these organs of government into the same space. The precinct includes the press gallery, an area reserved for accredited journalists.[16] Conversely, Crown corporations are situated in independent buildings.

Democracy is embodied in the premier and ministers overseeing the bureaucracy. They seek to implement their election agenda and generally act as the people's representatives among the permanent public service. These politicians take credit for good news announcements and they bear the brunt of criticism when controversy arises. Unlike them, a public servant is not elected, typically has job security, and is not the public "face" of the department. Many if not most are hired through the merit principle, which is to say that individuals deemed the best candidates in publicly advertised job competitions are generally the ones hired. Public servants are non-partisan and follow a working premise that they should provide frank advice to ministers and loyally implement whatever a minister decides, within the boundaries of the law. They tend to have specialized training, finely honed skill sets, institutional memory, and, above all, a respect for following a chain of command and formalized process mechanisms. By comparison, their political masters may have no training in the departmental area whatsoever and an impatient desire to implement decisions quickly. But what a minister does have is the legitimate authority to make decisions. Moreover, a minister and political staff are highly in tune with political realities. It is common for public servants to become frustrated by the political agenda being pursued by cabinet or the lack of resources allocated to a file. Other times a department may find itself the centre of public attention and pressured to take action. No matter what the circumstance, a public servant is expected to separate personal political opinion from a duty to carry out directives. This long-standing principle is itself subject to question, given the importance of protecting whistleblowers, another area of reform that has been slow to emerge in Newfoundland and Labrador.

Across Canada, the size of provincial governments has been growing, which in large part is a reflection of the expanding importance of health care and education in particular — both of which are assigned as a provincial responsibility by the Constitution. Another major area of provincial jurisdiction is non-renewable natural resources. Other responsibilities include lands, licensing, some forms of taxation, and overseeing municipalities. At any given time the number and names of departments and agencies vary. Among the most prominent are health, finance, education, natural resources, justice, and public works. Others ebb and flow, such as environment or tourism, and the federal government plays varying roles in some areas, such as the fishery. A reader interested in the latest configuration of government departments need only visit the relevant area of the Government of Newfoundland and Labrador website.[17]

Space prevents a deeper discussion about public administration and politics in the province; for a good overview, see work by Christopher Dunn and the publications of the 2003 Royal Commission on Renewing and

Strengthening Our Place in Canada (2003).[18] Historical perspective is also instructive, such as publications authored by Sean Cadigan, Henry Bertram Mayo, Susan McCorquodale, and S.J.R. Noel.[19] Equally, to get a sense of the problems that result when transparency is lacking in political decision-making, a reader might consult the 2007 report of the Review Commission on Constituency Allowances and Related Matters.[20] While there is little point in fixating on singular events, it is worth pointing out that even though institutional reforms contribute to better governance, bad habits are prone to creep back.[21]

How the Government Decides

So how is government policy formulated? Primarily through the implementation of the governing party's election platform. Those promises are formalized in the Speech from the Throne, which is prepared by the governing party and read by the lieutenant governor on the floor of the House of Assembly. The speech is peppered with "My government will . . ." statements that provide direction to the public service about the government's immediate agenda. At the start of every fiscal year, roughly in March or April, the finance minister delivers a budget that identifies how the government proposes to raise and spend money. Figures 3.2 and 3.3 provide a snapshot of where the government obtains its revenues and where the money goes. The budget tends to be the centrepiece of implementing aspects of the election platform and Throne Speech, though it may equally adapt to emerging political circumstances. The budget must be supported by a majority of MHAs; otherwise, the government falls and there must be a general election. Time is devoted to MHAs debating the budget and reviewing financial estimates. Other routine activities in the legislature include debates over issues of the day during Question Period and the introduction of new bills. The cycle repeats itself each year, with the House meeting roughly in March, April, May, November, and December — a bit more in years when there is urgent business and quite a bit less in election years.

Figure 3.2: Government of Newfoundland and Labrador Revenues (% of total, 2016–17 estimates)

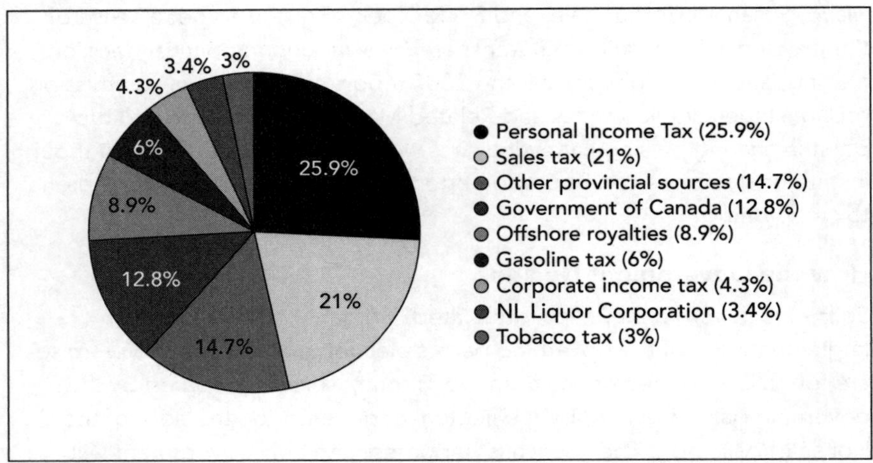

Source: Government of Newfoundland and Labrador, Department of Finance, "Estimates of the Program Expenditure and Revenue of the Consolidated Revenue Fund" (St. John's, 2017), ix, at: http://www.budget.gov.nl.ca/budget2017/estimates/estimates.pdf.

Figure 3.3: Government of Newfoundland and Labrador Spending (% of total, 2016–17 estimates)

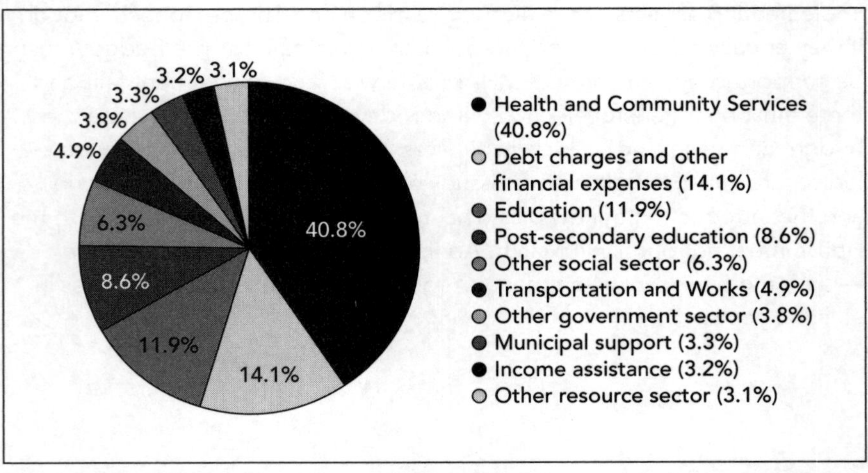

Source: Government of Newfoundland and Labrador, Department of Finance, "Estimates of the Program Expenditure and Revenue of the Consolidated Revenue Fund" (St. John's, 2017), x, at: http://www.budget.gov.nl.ca/budget2017/estimates/estimates.pdf.

Issues in the news are more likely to command political attention, to enter what is known as the public policy cycle, and to get on the public agenda.[22] Within the government there are many instruments used to manage information flow. Chief among them is a memorandum to cabinet, which is advanced by a minister to request that cabinet authorize a course of action. A cabinet memo applies all sorts of policy lenses on proposed actions to help ministers consider a plethora of perspectives. When submitted to cabinet it is normally referred to a committee of ministers, which invokes review by staff in the Cabinet Secretariat. This process brings a government-wide perspective to departmental initiatives. Government announcements are formally communicated through news releases and speeches. Increasingly, the government is availing of communications technology, such as social media and so-called "open government"[23] to make information publicly available online. Other matters occur behind closed doors and go undocumented, such as meetings between ministers and interest group leaders.

Communications technology is at the heart of reasons why traditional ways of governing suddenly seem outdated. It is one thing to be able to get a minister to respond to public concerns on local call-in radio programming, a phenomenon more prevalent in Newfoundland and Labrador than in other provinces.[24] It is quite another to exchange information around the world in real time via Internet-enabled portable devices. Media elites no longer act as gatekeepers who control what information can be circulated, though government elites continue to spin messages and obscure information. The tiniest of details are now pounced upon in the online public square. Events in remote areas of the province can be documented by citizens who have the technological means to share their stories. Interest group leaders can quickly co-ordinate a public protest. Journalists tweeting news and public opinion polls act as barometers of the public mood. Even so, traditional television news still dominates, though the intersection with Internet video means that exposure to local media and engagement in local public affairs are changing.[25]

A strong, vibrant democratic society is characterized by pluralism — the "marketplace of ideas," to use a long-standing expression featured in VOCM radio's promotion of its call-in shows. Information about government should be publicly available and the public should welcome spirited conversations about a full range of policy options. An ideal democracy would treat its citizens reasonably equally and welcome competing points of view. In such a society, coffee houses and talk radio shows, as well as public consultation forums and the Twitterverse, should engage the public towards coming up with thoughtful solutions to public problems. Citizens and their leaders should be sufficiently open-minded to consider new ways of doing things and to balance compromise with bold decision-making.

Reforming Democratic Governance in Newfoundland and Labrador

Is democratic governance working for Newfoundland and Labrador? Is it the best it could be? What is the ideal process for premiers, ministers, and MHAs to make decisions on behalf of the public, particularly when those decisions are difficult and potentially unpopular? These are questions without definitive answers.

Echoing themes of their federal counterparts' interest in promoting democratic reform, a core plank of the provincial Liberals' election platform in 2015 was better government through "openness, transparency and accountability."[26] On the surface, some themes were alternately well intentioned or mostly campaign rhetoric, such as a pledge to "respect" the House of Assembly, to "encourage co-operation," and to "respect diversity." Specific promises included creating a non-partisan Independent Appointments Commission; amending the House of Assembly Act to set a schedule for House sittings; reforming the standing orders of the House; implementing "family-friendly policies" to support gender diversity in the workforce; discontinuing the salary top-up for parliamentary secretaries; and regularly holding town halls across the province. Others were less concrete, such as a pledge to "make better use of existing committees" and a commitment "to open communication, consultation, and collaboration with Aboriginal communities." Moreover, the platform was silent on many aspects of democratic reform. By comparison, the federal Liberals proposed action on electoral reform, free votes by parliamentarians, leaders' debates, government advertising, judicial appointments, officers of the legislature, omnibus bills, parliamentary committees, political financing, Question Period, greater diversity and engagement in government, and more.[27]

The Liberal Party of Newfoundland and Labrador left open these possibilities by promising to create a committee on democratic reform that would be comprised of MHAs from all three political parties in the legislature. *A Stronger Tomorrow: Our Five Point Plan* states:

> A New Liberal Government will form an all-party committee on democratic reform. This committee will consult extensively with the public to gather perspectives on democracy in Newfoundland and Labrador, and make recommendations

> for ways to improve. The committee will consider a number of options to improve democracy, such as changing or broadening methods of voting to increase participation in elections, reforming campaign finance laws to cover leadership contests, and requiring provincial parties to report their finances on a bi-annual basis.[28]

Aspects of the election platform were formalized in mandate letters from the premier to ministers. The minister responsible for the Office of Public Engagement was directed to "host regular engagement activities including town hall meetings in communities throughout the province and use technology to expand the options to participate."[29] The government House Leader was instructed to "modernize the province's legislative process and engage elected representatives from all political parties" and to "make better use of existing committees and seek opportunities for further nonpartisan cooperation, including establishing legislative review committees to review proposed legislation."[30] Most significantly, the House Leader was expected to "*Bring a resolution to the House of Assembly to establish an All Party Committee on Democratic Reform*" (emphasis added). While the March 2016 Speech from the Throne further formalized some commitments, such as creating the Independent Appointments Commission, it did not mention the all-party committee on democratic reform.[31] Nor did the 2017 Throne Speech.

In the current context a barrier to change is limited resources. Deep research is required on the scale of the aforementioned Review Commission on Constituency Allowances and Related Matters, commonly known as the Green Report after its namesake, Judge Derek Green.[32] The constituency allowance scandal involved a systemic misappropriation of funds allocated to MHAs for work-related expenses. Thanks to the Green Report, considerable reforms to the internal financial management of the House of Assembly were implemented, through the creation of the House of Assembly Accountability, Integrity and Administration Act (2007).[33] After the reforms, Newfoundland and Labrador became a model for legislatures in Nova Scotia, the United Kingdom, and the Parliament of Canada when those institutions were embroiled in similar scandal. "For true transparency and openness, the House of Commons should follow Newfoundland's example," concluded parliamentary scholar C.E.S. Franks.[34] More recently, Rob Antle, a seasoned journalist who followed the constituency scandal, observed that "the current system is working" in the province because the Act required transparency of otherwise hidden political decisions.[35] Those reforms are evidence that high standards of professionalism and open government are possible.

Meaningful democratic reform is possible no matter what the financial circumstances of the province. We must not be satisfied with Churchill's notion that democracy is automatically better than the alternatives.[36] Improvements must constantly be made for that to ring true. The short essays in *The Democracy Cookbook* offer some suggestions. ★

Notes

1. See, for instance, J.G. Channing, *The Effects of Transition to Confederation on Public Administration in Newfoundland* (Toronto: Institute of Public Administration of Canada, 1982), 5.
2. Christopher Dunn, "The Persistence of the Institutionalized Cabinet: The Central Executive in Newfoundland and Labrador," in Luc Bernier, Keith Brownsey, and Michael Howlett, eds., *Executive Styles in Canada: Cabinet Structures and Leadership Practices in Canadian Government* (Toronto: University of Toronto Press, 2005), 48.
3. Heather Bastedo, Wayne Chu, Jane Hilderman, and André Turcotte, "The Real Outsiders: Politically Disengaged Views on Politics and Democracy," Samara Canada, 7 Dec. 2011, at: http://www.samaracanada.com/docs/default-document-library/sam_therealoutsiders.pdf.
4. José Antonio Cheibub, Jennifer Gandhi, and James Raymond Vreeland, "Democracy and Dictatorship Revisited," *Public Choice* 143 (2010): 67–101.
5. James McLeod, *Turmoil as Usual: Politics in Newfoundland and Labrador and the Road to the 2015 Election* (St. John's: Creative Publishers, 2016).
6. What Churchill said in the British House of Commons was: "Many forms of government have been tried, and will be tried in this world of sin and woe. No one pretends that democracy is perfect or all-wise. Indeed, it has been said that democracy is the worst form of government except all those other forms that have been tried from time to time; but there is the broad feeling in our country that the people should rule, continuously rule, and that public opinion, expressed by all constitutional means, should shape, guide, and control the actions of ministers who are their servants and not their masters." Hansard, *Debates,* 11 Nov. 1947, vol. 444, cc. 203–321, at: http://hansard.millbanksystems.com/commons/1947/nov/11/parliament-bill.
7. John Mueller, *Capitalism, Democracy, and Ralph's Pretty Good Grocery* (Princeton, N.J.: Princeton University Press, 1999), 8, 154.
8. Robert J. Barro, "Determinants of Democracy," *Journal of Political Economy* 107 (1999): S158–S183.
9. This discussion does not include the federal level of government, which

involves sending Members of Parliament and Senators to Ottawa, or municipal matters, or Nunatsiavut. For information about how the federal government works, see Eugene Forsey, How Canadians Govern Themselves, 6th ed. (Ottawa: Library of Parliament, 2005), at: http://www.lop.parl.gc.ca/About/Parliament/SenatorEugeneForsey/book/assets/pdf/How_Canadians_Govern_Themselves9.pdf or any works by David E. Smith, such as *The People's House of Commons: Theories of Democracy in Contention* (Toronto: University of Toronto Press, 2007); for information about the province's municipalities, visit the website of Municipalities Newfoundland and Labrador (www.municipalnl.ca); and for information about Indigenous self-government, see the Nunatsiavut website (www.nunatsiavut.com).

10. Amanda Bittner and Elizabeth Goodyear-Grant, "A Laggard No More? Women in Newfoundland and Labrador Politics," in Linda Trimble, Jane Arscott, and Manon Tremblay, eds., *Stalled: The Representation of Women in Canadian Governments* (Vancouver: University of British Columbia Press, 2013), 115–34.
11. Matthew Kerby and Kelly Blidook, "Party Positions in Newfoundland and Labrador: Expert Survey Results in the Buildup to the 2011 Provincial Election," *American Review of Canadian Studies* 44, 4 (2014): 411.
12. In the 2008 federal election, PC Premier Danny Williams advocated voting "ABC" (anything but Conservative), followed by PC Premier Kathy Dunderdale's public endorsement of the federal party in the 2011 contest, and then in 2015 PC Premier Paul Davis arguing that the province would benefit from MPs from all three national parties being elected.
13. For more on party discipline, see Christopher J. Kam, *Party Discipline and Parliamentary Politics* (New York: Cambridge University Press, 2009).
14. The process of judicial appointments has been controversial at the federal level for many years. See, for example, Erin Crandall, "Defeat and Ambiguity: The Pursuit of Judicial Selection Reform for the Supreme Court of Canada," *Queen's Law Journal* 41, 1 (2015): 73–104.
15. For instance, see Emmett Macfarlane, ed., *Constitutional Amendment in Canada* (Toronto: University of Toronto Press, 2016).
16. For an overview of the operations of the House of Assembly, see Alex Marland, "Order, Please! The Newfoundland and Labrador House of Assembly," *Studies of Provincial and Territorial Legislatures*, Canadian Study of Parliament Group (2011): 1–48, at: http://cspg-gcep.ca/pdf/Newfoundland_Marland-e.pdf, and the House of Assembly website at: www.assembly.nl.ca.
17. See www.gov.nl.ca/departments.html.

18. Christopher Dunn, "The Public Sector of Newfoundland and Labrador," in Alex Marland and Matthew Kerby, eds., *First Among Unequals? The Premier, Politics, and Policy in Newfoundland and Labrador* (Montreal and Kingston: McGill-Queen's University Press, 2014), 32–66; Government of Newfoundland and Labrador, Royal Commission on Renewing and Strengthening Our Place in Canada, *Our Place in Canada* (St. John's, 2003), at: http://www.exec.gov.nl.ca/royalcomm/.
19. Sean Cadigan, *Newfoundland and Labrador: A History* (Toronto: University of Toronto Press, 2009); H.B. Mayo, "Newfoundland's Entry into the Dominion," *Canadian Journal of Economics and Political Science* 15, 4 (1949): 505–22; Susan McCorquodale, "Newfoundland: Personality, Party, and Politics," in Gary Levy and Graham White, eds., *Provincial and Territorial Legislatures in Canada* (Toronto: University of Toronto Press, 1989); S.J.R. Noel, *Politics in Newfoundland* (Toronto: University of Toronto Press, 1971). See also survey research data compiled by Mark Graesser on file in the Centre for Newfoundland Studies, MUN.
20. Derek J. Green, *Rebuilding Confidence: Review Commission on Constituency Allowances and Related Matters* (St. John's: Government of Newfoundland and Labrador, May 2007), at: http://www.gov.nl.ca/publicat/greenreport/.
21. A recent example is the House of Assembly management commission initially overruling an independent committee's recommendation to curtail MHA pensions. See Rob Antle, "Why the MHA Pension Debate Is Proof the System Overseeing N.L. Politicians Now Works." CBC News, 18 Dec. 2016, at: http://www.cbc.ca/news/canada/newfoundland-labrador/analysis-mha-pension-debate-transparency-1.3898650.
22. For more on this, see the government's Policy NL site: www.policynl.ca.
23. See www.open.gov.nl.ca.
24. Alex Marland, "Public Opinion Monitoring by Provincial Governments: The Prevalence of Open Line Radio in Newfoundland and Labrador," *Canadian Journal of Communication* 38 (2013): 649–61.
25. For instance, see IAB Canada, "Canadian Media Usage Trends Total Canada Report: Canada's Media Landscape," 3 Dec. 2015, at: https://iabcanada.com/wp-content/uploads/2015/12/V2-Total-Canada-Exec-Summary-Nov-25-2015.pdf.
26. Liberal Party of Newfoundland and Labrador, *A Stronger Tomorrow: Our Five Point Plan*. Election platform (2015), at: https://nlliberals.ca/wp-content/uploads/2015/11/Liberal-Five-Point-Plan_Web.pdf.
27. Liberal Party of Canada, *Real Change: A Fair and Open Government*. Election platform backgrounder (2015), at: https://www.liberal.ca/wp-

content/uploads/2015/08/a-fair-and-open-government.pdf.

28. Liberal Party of Newfoundland and Labrador, *A Stronger Tomorrow*, 8.
29. Dwight Ball, "Letter to Minister Siobhan Coady," 14 Dec. 2015, at: http://www.exec.gov.nl.ca/exec/cabinet/ministers/pdf/Minister_Coady_Mandate.pdf.
30. Dwight Ball, "Letter to Minister Andrew Parsons," 14 Dec. 2015, at: http://www.exec.gov.nl.ca/exec/cabinet/ministers/pdf/Minister_Parsons_Mandate.pdf.
31. Frank F. Fagan, Speech from the Throne, 8 Mar. 2016, at: http://www.exec.gov.nl.ca/thronespeech/2016/speech.html.
32. Green, *Rebuilding Confidence*.
33. Government of Newfoundland and Labrador. *An Act Respecting the Effective Administration of the House of Assembly, the Standards of Conduct of Elected Members, and their Ethical and Accountable Behaviour* (St. John's, 2007), at: http://www.assembly.nl.ca/legislation/sr/statutes/h10-1.htm.
34. C.E.S. Franks, "*Quis Custodiet Ipsos Custodes?* The Contribution of Newfoundland and Labrador to the Reform of Management of Canadian Legislatures," *Canadian Public Administration* 51, 1 (2008): 167.
35. Antle, "Why the MHA Pension Debate Is Proof."
36. Hansard, *Debates*, 11 Nov. 1947.

4 Why Focus on Provincial Politics?

Jared Wesley

Provincial politics drive Canadian democracy. It's time for #cdnpoli to move beyond Ottawa: @ipracademic #DemocraticReformNL

Studying Canadian democracy without an eye to provincial politics is like trying to understand the Atlantic Ocean from a floatplane: the view is interesting, but you miss most of the elements that give it life. Look closely and you will see its strongest undercurrents, its contours, its depths, and its most colourful characters.

Like the ocean, most of Canada's politics take place below the surface of federal developments. Few countries have regional governments as influential. Most of the highest-profile issues impacting Canadians, from health and education to community safety and social services, fall squarely within provincial jurisdiction. Others, such as Indigenous relations, the environment, infrastructure, and economic development, require significant coordination between federal and provincial governments.

Domestic observers may be forgiven for missing the importance of provincial politics, given the media's fascination with all things Ottawa and certain global affairs, in particular the politics of the United States. Grand national policy plans, regardless of whether they come to fruition, often seem more attractive to the national consciousness than are provincial initiatives. This public focus does not give licence to conflate "Canadian politics" with "federal politics." Forces at play at the national level are not necessarily at play in the provinces. A cursory glance at the distinct political party systems, voter turnout rates, and proportions of women in legislatures reveals as much. We cannot simply learn about federal politics and expect to apply the same lessons at the subnational level.

By the same token, we cannot understand pan-Canadian institutions and dynamics without due attention to the goings-on provincially. Just ask Prime Minister Justin Trudeau, whose top policy priorities have run headlong into the quagmire of federal-provincial negotiations. The federal Liberal government is unable meet its commitments to Canadians on issues such as legalizing marijuana, constructing pipelines, reducing carbon emissions, enhancing infrastructure, improving health care and child care, or many other areas without co-operation or acquiescence (if not consensus) among (most) provincial premiers. Beyond Canada's borders, provincial governments played a leading role in the negotiation of the Comprehensive Economic Trade Agreement (CETA) with the European Union and the Paris climate agreement, for instance. They are also at the centre of trade disputes with the United States over industries such as softwood lumber and dairy.

Studying provincial politics and governance is arguably more important than ever. In recent years, political scientists have realized the importance of studying provincial politics in Canada. After decades of relative quiet -- with some notable exceptions particularly works by Rand Dyck and Christopher Dunn and his contributors[1] — a series of new edited volumes[2] and pan-Canadian studies such as Vote Compass, Making Democracy Work, and the Comparative Provincial Elections Project have reinvigorated interest in provincial governance among scholars and students.

Here are two reasons why this cutting-edge research is important, and why Canadians beyond the academy, including citizens, public servants, and legislators, should take note.

First, a lot has changed in the arenas of provincial politics. We cannot rely on the accepted wisdom of the last wave of provincial scholarship produced in the 1980s. New Democratic Party (NDP) governments were formed in Nova Scotia and Alberta — two bastions of Canadian conservatism, albeit of different flavours. Eight women have led provincial governments as premiers: two in the 1990s and six in the twenty-first century. A Progressive Conservative Premier (Danny Williams) openly campaigned to defeat a Conservative Prime Minister (Stephen Harper). That same Prime Minister granted plum foreign affairs appointments to two former premiers, neither of whom was from his own party. These are just some of the many ways that provincial politics has evolved considerably over the past three decades. Scholarship is beginning to catch up.

Second, provinces are the primary sites of policy innovation. They routinely experiment with approaches that often find their way across borders and to the national level. This is particularly true in the areas of democratic reform, climate change, and reconciliation. Some provincial governments have driven the movement towards gradual tightening of campaign finance rules. They have led a push to ban union and corporate donations and to restrict partisan government advertising. Some have led efforts to increase government transparency, through open-data initiatives and freedom-of-information reforms. Provincial governments across Canada have established fixed election dates, and struck numerous democratic reform commissions. To date, four province-wide referendums have been held on electoral reform, although none of the proposed changes came to fruition. In terms of environmental policy, provinces are at the forefront of efforts to place a price on carbon, experimenting with a variety of mechanisms including cap-and-trade and carbon taxes. To advance reconciliation with Indigenous peoples, provincial premiers meet annually with the leaders of the national Indigenous organizations on issues ranging from education and child care to resource development and violence against Indigenous women and girls. At annual Council of the Federation meetings, premiers assert collective leadership over pan-Canadian issues such as Indigenous children in care, health care, disaster response and recovery, energy development, climate change, and internal trade.

In sum, while the federal government has vacated certain areas of pan-Canadian policymaking, provincial governments are leading the response to many of the most pressing issues facing Canadians. For these and other reasons, observers of Canadian politics must cast their eyes below the glossy surface of the federal level. Volumes such as *The Democracy Cookbook* are crucial in that endeavour. ★

About the Author

Jared Wesley (Political Science, University of Alberta) is co-author of *Inside Canadian Politics* (Oxford University Press, 2016) and editor of *Big Worlds: Politics and Elections in the Canadian Provinces and Territories* (University of Toronto Press, 2016). His research interests are in the areas of comparative provincial public policy and the politics of bureaucracy.

Notes

1. Rand Dyck, *Provincial Politics in Canada: Towards the Turn of the Century*, 3rd ed. (Scarborough: Prentice Hall Canada, 1995); Christopher Dunn, ed., Provinces: Canadian Provincial Politics, 3rd ed. (Toronto: University of Toronto Press, 2015).

2. Jared J. Wesley, ed., *Big Worlds: Politics and Elections in the Canadian Provinces and Territories* (Toronto: University of Toronto Press, 2016); Bryan M. Evans and Charles W. Smith, eds., *Transforming Provincial Politics: The Political Economy of Canada's Provinces and Territories in the Neoliberal Era* (Toronto: University of Toronto Press, 2015); Michael M. Atkinson et al., eds., *Governance and Public Policy in Canada: A View from the Provinces* (Toronto: University of Toronto Press, 2013).

5 Patriotic Correctness in Newfoundland and Labrador

David Cochrane
Reprinted with permission

To what extent does "patriotic correctness" exist in #NLpoli? Coined by @CochraneCBC, how has the term evolved? #DemocraticReformNL

Editors' note: *The following is an excerpt from a speech David Cochrane delivered to the St. John's Board of Trade on 21 February 2007. Within Newfoundland and Labrador it led to the term "patriotic correctness" being used to refer to the stifling of pluralistic public debate on topics that go against a nationalistic ethos and/or the will of populist premiers. The speech is a snapshot in time whose content arguably remains relevant today.*

There exists in Newfoundland and Labrador a phenomenon I like to call "patriotic correctness." Like political correctness, it makes certain words or expressions unacceptable. But most significantly, it has fostered an environment where informed dissent is seen as nothing short of treason. Where the simple questioning or criticism of the government or the premier is viewed as an unpatriotic assault upon the very fabric of Newfoundland and Labrador.

Patriotic correctness manifests itself in times of conflict. Usually it pits the premier and the government against an outside force such as the federal government, a nickel company, Big Oil, or a fish company that happens to be run by a Nova Scotian. It creates an incredibly lopsided public debate, one where all good Newfoundlanders and Labradorians must rally to the side of the government.

What matters most is a public display of loyalty; of being on side with the stated goal of getting the best deal, best return, and most benefits for the province. What matters least is a public debate about the merits of this stance. Or whether these goals are even reasonable or achievable. Or whether the government is acting in a way that is fair to all parties. . . . When a particular political issue is causing the government grief, it dispatches hit squads to the open line. Armed with talking points, they seek to hijack the debate. And if someone questions the government on an issue . . . the Us versus Them argument is reopened. . . .

I'm not saying people should vote against the government. I'm not suggesting they should vote for one party over another. But people should be free to make up their mind and vote in an election without having their patriotism questioned, before they step into the voting booth. Just as they should be free to question this government — and any other government — without having their love of place put to some sort of test. . . .

The sad reality is that for my entire adult life the intellectual leadership of this province has been confined to the legislature and the open line. I believe this has to change. The broader elements of our society need to participate in the larger discussion on how the government conducts itself and how it manages the economy. People need to be free to question, challenge, and criticize their government without fear of reprisal or of facing a public challenge to their patriotism. . . .

A society cannot progress unless it does so on the strength of its ideas. And good ideas require the courage and the intellectual leadership that aren't always found in the legislature or from the caller on line 3. Public debate cannot be ceded to the mob. Because when it is, the mob almost always chooses to free Barabbas and send the good man to the cross.

About the Author

David Cochrane (CBC) is a senior reporter with the CBC's parliamentary bureau. Previously he was a political reporter for *Here and Now* and CBC-NL radio. He is the former host of *On Point with David Cochrane*, a political discussion program that aired on CBC-NL.

Editor's note: *To understand the confines of expressed opinion in public debate in Newfoundland and Labrador one needs to consider different forums. In all cases — news coverage, talk radio call-in shows, letters to the editor in newspapers, opinion editorials, debate in the House of Assembly, local opinion blogs, #nlpoli tweets — there is often an undercurrent of patriotic correctness. But what does this mean, exactly? Table 5.1 (page 63) provides some examples. It is not definitive and does not render judgment, and may not be exactly what David Cochrane had in mind in 2007 or today. It is presented to illustrate that stronger public policy and improved democratic governance require institutional mechanisms to encourage, rather than suppress, diversity of opinion in Newfoundland and Labrador.*

Table 5.1: Illustrating Patriotic Correctness in Newfoundland and Labrador

Actions, Beliefs, or Ideas that Cause Offence	Socially Approved Actions, Beliefs, or Ideas
Democracy/Governance	
Stand up to a popular premier	Stand up for a popular premier
Lean, efficient government	Government should solve societal problems
Take local responsibility for problems	Blame outsiders for problems
Question organized labour	Don't criticize organized labour
Small government	Big government
Economy	
Economic productivity needs to improve	Newfoundlanders are hardworking
Free market forces are good	Government must help
Business is an economic engine	Capitalism is an exploiter
Privatize some areas of the public sector	Defend public ownership/delivery of services
Cut government jobs	Create more government jobs
NL has high unemployment	Government needs to tackle poverty
NL has high use of Employment Insurance (EI)	Distribute work hours so people qualify for EI
Society	
Centralize health-care services	Localize health-care services
Close small schools	Keep local schools open
Drivers should pay more for roads upkeep	Government should fix roads
The provincial ferry system is irrational	Government should provide better ferries
Resettle remote communities	"Save rural Newfoundland!"
Rural NL is decaying	Rural NL success stories
Conservation/Science	
Scientific evidence shows fish stocks are low	Fishermen say there are plenty of fish in our bay
End the seal hunt	Defend the seal hunt
Introduce tougher environmental regulation	Develop natural resources for economic gain
Local consultation practices are imprecise	Local "question of the day" straw polls matter

Source: Prepared by Alex Marland. ★

6 Begging to Differ in a Small Place

Robin Whitaker

Is there pressure to be silent in a small place like Newfoundland & Labrador? @rgwhitaker thinks so. #DemocraticReformNL

A few years back, I asked an exceptionally able undergraduate seminar to read Gerald Sider's "Between Silences and Culture."[1] Here, Sider recounts being struck during fieldwork in post-moratorium Newfoundland by an increasingly romanticized view of the pre-1960s inshore fishery. "Life was hard, bye, but we did it," people told him.[2] In contrast, when Sider started visiting the region in 1972 people who had worked in that fishery, the parents and grandparents of his later interlocutors, talked explicitly about hardship and vulnerability. Sider wonders if the late twentieth-century narrative — he calls it a "tourist" version — reflects people's desire to shield their children from expropriation and humiliation. But, he adds, such silences must be understood as political. They give culture its simultaneously inclusive and exclusionary character, marking the boundary between continuity and chaos. Or, we might say, such silences underpin the ability to speak as the "we" that "did it," even as they hide the specifics of what "we did" and the conditions that compelled the doing. To the extent that these conditions extend into the present and its intensified inequalities, such silences also frustrate attempts to make the future different.

While my students were intrigued by this essay, some were also discomfited by it. After all, it unsettled a version of their history that at least partly informed who they understood themselves to be. Was that the business of anthropologists? Besides, if the narrative Sider targets reflects a tourist industry version of Newfoundland heritage, it is inseparable from public discourses of collective pride and grievance against an arch-other: mainland contempt for a place "derided for decades as the fish-dependent fiscal laughingstock of Canada," as the *National Post* put it in 2012.[3]

When I pushed the class on where they thought "our" history was comfortably free of politically salient silences about who and what were at stake, several suggested the seal hunt. They meant the commercial hunt that became the international target of animal rights activists in the 1970s and, by extension, a platform for populist nationalism, to be defended in the name of Newfoundland culture. As the popularity of sealskin apparel among local politicians suggests, it also provides a handily wearable badge of Newfoundland patriotism. (Labrador patriotism too — another story, and one that points to just how much "our" identity as "Newfoundlanders and Labradorians" is hedged by especially consequential silences.)

And yet, Ray Guy reminds us that, prior to the early 1970s: "In the communal consciousness, sealing was relegated to folk song and story of a bleak and tragic cast. . . . E.J. Pratt's . . . doleful lines on sealing tragedy — 'ring out the toll for a hundred dead, who tried to lower the price of bread' — were to be memorized [by schoolchildren]. . . . The only virtue salvaged from a couple of centuries of seal killing was stoicism in the face of misery and calamity."[4]

If my students' sense of the seal hunt as a marker of cultural identity was largely silent on its exploitative history, the example points to another way that silences mark political culture here. In a small place, where "everyone knows everyone," saying nothing can be the price both of acceptance and acceptability. Such counsel-keeping often reflects a desire to keep the peace, to avoid insulting people who may be your neighbours, friends, even family. But that doesn't mitigate the anti-democratic effect. Laura Nader names this "coercive harmony," where good manners and civility dampen outrage against injustice.[5]

Thus, even as I pushed my students on whether the seal hunt was really so straightforward, I reassured them: I am not opposed; I have been known to consume seal products. Similarly, the odd politician who wonders in public about sealing's commercial viability is liable to be seen about town in a sealskin vest inside of a week.

Teresa Caldeira and James Holston argue that all democracies are "disjunctive" insofar as democratic political institutions coexist with significant gaps in the social conditions required for fully democratic citizenship.[6] When democratic engagement is blocked by inadequate education or health services or a corrupt legal system, remedies are easy to identify if not to achieve. It is much harder to get to grips with political culture, partly because the best way to get at the problems is to get caught up in them.

The "deep background" to my contribution to this project on "fixing" local democracy lies in my own attempts to negotiate silences edging our political culture: silences central to the twin crises of environment and capitalism. At least these seem most urgent to me; observations by David Cochrane[7] suggest that "patriotic correctness" works to mute dissent from substantively different positions too. But Cochrane and I occupy positions of privilege — press and academic freedom, relative financial security — so the direct risks are small. The real question, for which there is no obvious answer, is how citizens can be empowered to take on the public silences that encircle lives much more vulnerable to chaos. For that, there is no revenue-neutral policy remedy. Suggestions from other contributors in this book may help. Perhaps the matter requires deeper academic research, drawing insights from other small polities. But ultimately, the challenge is less to fix what passes for democratic discourse here than to break it open, to unfix it. And that is a matter of unsettling politics, not policy. ★

About the Author

Robin Whitaker (Anthropology, Memorial University of Newfoundland) has published on democracy, citizenship, human rights, and gender politics in post-conflict Northern Ireland, most recently in a chapter entitled "Abortion Governance in the New Northern Ireland," co-authored with Goretti Horgan, in Silvia de Zordo, Joanna Mishtal, and Lorena Anton, eds., *A Fragmented Landscape: Abortion Governance and Protest Logics in Europe* (2017). She is currently conducting new research on household debt in Newfoundland. She also contributes an irregular column ("Gadfly") to the *Independent.ca* and is a known troublemaker.

Notes

1. Gerald Sider, "Between Silences and Culture: A Partisan Anthropology," in Maria-Luisa Achino-Loeb, ed., *Silence: The Currency of Power* (New York: Berghahn Books, 2006).
2. Ibid., 148.
3. "Quebec on Pace to Become Canada's Poorest Province," *National Post*, 8 Feb. 2012, at: http://news.nationalpost.com/news/canada/quebec-on-pace-to-become-canadas-poorest-province (accessed 16 Oct. 2016).
4. Ray Guy, "Seal Wars," *Canadian Geographic* 120, 2 (2000): 36–48.

5. Laura Nader, "Harmony Coerced Is Freedom Denied," *Chronicle of Higher Education* 47, 44 (2001): B13.
6. Teresa Caldeira and James Holston, "Democracy and Violence in Brazil," *Comparative Studies in Society and History* 41, 4 (1999): 691–729.
7. David Cochrane, "Speech on 'Patriotic Correctness,'" 2007, at: http://meekermedia.blogspot.ca/2007/02/david-cochranes-speech-on-patriotic.html (accessed 1 Nov. 2016).

7 Can Newfoundlanders and Labradorians Govern Themselves?

Drew Brown

Reforming Newfoundland's democracy is inseparable from tackling its melancholic political culture, says @drewfoundland. #cdnpoli #DemocraticReformNL

In the concluding remarks to a recent collection of case studies about public policy and politics in twenty-first-century Newfoundland and Labrador, Alex Marland broaches the million-dollar question of the province's political history: "what can be done to limit . . . Newfoundlanders' tacit acceptance of an imperfect democratic system?"[1] I would like to venture that this is largely a question of political culture. For the sake of argument, let's follow theorist Lauren Berlant here and call it "national character." National character is not simply a shared history or political allegiance but is rather what structures our collective forms of social life, what attaches us to them, and what makes them meaningful.[2]

Understanding and addressing Newfoundland's national character is central to any genuine effort towards democratic reform. We need to take it seriously as a structuring force in provincial politics.

We do not have time to go into it in any depth here, but I think any serious survey of Newfoundland's political history will establish that its national character is profoundly melancholic. Melancholia[3] is the maladaptive cousin of mourning, characterized by despondency and exaggerated self-depreciation, punctuated by bouts of mania. It is generally best described as "pathological self-absorption."

Mourning and loss figure heavily in Newfoundlanders' cultural memory;

philosopher F.L. Jackson has argued that Newfoundland's history, as popularly understood, represents a kind of post-traumatic stress disorder.[4] This is also, perhaps especially, true in the last century of politics — the "lost generation" at Beaumont Hamel; the loss of self-government in 1934; the loss of independence in 1949; the loss of our traditional way of life through resettlement and the cod moratorium; and even now, the loss of our short-lived prosperity.

Politically, our national character is melancholic precisely insofar as it has never appropriately reconciled itself to these losses and indeed remains haunted by Baron Amulree's basic diagnosis of our condition: that Newfoundlanders are ultimately, perhaps inherently, incapable of self-government. As R.M. Kennedy has written, Newfoundlanders are traumatized and taunted "by the shame and humiliation . . . [of] the legacy of our inability to fulfill the modern dream of political autonomy."[5]

This is the horizon of the problem(s) in our political culture. There is no immediate way to resolve this complex in its entirety without sustained reflection, analysis, and a genuine collective desire to change. Ironically, it is mostly Newfoundland nationalists who have been keeping this psychic wound open from the 1970s onward; as Ed Hollett has observed, "Newfoundlanders do not even know themselves. They must struggle daily with the gaps between their own history and the history as other Newfoundlanders tell it to them, wrongly, repeatedly."[6]

There are, however, institutional changes the government can make to start breaking the chains of our national character. After all, character is largely the accumulation of *habit* — actions and responses to stimuli repeated over enough time that they crystallize into regular patterns of behaviour, feeling, and thinking. Small interventions into political behaviour will go some way into dislodging bad democratic habits and encouraging new ones. Newfoundlanders must be reminded that they have always been able to govern themselves if provided with the tools and opportunities for doing so.

Parliamentary committees are one such simple (but effective) mechanism for empowering citizens as democratic actors. Committee hearings are spaces where citizens — experts, stakeholders, and lay people — are able to come before their elected officials and provide direct testimony and insight into a legislative concern, on the record. Establishing smaller committees also has the upshot of cutting down on the childish political theatrics of the Committee of the Whole that tend to alienate people from following or participating in provincial politics.

The House of Assembly is so small that putting parliamentarians in direct official contact with citizens will both generate better legislation as well as bring the daily grind of democratic governance down to earth for the average person.

The problems with the province's political culture that I have sketched here appear daunting in their scope and seeming abstraction. Culture — the realm of emotion, meaning, memory, affect, habit — is by its very nature suprarational, which makes directed, rational, and/or institutional intervention difficult. It is not a question of righting historical wrongs or dispelling false memories of Newfoundland's victimhood. Democratic reform should instead focus on building more robust civic and cultural institutions that have no room for the ghosts of Newfoundland and Labrador's failed national project.

Democracy is a way of life that must be practised, and there are many basic practices that the provincial state can encourage and foster to help Newfoundlanders and Labradorians live more like citizens and less like subjects. It is my hope that by providing and producing new modes of democratic political action, this contribution will in turn generate new modes of democratic thoughts and feelings and, ultimately, a healthier, more democratic national character. ★

About the Author

Drew Brown (writer) lives in St. John's. He is a former PhD candidate in Political Science at the University of Alberta whose work focused on Canadian nationalism. His columns appear regularly at VICE Canada and he is a contributor to many other local and national publications.

Notes

1. Alex Marland, "Conclusion: Inferiority or Superiority Complex? Leadership and Public Policy in Newfoundland and Labrador," in Alex Marland and Matthew Kerby, eds., *First Among Unequals: The Premier, Politics, and Policy in Newfoundland and Labrador* (Montreal and Kingston: McGill-Queen's University Press, 2014), 280.
2. Lauren Berlant, *The Anatomy of National Fantasy: Hawthorne, Utopia, and Everyday Life* (Chicago: University of Chicago Press, 1991).
3. See Sigmund Freud, "Mourning and Melancholia (1917)," in *General Psychological Theory: Papers on Metapsychology* (New York: Touchstone, 2008).
4. F.L. Jackson, "Is Newfoundland a Retrograde Society?" in *Surviving Confederation* (St. John's: Harry Cuff Publications, 1986).
5. R.M. Kennedy, "National Dreams and Inconsolable Losses: The Burden of

Melancholia in Newfoundland Culture," in Ursula A. Kelly and Elizabeth Yeoman, eds., *Despite This Loss: Essays on Culture, Memory, and Identity in Newfoundland and Labrador* (St. John's: ISER Books, 2010). 109.

6. Ed Hollett, "Two Solitudes," *The Dorchester Review* 6, 1 (Spring/Summer 2016): 17.

8 Decolonizing Newfoundland and Labrador's Democracy

Vicki Hallett

Storytelling can help decolonize democracy in Newfoundland & Labrador. #Aboriginal #DemocraticReformNL

At a time when the Newfoundland and Labrador government's relationships with Indigenous peoples are fraught with the continuing colonial legacies of land use and ownership, education access, residential schools, and more, a key commitment of the provincial government should be to provide insights into how these complex relationships formed and leadership on how they can be *transformed*. Thus, my suggestion for improving democratic governance in the province is to enable the peoples of Newfoundland and Labrador to more clearly understand ourselves as continually (and differentially) impacted by our complex history of colonization, and in turn to help us move towards a more ethical and equitable future together.

Indeed, Newfoundland and Labrador is unlike any other place in Canada, and its history, cultures, and peoples cannot be subsumed under the banner of Canada. For example, in Labrador the term "Settler" does not refer to white European Canadians. Instead, it has referred to people whose ancestors are both Indigenous and European, and who have become another sector of Labrador's population. In some cases, people who had been identified as Settlers now identify as members of the NunatuKavut (Southern Inuit) community, while others do not. Thus, the realities of what Mary Louise Pratt talks about as "transculturation" in "contact zones," that is, social spaces where "disparate cultures meet, clash, and grapple with each other, often in highly asymmetrical relations of domination and subordination,"[1] have particular resonances in this place.

Keeping in mind the province's unique background and history, we can move towards reconciliation in ways that honour that while also respecting our role in the larger Canadian community. The final report of the Truth and Reconciliation Commission of Canada recognizes the importance of sharing stories as part of the reconciliation process between Indigenous and non-Indigenous Canadians. As the report, *Honouring the Truth, Reconciling for the Future*, puts it, "While the past cannot be changed, together we can create a new understanding of our shared history — this knowledge can lead to respectful relations for the future."[2] One of the most common ways we share our experiences, and so create understanding of those experiences, is through storytelling. It is a practice that all cultures share, and one that resonates on multiple levels of identity, culture, and history. In Newfoundland and Labrador, we take pride in our dedication to storytelling, both written and oral.

Invoking this proud tradition in our education systems, a tradition shared by the Indigenous and non-Indigenous peoples of the province and manifested beautifully in local publications such as Labrador's *Them Days* magazine,[3] will have three key outcomes. It will showcase the ways that the peoples of the province have created communities through storytelling, and it will allow the peoples of the province to hear one another's stories of shared history and to take a small step on the road to reconciliation and decolonization. Ultimately, it will create a more critically engaged citizenry that is better able, and more willing, to participate in the democratic processes that shape the province.

The ultimate goal of decolonization is the independence of formerly colonized peoples from colonial rule: there will be multiple pathways to this goal. According to some Indigenous scholars, one is "being theorized and enacted . . . through practices such as storytelling."[4] Thus, it has never been more crucial to share our stories.

The Office of Labrador and Aboriginal Affairs could co-ordinate a set of initiatives that would constitute the first steps on this journey. Such initiatives could include: encouraging the use of existing resources such as *Them Days* in school libraries and classrooms across the province; enabling schools to develop links with local Indigenous communities and organizations such as the Labrador Friendship Centre and the St. John's Native Friendship Centre, so that they might undertake community projects (such as planting gardens and creating cultural fairs) together; creating a database of willing elders (Indigenous and non-Indigenous) who would volunteer to come into local schools to share stories with the students; and organizing storytelling festivals in which students and community members participate in telling traditional and newly created stories about the province and its peoples.

These steps use existing resources while integrating them in new ways. They are not the ultimate solution to reconciliation and revitalizing our democracy, but they are a way in which we may start new conversations and perhaps create new narratives that engage the citizens of the province as agents of change. ★

About the Author

Vicki Hallett (Gender Studies, Memorial University of Newfoundland) has studied the inter-relationship between people, places, and life stories in Newfoundland and Labrador for over a decade. Her most recent publications include *Mistress of the Blue Castle: The Writing Life of Phebe Florence Miller* (ISER Books, forthcoming) and "Fluid Possibilities: Theorizing Life Writing at the Confluence of Decolonial and Post-Colonial Approaches in Newfoundland and Labrador," *Newfoundland and Labrador Studies* 31, 2 (Fall 2016): 316–28.

Notes

1. Mary Louise Pratt, *Imperial Eyes: Travel Writing and Transculturation*, 2nd ed. (New York: Routledge, 2008), 7.
2. Truth and Reconciliation Commission of Canada, *Honouring the Truth, Reconciling for the Future*. Summary of the Final Report of the Truth and Reconciliation Commission of Canada, 2015, at: www.trc.ca/websites/trcinstitution/index.php?p=3 (accessed 14 Dec. 2015).
3. *Them Days*, at: www.themdays.com/ (accessed 25 Apr. 2014).
4. Aman Sium and Eric Ritskes, "Speaking Truth to Power: Indigenous Storytelling as an Act of Living Resistance," *Decolonization: Indigeneity, Education & Society* 2, 1 (2013): i.

PART 2: ALL POLITICS IS LOCAL, B'Y

Typical Newfoundland house: woodpile at right, early 1900s. Saltbox house surrounded by three types of fences. (Source: Provincial Archives)

Democracy is like butter on toast: it must uniformly spread to the crusts. In this section, we are reminded of the need to enact democracy in our daily lives by widening our social networks to include others and, where possible, by transferring decision-making to local areas. This focus on individual action radiates outward, recognizing the roles of grassroots neighbourhood coalitions and the challenges of governing hundreds of geographically dispersed communities, as well as generating participation in municipal politics.

Karen Stanbridge begins by arguing that citizens need to get involved with their communities and practise democracy. Ken Carter, Reeta Chowdahri Tremblay, and Kelly Vodden contemplate how rural areas can be resilient and self-reliant in the face of global economic forces and demographic change. Clifford Grinling and Kathryn Simonsen explain that local community groups and not-for-profits play an important role in democratic society. Alison Shott explores ways that municipalities and regional governance can be organized. Elizabeth Yeoman wraps up Part 2 by turning localism on its head, asking if ministers can make time to go for weekly walks with citizens. Lots of potential for crusty conversation there!

9 Renewing Democracy through Practice

Karen Stanbridge

Do we practice democracy enough in Newfoundland and Labrador? How can we do better? #DemocraticReformNL

Democracy is a skill and we're out of practice. Not just Newfoundlanders and Labradorians, mind you, but everyone who has become accustomed to expecting, and allowing, elected officials to take decisions on their behalf, and elected officials who expect to be allowed to do so. There are lots of reasons for this situation, some of which are unique to the province, most of which are not. All of them add up to the same thing: we've not been practising democracy nearly enough, especially in our daily lives, to be any good at it.

Political scientist Robert Putnam noticed this happening in the United States some years ago. In *Bowling Alone* (2000),[1] Putnam looked at how Americans' participation in groups with varied membership like bowling leagues, bridge clubs, and the like had declined over time. He said that, as a result, people's stock of "social capital," or the number and breadth of their social networks, had declined considerably over the past 50 years. Consequently, people were not cultivating the dispositions needed to sustain democratic political cultures, things like trust in others, knowledge of and adherence to norms of reciprocity, and the ability (and humility) to negotiate, co-operate, and compromise with others who share different views.

Notice here that Putnam was not blaming the usual suspects for the deterioration of our democratic processes: political apathy; corrupt government officials who misspend taxpayer dollars; the sense that the political game is "rigged" to service big business or "bleeding heart" liberals; and so forth. These are real concerns, but they are largely symptoms of broader processes that have manifested in people's withdrawal from public life. And as we've withdrawn, we've become less and less able to conceive, let alone undertake, the hard work involved in cultivating consensus among people holding views different than our own.[2]

Almost 20 years later, things have just gotten worse. Social media have the potential to expand people's social capital to encompass associations with those who have very different world views. However, it is often a means to block opposing perspectives and stoke exclusive ones. Technologies like smart phones have made it possible for us to communicate immediately through time and space, but these devices also let us avoid contact with others in our immediate surroundings. Although we've never had so many opportunities to interact with people who aren't like us, we just don't need to, nor are there the same kinds of social pressures to belong to the associations that used to bring us together. As a result, our democratic muscles have atrophied, and our political cultures have suffered for it.

But it's possible to get our democratic "chops" back, or at least in better shape: through practice. Of course, this takes time and effort and the will to stick to the task even when it's easier not to. Those of us who do not occupy political office have to work against all the forces that encourage us to turn inward, to disappear into our homes and into the echo chambers of our member forums and Facebook feeds, and become accustomed to living more "open" lives. Those of us in government have to overcome institutional imperatives that foster contention over negotiation and consensus-building. Together this amounts to all of us giving over some of the control that we exercise over our own circumstances so that we can develop capacities that help us to condemn less and trust each other more.

Let me add quickly that I'm not advocating for a "return" to some folksy, tech-free (and imaginary) past where people were more accepting of difference and elected officials were more accessible and willing to act on the desires of their constituents. I'd just like that more of us commit to practising democracy. We can do this by involving ourselves in activities that will help us to develop our democratic dispositions. If we focus our efforts on our immediate communities, we can even help shape them in innovative ways.

In this respect, there are models we can follow. The Transition Towns (TT) movement,[3] for example, provides guidance to people who are tired of waiting for governments to act and who just want to get on with transitioning to low(er) carbon, to more ecologically sustainable ways of living. Whatever location-specific, grassroots-led initiative you and your neighbours might devise — establishing a food-growing network, creating a neighbourhood transportation system, or generating community-owned energy — TT can give you advice on how to proceed. The key is that all decisions are taken collectively, which gives participants the chance to practise real democracy while contributing to their well-being and to that of their neighbours.

Although TT-type initiatives are about people on the ground "just doing stuff,"[4] governments can help too. They can, for example, make advisers available who will consolidate information on the administrative and legal requirements around ventures like these, for example, the approvals groups need if they want to start a community-owned bakery or establish a local reuse and repair service. These "bureaucracy wranglers" can help community groups struggling to negotiate with multiple government offices to navigate these networks. Democracy-enabling activities like these don't cost a lot of money; they just take the will to do them. Indeed, these things are right in the wheelhouse of the provincial government's Office of Public Engagement. By helping smooth the processes by which local undertakings are put into effect, the province can show that it supports our efforts to practise democracy and is willing to guide us as we work to renew our democratic proclivities.

Or maybe we just need to join a neighbourhood bowling league. Really, it doesn't matter how we start, as long as whatever we do lets us stretch our democratic muscles. Democracy is hard work and we're out of practice; we can start slowly or aim higher, but it's time we get to it. ★

About the Author

Karen Stanbridge (Sociology, Memorial University of Newfoundland) is a political sociologist who studies the state, social movements, and nationalism. Among her recent publications are "Political Sociology Is Dead. Long Live Political Sociology?" (with D. Béland and H. Ramos), *Canadian Review of Sociology* 53, 3 (2016): 337–9, and "Thrift and the Good Child Citizen: The Junior Thrift Clubs in Confederation-era Newfoundland" (with Jonathan Luedee), in L. Cullum and M. Porter, eds., *Creating This Place* (Montreal and Kingston: McGill-Queen's University Press, 2014).

Notes

1. Robert Putnam, *Bowling Alone: The Collapse and Revival of American Community* (New York: Simon & Shuster, 2000).
2. See also Robert Putnam, with Robert Leonardi and Rafaella Y. Nanetti.

Making Democracy Work: Civic Traditions in Modern Italy (Princeton, NJ: Princeton University Press, 1993).

3. See transitionnetwork.org.
4. Rob Hopkins, *The Power of Just Doing Stuff: How Local Action Can Change the World* (Cambridge: UIT Cambridge Ltd., 2013).

10 Governance for the Rural Knowledge Economy

Ken Carter and Reeta Chowdhari Tremblay

Here's an idea for how to improve governance in rural economies. #DemocraticReformNL

The emergence of the knowledge-based economy, characterized by rapid technological change and the onset of globalization, has had profound impacts on the organization of developed economies. These changes have obliged developed economies to adapt and, indeed, the forces of innovation and creative destruction have highlighted the importance of economic agility, learning, and innovation. Not surprisingly, the era of what some call "dynamic capitalism"[1] has thus far largely favoured central urban spaces with their agglomeration economies, knowledge infrastructure, and ability to attract the creative class.

But rapid change has also become a hallmark of peripheral or rural resource-based economies during recent decades with demographic shifts, out-migration, declining resource employment, and economic upheaval. The onslaught of dynamic capitalism in many rural places has had negative outcomes, which calls into question the ability of rural spaces to adapt to technological change, globalization, and the entrepreneurial economy.

Rural adaptation, change, and resilience are needed in the face of the challenges presented by globalization, the knowledge-based economy, and resource-based rural dependency. New approaches are needed to build resilience in the rural areas of our province. Rural areas need external support through stronger relationships between government, university, community, and business. Academic research suggests that "new forms of governance focus on the integration of actors across public and private sectors rather than on 'government' as the only component of the process."[2] Our suggestion is that government support building collaboration across a broad group of partners to enhance extra-local resources to support community development.

"New regionalism" is an academic concept focused strongly on the local as the appropriate scale for planning and economic development. While this was an important advance, new regionalism has been criticized for ignoring important connections beyond the local and for implying that regions can prosper simply by shifting governance of the economy to the local level.[3] However, important policy levers and resources, as well as knowledge infrastructure, do not always exist at the local level and this underscores the need instead for inclusive multi-scale governance. One stream of new regionalist literature related to innovation and learning has focused on regional innovation systems approaches that closely tie regional firms to local as well as external knowledge capacity. These linkages are increasingly seen as essential to allow regions more fully to participate in the knowledge economy. The governance implications of this approach need further unpacking.

Recent approaches to regional innovation systems have focused on building "quadruple helix" relationships: an inclusive multi-scale collaborative approach to innovation governance that brings together universities/colleges, businesses, governments, and community leaders to support resilience and adaptation to change at the regional level. Thus, regional systems involve local actors working with non-local levels of government, non-local knowledge institutions, and other external partners. The European Union and the Organization for Economic Co-operation and Development (OECD) have focused on such a regional innovation approach, the Research and Innovation Strategies for Smart Specialization or RIS3.[4] Its goal is integrated, place-based economic transformation.

Supporting these approaches to innovation systems requires that governments shift important elements of leadership for sustainability to the local level. However, these approaches also bring extra-local resources, knowledge capacity, and global linkages to local places. In effect, such regional innovation strategies become the basis for generating collaborative methods to community development based on local initiative, but with key institutional supports from outside the region.

RIS3 focuses on an entrepreneurial approach to challenges regions face. This entails a twofold process: a process of discovery whereby the region undertakes an assessment of local strengths that can be supported by research and innovation within a coalition of firms, universities/colleges, governments, and community players; and addressing the need for strategies that drive research and development to support entrepreneurship and university/college connections to regions. Harnessing an entrepreneurial spirit across the key regional actors can drive new business activity.[5] Entrepreneurs are central to this process as they are best suited to identify research and development and innovation needed in the region.

Local firms and universities/colleges are important players in regional innovation systems. Two key elements are needed for the entrepreneurial process of discovery to be successful: the alignment of research efforts at universities and colleges to regional needs; and the building of the capacity of local firms to absorb this research. University engagement, while critical to the process, requires support from governments and other community development organizations. Along with universities and firms, governments are an important convener and funder of these processes as well as critical to ensuring public policy supports local entrepreneurial innovation.

These approaches also require local organizations not only to participate, but to take ownership of leading regional development efforts while engaging external support institutions. Local governance of the knowledge economy is about building working relationships both within the community and, more broadly, with external knowledge institutions that can drive innovation at the regional level.

The challenges facing rural regions are significant, and demographic change, out-migration, and declining resource employment will likely continue. RIS3 offers a way for a broad coalition of entrepreneurs, researchers, public policy-makers, and community leaders to come together to build regional strategies. These strategies use research and an entrepreneurial spirit to allow rural regions to more fully and successfully participate in the knowledge economy. ★

About the Authors

Ken Carter (Office of Engagement, Grenfell Campus, Memorial University of Newfoundland) previously worked for the Government of Newfoundland and Labrador in rural development and rural policy, most recently as Director of Research and Analysis with the Office of Public Engagement, Executive Council. He is currently a Ph.D. candidate in the Department of Geography at MUN where he is researching the applicability of territorial innovation systems and entrepreneurial ecosystems to rural regions.

Reeta Chowdahri Tremblay (Political Science, University of Victoria) researches identity-based politics and secessionist movements (Kashmir) in South Asia, the politics of subaltern resistance and accommodation in post-colonial societies, democracy and governance, and comparative federalism. During her career, she has held several administrative positions, including at Memorial University as Pro Vice-Chancellor (Pro Tem) and as Dean of Arts.

Notes

1. A. Thurik, E. Stam, and D. Audretsch, "The Rise of the Entrepreneurial Economy and the Future of Dynamic Capitalism," *Technovation* 33, 8/9 (2013): 302–20.
2. Kevin O'Toole, and Neil Burdess, "New Community Governance in Small Rural Towns: The Australian Experience," *Journal of Rural Studies* 20, 4 (2004): 433–43.
3. E. Uyarra, "Key Dilemmas of Regional Innovation Policies," *European Journal of Social Science Research* 20, 3 (2007): 243–61.
4. D. Foray, J. Goddard, X. Goenaga Beldarrain, M. Landabaso, P. McCann, K. Morgan, C. Nauwelaers, and R. Ortega-Argiles, *Guide to Research and Innovation Strategies for Smart Specialization (RIS 3)* (Luxembourg: European Commission, 2012), at: http://ec.europa.eu/regional_policy/sources/docgener/presenta/smart_specialisation/smart_ris3_2012.pdf.
5. H.M. Hall and J. Walsh, *Advancing Innovation in Newfoundland and Labrador: Knowledge Synthesis* (St. John's: Harris Centre, Memorial University of Newfoundland, 2013), at: http://innovationnl.ca/wp-content/uploads/2013/08/Advancing-Innovation-Knowledge-Synthesis.pdf.

11 Enhancing Democracy in Rural and Regional Development Governance

Kelly Vodden

Come Gather All Around Me Now I'll Sing To You a Tale about Governing in Rural NL. #DemocraticReformNL

Citizen engagement and collective action are essential elements of a well-functioning democracy and of community-level social capital. Social capital is a critical community asset that enables other types of community assets to be mobilized in the pursuit of common goals or in response to stresses. An important task of rural and regional development, therefore, is to protect and build social capital.

While rural Newfoundland and Labrador has a rich history of organizing on one hand (e.g., through co-operatives and development associations), the need to support and encourage such mobilization is particularly important in a political culture that I and others have characterized as clientelistic, conservative, highly centralized, and reliant on political favours and vote buying.[1] The relative prosperity of recent years is likely to have exacerbated this situation. Looking to Alberta, for example, Epp describes how increased dependency on the oil industry, its outside capital and expertise, and related state largesse led to "political deskilling" and "paralyzing patron–client politics" after an era of local institution-building.[2]

Local leaders in the St. Anthony–Port au Choix region describe a situation of complacency because "people are not hurting enough" in a region where personal income has grown and lies only slightly below the provincial average with the help of energy megaproject-related employment and, consequently, geographical mobility, the public sector, and, for some, high incomes in the fishery. Yet the region's demographic situation is among the bleakest in the province. Among other challenges, employment rates are well below the provincial average and have fallen even as individual incomes have risen. Engagement rather than complacency is required, with a role for public policy and programs in encouraging this shift.

Formal and informal associations enable citizen involvement in planning and development. Opportunities for effective citizen engagement, including personal involvement in processes that visibly influence policy outcomes and in associations working towards collective aims, can build political capacity and help overcome barriers to collective action, such as apathy and feelings of powerlessness and social isolation. Investments in education and efforts to co-ordinate community organizations can also facilitate social capital and engagement.[3] Unfortunately, ample evidence suggests that provincial policy in recent years has weakened rather than strengthened civil society and social capital in rural regions.

A recent paper[4] describes rural and regional development in Newfoundland and Labrador as having gone from dysfunctional to destitute. Funding cuts and continued concentration of decision-making have resulted in the loss of local voices in what remains of regional development planning, policy, and programming in the province. The choice by provincial and federal governments to eliminate all support for Regional Economic Development Boards rather than continuing to work to improve and co-construct them, or to put in place a process to replace them with something new, suggests a hands-off, laissez-faire approach consistent with a free market-style of governance that Wolin and others warn of in their writing on the demise of democracy.[5] We have also lost employment assistance offices, regional school boards, and the model forest, among other withdrawals by a centralized state. Each of these entities was run by volunteers and provided community members and leaders with a voice and active role in development within their regions. Democratic engagement is most likely to occur at this local level, but the mechanisms to allow for this engagement have been significantly reduced.

The Office of Public Engagement was established by the Government of Newfoundland and Labrador to facilitate collaboration among rural stakeholders and to engage the public in deliberative dialogue related to sustainability issues. The Office is made up of a trained and well-intentioned staff attempting to construct meaningful engagement processes, but to what end? There is weak evidence (at best) that the input they gather is being taken into account by decision-makers. This leaves the Office subject to common critiques of government-run engagement processes as forms of "managed democracy" that favour efficiency and competition over deliberation, that offer largely one-way versus two-way exchange, and lends "a certain sheen of legitimacy to a system of complicitous democracy."[6] The Office of Public Engagement's nine regional councils were criticized for being appointed rather than elected, but nonetheless these councils offered a local voice to provincial decision-makers. They, too, have been cut.

One much discussed option has been to turn to the municipal sector, where democratically elected officials might extend their current range of activities and fill the gap left by declines in non-government rural and regional development organizations. Municipal government in its current form, however, lacks the regional structure, resources, and capacity to take this on. Further, municipalities often fail to engage citizens in planning and decision-making, thus making themselves anti-democratic. New regional development structures and related processes must be established that are combined and/or work in concert with a new level of regional government. At the same time, such structures must ensure inclusivity and ongoing, active creation of opportunities for participation by citizens, associations (formal and informal), and the private sector. Such regional structures should be regionally driven but work side by side with (and with support from) all levels of government that share an aspiration of healthy, sustainable rural communities and regions in the Newfoundland and Labrador of the future. ★

About the Author

Kelly Vodden (Environmental Policy Institute, Grenfell Campus, Memorial University of Newfoundland) has been actively involved in community and regional development research, policy, and practice in Canadian rural communities for over 20 years, including on projects related to collaborative governance and community involvement in resource management, regional planning, and developing sustainable local economies. She has led several major, multi-year research projects on these topics and has published and presented widely on her work.

Notes

1. K. Vodden, "Heroes, Hope and Resource Development," in G. Halseth, S. Markey, and D. Bruce, eds., *The Next Rural Economies: Constructing Rural Place in a Global Economy* (Oxfordshire, UK: CABI International, 2010), 223–38.
2. R. Epp, "Off-Road Democracy: The Politics of Land, Water, and Community in Alberta," in D. Taras and C. Waddell, eds., *How Canadians Communicate*

IV: Media and Politics (Edmonton: Athabasca University Press, 2012), 265.
3. Atlantic Health Promotion Research Centre (AHPRC), *A Study of Resiliency in Communities.* Prepared for Health Canada, Catalogue no. H39-470/1999E (Ottawa: Minister of Public Works and Government Services Canada, 1999); S. Wilson-Forsberg, "The Adaptation of Rural Communities to Socio-economic Change: Theoretical Insights from Atlantic Canada," *Journal of Rural and Community Development* 8, 1 (2013): 160–77.
4. H. Hall, K. Vodden, and R. Greenwood, "From Dysfunctional to Destitute: The Governance of Regional Economic Development in Newfoundland and Labrador," *International Planning Studies* (Apr. 2016), at: http://dx.doi.org/10.1080/13563475.2016.1167585.
5. S. Wolin, *Democracy, Inc.: Managed Democracy and the Specter of Inverted Totalitarianism* (Princeton, NJ: Princeton University Press, 2008).
6. Ibid., 274.

12 Non-Profits Are a Resource Waiting in the Wings

Clifford Grinling

If the Govt of NL needs skilled help, what about turning to volunteers? #DemocraticReformNL

While the political system in Newfoundland and Labrador is primarily a two-party system, the parties seldom share power. When voters go to the polls, often their primary purpose is not to vote for the representative of their choice, but to get whichever party is in power out. Consequently, every six to eight years, a landslide vote occurs and a new administration moves into the Confederation Building, often with very little experience in governing. The new administration, keen to undo the mistakes of the previous incumbent, generally sets out a bold new strategy — forgetting that politics is the art of the possible. Despite the cautions of civil servants who have seen it all before, the new administration makes brave promises and plans only to discover they lack the resources to carry out their ideas even though help is available.

Good leaders use every resource at their disposal. In Newfoundland and Labrador, there are thousands of capable, experienced, knowledgeable, and hard-working people who yearn to make their province a better place. These people are called volunteers and they operate more than 3,000 non-profit organizations across the province. Almost half of all Newfoundlanders and Labradorians over 15 years old volunteer. On average, each volunteer donates 151 hours a year to social causes, a total of more than 30 million hours.[1] These efforts have huge economic effects. In 2015, The

Community Sector Council Newfoundland and Labrador, in conjunction with Memorial University, analyzed the economic contributions of 45 non-profit organizations around St. John's. They found that these organizations spent almost $61 million annually, creating 1,200 full-time jobs, and that this resulted in more than $169 million being spent on sales, goods, and services.[2] This is not chump change. Non-profits have knowledge and expertise of which governments could make use.

Volunteers working through non-profit organizations work in schools, hospitals, libraries, community development organizations, tourism, youth recreational groups, environmental groups, social clubs, and more. Voluntary organizations are central to prosperous and successful democracies. They build networks of trust and reciprocity, they reflect common aspirations, and they are skilled at raising money and using it to good effect. While governments impose taxes and decide how to spend them, non-profits appeal to donors' better selves to raise funds and then democratically decide how to use them. Yet, there is sometimes a social stigma attached to the term "volunteer," as though volunteers are well-meaning amateurs but not up to the skill levels of professionals. This disparity is most common when governments are dealing with volunteer organizations; their attitude is often tainted with ideas like: "We are the government and we know what is best for you. We welcome your help but we are in charge."

The lead organization for non-profits in Newfoundland and Labrador is the Community Sector Council (CSC), whose mission is to integrate social and economic development and provide leadership in shaping public policies. For 40 years the CSC has worked to increase its members' knowledge and abilities through training sessions and seminars with leaders in the field of community development. Now non-profits have reached a tipping point in their development. CSC Chief Executive Officer Penelope Rowe says:

> Non-profit groups collectively are coming-of-age. For years working in the trenches addressing client needs, existing on a shoestring-and-a-half, apologizing for seeking adequate resources while being expected to do extraordinary services without a steady flow of income, non-profits are now assertively articulating policy directions and espousing fresh ideas to address complex problems. If ever there was a time when the ingenuity of non-profit organizations should be paramount, it is now.[3]

The problem is that the private and public sectors are too often considered the essential players and non-profits a peripheral sector. Rowe says it's a view that is out of date. The community sector has thousands of people who are knowledgeable, savvy, nimble, adaptable, efficient, and effective — qualities one seldom hears in describing government.

Non-profits are an army of volunteers who want to see their province grow. But they want to do more than throw ideas and suggestions over the garden wall in the hope that government might act on them. Non-profits want to be part of the economic process. They want a formal framework, a partnership with government through which they can bring their ideas to the table and be integrated into government policy. This should not be difficult. Community volunteers could be appointed to a special democracy advisory board or play a role in revitalizing legislative committees. Bringing volunteers and civil servants together to explore common aims could benefit both groups and result in huge exchanges of useful knowledge.

What is needed is the political will to integrate volunteers. Fortunately, politicians are well aware of the value of volunteers. If it were not for volunteers, how would politicians seeking election organize their efforts? How would they find people to put up signs, do fundraising, phone canvass, knock on doors, liaise with the media, or drive the house-bound to polling stations? Volunteers have their own mature organizations and want to use their knowledge in the governance of their province. Who better to champion their desire than politicians? Non-profit volunteers are a group whose time has come. They are waiting in the wings. ★

About the Author

Clifford Grinling (retired public servant) has written magazines and newsletters about Newfoundland and Labrador for 30 years. He was a writer of the community magazine, *Decks Awash*; editor and writer of the business publication, *The Networker*; Newfoundland correspondent for *Northern Aquaculture*; communications director for Enterprise Newfoundland and Labrador; and a Government of Newfoundland and Labrador speechwriter. He is also a former Jaguar mechanic and antique reproduction cabinetmaker.

Notes

1. Community Sector Council Newfoundland and Labrador, "The Community Sector in Newfoundland and Labrador" (2016), at: http://communitysector.nl.ca/resource-centre/about-community-sector/community-sector-newfoundland-and-labrador.

2. Wade Locke, Penelope Rowe, and Darlene Scott, "Demonstrating the Economic Contribution of Community Organizations in the St. John's Region: A Pilot Study," PowerPoint file, 30 Sept. 2015, at: http://www.mun.ca/care/CSC_NL_and_CARE_30_Sept._30.pdf.
3. Community Sector Council Newfoundland and Labrador, *Annual Impact Report* (2015), p. 4, at: http://communitysector.nl.ca/f/CSC%20Annual%20Report%202015.pdf.

13 The Role of Neighbourhood and Community Groups

Kathryn Simonsen

Want democratic renewal and a stronger civil society in #NLpoli? Support your local organizations! #DemocraticReformNL

"All politics is local"[1]: neighbourhood and community groups ought to be the front line of any concept of democratic renewal. Few things touch us more closely than the street that we live on. The more that we are aware of and concerned with local matters, the more we can see how those same things affect us and others on a broader scale. In fact, in British Columbia, several reports produced by provincial task forces observed that engaged citizens are "the key to responding more effectively to large scale public issues."[2] Community groups are often a citizen's first encounter with social activism and community engagement, and they can provide opportunities for citizen participation in many different areas and on many different levels.

In the 1970s, an initiative on the part of the City of St. John's led to the creation of several neighbourhood improvement programs (or NIPs). The goal of the NIPs was to "conserve and improve older run-down neighbourhoods and to encourage development of higher quality community environments."[3] This led to the creation of conceptual plans for the neighbourhoods. Boards of directors, who were members of the neighbourhoods, developed these plans together with consultants and city employees. Funding came from all three levels of government, and the NIPs were accompanied by a Residential Rehabilitation Assistance Program, which provided homeowners with loans for repairs and upgrades.[4] The conceptual plans were comprehensive and did lead to a number of changes to neighbourhood green spaces and parking areas. The NIPs demonstrated that, with sound support, an association of volunteers, dedicated to the well-being of their community, could put together a credible plan for urban renewal in less than a year.[5]

More recent neighbourhood groups tend to come into existence when neighbourhoods feel threatened (usually by new developments) or feel that their interests have been ignored in the decision-making process. These are truly "grassroots" organizations and do not have the level of civic support and funding that NIPs did; they may, in fact, be at odds with local politicians on specific issues. As manifestations of local views, however, these organizations should be taken seriously: the creation of an organization to lobby against a proposal or to co-ordinate protest is a sign that discontent is high. The citizens of a neighbourhood know their neighbourhood best. They have the clearest ideas of what is needed and how it can be fixed. The concept of "livability" is tied to citizen involvement. Portland, Oregon, which has a long tradition of partnerships between the civic government and its neighbourhoods, is considered one of the most livable cities in the United States.[6] Similarly, the Georgestown neighbourhood in St. John's, which has a vibrant neighbourhood association, was voted the "best neighbourhood" in St. John's by *The Scope*, an alternative local newspaper.[7]

Community groups of all sorts need to have a place in democratic renewal. The evidence shows that the more people are involved in their communities, the better those communities are: "When people decide that they are going to be part of the solution, local problems start getting solved."[8] How, then, are community groups to become part of the fabric of the democratic system in Newfoundland and Labrador?

First, citizens and political leaders need to recognize the value of these organizations. Community groups represent the best opportunity for grassroots civic involvement and for developing a culture of engagement in the wider population. The recognition of community groups as means of accessing public opinion and local knowledge on specific, local problems will improve politicians' ability to make well-informed decisions. Treating groups with respect (such as attending their events), understanding what they are good at, and including them in decision-making is either free of cost or a form of cost-saving, as decisions are made with community input and support from the beginning. Fewer confrontations between communities and government are likely to occur.

Second, social and political support for community groups will help community groups with their particular problems. Many community groups find it hard to recruit organizers and volunteers. If groups are seen to be playing a significant role in the democratic culture of the province, more people will be involved because they will see that their participation is valued. Community groups also wrestle with the problem of inclusion and representativeness: participants tend to be middle class and better educated.[9] A conscious effort to recruit a more diverse membership can overcome this, but it also helps if the broader good caused by community groups is recognized.

In short, a strong civil society, supported by citizens and politicians, will improve the overall political culture of the province from the grassroots up. ★

About the Author

Kathryn Simonsen (Classics, Memorial University of Newfoundland) is a historian whose research interests include the development of the city-state in ancient Greece and the creation of civic memory and its role in the politics and historiography of ancient Athens. Her publications include "Demaenetus and the Trireme," *Mouseion* 9, 3 (2009). She is also currently co-editor of *Mouseion*, a journal published by the Classical Association of Canada.

Notes

1. Attributed to the late US congressman Tip O'Neill.
2. Charles Dobson and Vancouver Citizens Committee, *The Citizen's Handbook* (n.d.), 7, at: www.vcn.bc.ca/citizens-handbook.
3. Sheppard/Burt/Pratt Architects and Engineers, *Conceptual Plan: Georgestown Neighbourhood Improvement Program, City of St. John's* (1978), 1.
4. Ibid., 1–2.
5. Ibid., iii.
6. Dobson and Vancouver Citizens Committee, *The Citizen's Handbook*, 7.
7. See http://www.stjohns.ca/living-st-johns/newcomers/about-st-johns/neighbourhoods (accessed 9 Mar. 2017).
8. Dobson and Vancouver Citizens Committee, *The Citizen's Handbook*, 7.
9. See, for example, P. Lichterman, "Piecing Together Multicultural Community: Cultural Differences in Community Building among Grass-Roots Environmentalists," *Social Problems* 42 (1995): 513–34; S. Escandon, "Theoretical versus Grass-Roots Development of a Community Partnership," *The Qualitative Report* 15 (2010): 142–55.

14 Increasing the Competitiveness of Municipal Council Elections

Alison Shott

Electoral reform can strengthen municipalities and integrate community interests. #DemocraticReformNL

Municipal associations, like Municipalities Newfoundland and Labrador (MNL), are membership organizations for elected municipal officials (mayors and councillors) within a geographic area, such as a province. They were established in Canada as forums for the representatives of municipal governments to discuss common concerns and lobby for policy changes. Municipal associations have the potential to exert considerable influence on provincial governments because their members cannot belong without being directly elected to municipal office by the public. However, challenges faced by municipal governments limit an association's effectiveness. In Newfoundland and Labrador, MNL must confront the problems that arise from having a large number of municipalities for a small population.

Municipalities Newfoundland and Labrador has some key strengths — 98 per cent of municipalities belong to the association, representing nearly 90 per cent of the provincial population. It was founded just two years after Newfoundland joined Confederation and is one of only four provincial-level municipal associations in Canada that has remained unified and open to all municipalities since its formation, rather than fracturing along rural/urban or linguistic lines.[1] Conversely, MNL's leverage is weakened by the low-level of competitive municipal elections in the province. In 2013, only 46 per cent of municipalities had contested elections and only 54 per cent of municipal officials — MNL's members — faced opposition, reducing the legitimacy of the organization's democratic voice.[2]

The low level of competitive elections is not uniform. There is a strong relationship between the population of municipalities and the percentage of municipal seats that are acclaimed. In municipalities with less than 1,000 residents, 62 per cent of positions were acclaimed — compared to acclamation rates of 27 per cent in municipalities with a population between 1,000 and 2,500, and 9 per cent in municipalities with more than 2,500 residents.

Newfoundland and Labrador is not alone in this pattern. Across Canada, there is a clear relationship between municipal populations and acclamation rates (Table 14.1 and Figure 14.1). Municipal populations and officials per capita are both correlated with acclaimed seats rates. The recognition of this relationship has led MNL to hold forums on increasing competitiveness and spurred discussions of creating regional governments in the province, although the provincial government maintains that it will not force the creation of regional municipalities. However, a closer look at other provinces demonstrates that an increase in population size will not necessarily increase electoral competitiveness.

Table 14.1: Population and Municipal Election Statistics by Province

Province	Provincial Population (2011)	Number of Municipalities	Provincial Population per Municipality	Population per Municipal Official	Municipalities with a Pop. <1,000	Municipal Election Year	Officials Acclaimed
AB	3,645,257	354	10,297	1,896	44%	2007	38%
BC	4,400,057	191	23,037	4,331	17%	2008	8%
MB	1,208,268	137	8,819	1,222	2%	2014	34%
NB	751,171	107	7,020	600	37%	2008	25%
NL	514,536	281	1,831	293	78%	2012	46%
NS	921,727	54	17,069	2,104	11%	2012	28%
ON	12,851,821	444	28,946	4,484	18%	2006	9%
PEI	140,204	72	1,947	333	81%	2006	69%
QC	7,903,011	1,111	7,113	987	43%	2009	56%
SK	1,033,381	791	1,306	300	81%	2012	54%

Sources: Statistics Canada, "Population and Dwelling Counts, for Canada, Provinces and Territories, and Census Subdivisions (Municipalities), 2011 and 2006 Censuses" (2011), at: www.statscan.gc.ca; Intergovernmental Committee on Urban and Regional Research; other government sources.

Figure 14.1: Relationship between Population per Municipal Official and Rate of Officials Acclaimed

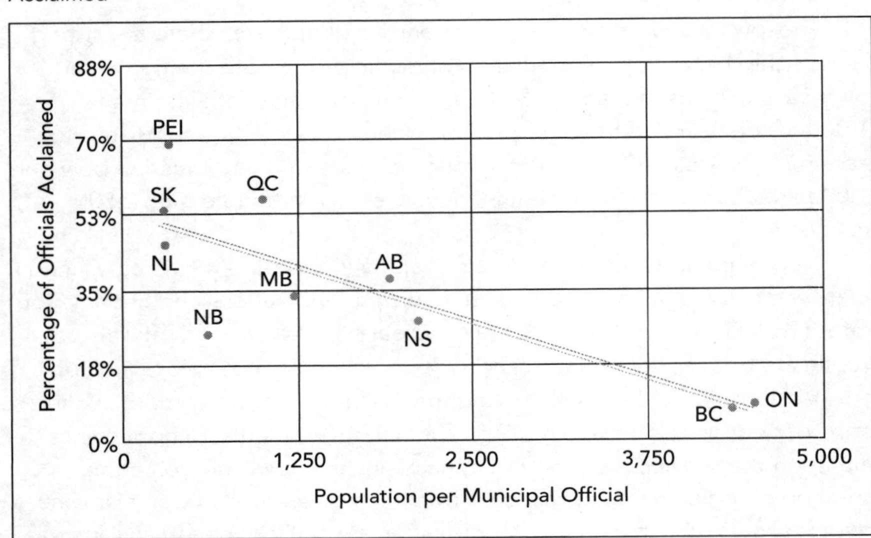

Sources: Statistics Canada, "Population and Dwelling Counts, for Canada, Provinces and Territories, and Census Subdivisions (Municipalities), 2011 and 2006 Censuses" (2011), at: www.statscan.gc.ca; Intergovernmental Committee on Urban and Regional Research; other government sources.

In 2013–14, municipalities in Manitoba were amalgamated to meet a provincially mandated minimum population requirement of 1,000 residents. The first post-amalgamation municipal elections were held in 2014, but the rate of acclamations was 34 per cent, only 6 percentage points lower than the pre-amalgamation rate of 40 per cent in 2010. A population of 1,000 residents is a major threshold for acclamation rates in Newfoundland and Labrador, but the minimum population requirement had minimal impact on Manitoba.[3]

Nova Scotia also demonstrates that larger populations do not always mean more competitive elections. The province's towns, with an average population of 3,500, have an acclamation rate of 16 per cent, compared to 44 per cent in counties, with an average population over 10,000.The low level of competitiveness in both provinces may be due to ward systems in Nova Scotia counties and some Manitoba municipalities. Wards are intended to ensure the interests of local communities are represented in a larger municipality, but they can drive down competition. Candidates may be more likely take the chance of being in the top six or eight candidates for at-large spots, rather than competing in a winner-takes-all race for a single ward seat.[4]

If Newfoundland and Labrador implements regional governments with the intention of increasing democratic legitimacy in the province, it will need to consider whether they will actually have that effect. Furthermore, the province will need to grapple with the balance of local issues and potential competitiveness. If regional governments are created, the residents of existing municipalities may feel reassured if their community is guaranteed a local representative under a ward system, rather than under an at-large system. Yet, wards may not address the acclamation problem that regional governments intend to solve.

One potential solution for balancing these competition forces is the multi-member ward system employed by 29 municipalities in Manitoba post-amalgamation. Under this system, municipalities are divided either into wards or along rural/urban lines, with two to four seats allocated to each section. This system enables greater local representation than an at-large system but produces greater competition for seats. In 2014, the municipalities using this system had an acclamation rate of 22 per cent, compared to 38 per cent in municipalities using an at-large system or assigning one seat per ward. This structure loses the finest grain of local representation but enables greater electoral competitiveness, which balances community interests and democratic health. This change would also be both enduring and cost-effective, thereby reducing the number of municipal positions in the province.

Municipalities in Newfoundland and Labrador can learn from Manitoba and Nova Scotia. Those provinces demonstrate that larger municipal populations do not necessarily mean greater electoral competitiveness. Foremost, they highlight the need to give careful consideration to what regional governments would mean for the province and, if implemented, how they would be structured. It is imperative for Newfoundland and Labrador to move towards more contested elections in order to renew municipal democracy in the province. This would create in MNL a stronger counterbalance for the provincial government and strengthen intergovernmental relations in the province. ★

About the Author

Alison Shott (Econsult Solutions, Inc.) received her Ph.D. from the University of Western Ontario after completing her MA at Acadia University and a Fulbright Fellowship at the University of Prince Edward Island. She is now an associate director at a public policy consulting firm in Philadelphia, but part of her heart will always remain in Atlantic Canada.

Notes

1. Alison Shott, "The Composition of Municipal Associations and Policy Requests to Provincial Governments: Selected Cases," *Canadian Public Administration/Administration publique du Canada* 60, 1 (2017): 111–34.
2. Government of Newfoundland and Labrador, Municipal and Intergovernmental Affairs, *Master Election Database* (St. John's: Government of Newfoundland and Labrador, 2013).
3. Manitoba Votes, "Municipal Elections" (2014), at: manitobavotes.ca.
4. Government of Nova Scotia Department of Municipal Affairs, *2008 and 2012 Election Results* (Halifax: Government of Nova Scotia, 2012).

15 Ministers and Citizens Walking Together

Elizabeth Yeoman

Take a walk on the wild side. Read about ministers and citizens walking together. #DemocraticReformNL

A few years ago I went for a very long walk. It was 30 below and the frozen landscape of Nitassinan was spectacularly beautiful. That walk changed my life. Trekking on snowshoes, pulling my belongings on a toboggan behind me, and learning from my Innu companions gave me a glimpse into another way of life. It helped me understand why they were willing to go to prison to protect their land during the 1980s protests against North Atlantic Treaty Organization (NATO) low-level flying training and what the land and the animals mean to them today. I rarely eat meat but it helped me see why hunting and fishing matter so much. Walking with someone and seeing the world through their eyes can change the way you think. If enough of us do it, it can help renew democracy in Newfoundland and Labrador.

We don't listen to each other enough. Most traditional ways of communicating in political contexts are either adversarial or "preaching to the choir." Debates, town halls, travelling road shows, and social media forums all have their place, but none of them make room for what cultural theorist Gayatri Spivak called "the mind-changing one-on-one responsible contact"[1] that can give us insight into the world of people who think differently from us. The simple act of going for a walk with someone can do that. (I use the word "walk" to mean moving around at a human pace, whether on foot or with a wheelchair or other mobility aids. Disability activist

Sunaura Taylor uses the word this way, asserting "I always tell people I'm going for a walk. I use that word."[2])

There are many famous walks in history. Mahatma Gandhi's pilgrimage to protest an unfair tax was a catalyst for the movement that led to Indian independence.[3] The civil rights movement was built by people walking together and talking to each other about things that mattered. We also have our own historic walks here in Newfoundland and Labrador. When Joey Smallwood trudged across the island to organize railway workers he talked to people and learned from them. More recently, Gemma Hickey followed the same 900-kilometre route to support victims of abuse. Though it was a run, not a walk, Terry Fox's Marathon of Hope began in St. John's, and he too met and talked to people along the way. Elizabeth Penashue's annual walk in Labrador (the one I joined) educates people about the natural world and traditional Innu values. These are dramatic examples but even an hour of really listening and seeing a person's world while walking with them can make a difference.

How would this work? First of all, it doesn't have to cost anything. Government representatives and citizens would simply commit to an hour-long walk once a week with someone from a different background, perspective, or political orientation. For example, a British research group interested in including disabled people's voices in discussions of sustainability paired people who self-identified as disabled or as sustainability practitioners. Each pair of co-researchers took two walks together with each partner choosing one of the routes. The research findings were made available to planning agencies and policy-makers.[4] The walks I'm proposing could use this format. People could be matched at random or request a partner representing a specific group or interest. Most matches would be in the participants' home region but if someone was travelling they could ask to meet someone at their destination. A little imagination suggests places to walk: along someone's daily route to work or school, at the mall, on a hiking trail, a highway, or a city street in winter. To ensure fairness of access, people requesting a walk with a minister would be selected at random in a supervised process and journalists or researchers could join some of the walks. It's a big commitment but it offers big rewards too: a chance to learn new things, to gain insight, to be truly listened to, and to get an hour of exercise at least once a week. The public act of walking would also promote sustainability and active living.

Participants would be offered strategies for listening — not as easy as it seems, but there's plenty of insight and advice available. Start by Googling "how to listen" and "active listening" for practical advice and then explore more deeply by reading research and theory about listening. We know that effective listening can be taught,[5] and its value and meaning have been examined in depth in fields ranging from philosophy to media studies.[6]

Most political interaction focuses on winning, but my proposal is about learning from each other. An American friend has always voted Republican. I have a completely different perspective. I'm not sure how she feels about the current situation in the US but I've been thinking about her a lot lately. She's a good person. Once she said to me, "I think we need to talk to each other more than we do." Let's talk. ★

About the Author

Elizabeth Yeoman (Education, Memorial University of Newfoundland) is the co-director and co-producer (with Sharon Roseman) of the documentary film, *Honk If You Want Me Off the Road*, about pedestrians' rights in winter. She recently edited a book by Innu elder and environmental activist Elizabeth Penashue and is currently working on a book about collaborative writing and translation.

Notes

1. Gayatri Chakravorty Spivak, *A Critique of Postcolonial Reason* (Cambridge, Mass.: Harvard University Press, 1999), 383.
2. This video clip of Sunaura Taylor and philosopher Judith Butler walking together is a good example of the kind of walk I'm suggesting here: https://www.youtube.com/watch?v=k0HZaPkF6qE. The clip and the quotation are from Astra Taylor, director, *The Examined Life* (documentary film, 2008), Sphinx Productions/National Film Board of Canada.
3. Dennis Dalton, "Civil Disobedience: The Salt Satyagraha," *Mahatma Gandhi: Nonviolent Power in Action* (New York: Columbia University Press, 2012), 91–138.
4. Walking Interconnections, "Walk in Someone Else's Shoes," *Walking Interconnections: Researching the Lived Experience of Disabled People for a Sustainable Society* (2016), at: http://walkinginterconnections.com (accessed 10 Nov. 2016).
5. David McNaughton, Dawn Hamlin, John McCarthy, Darlene Head-Reeves, and Mary Schreiner, "Learning to Listen: Teaching an Active Listening Strategy to Preservice Education Professionals," *Topics in Early Childhood Special Education* 27, 4 (2008): 223–31.
6. David Beard, "A Broader Understanding of the Ethics of Listening: Philosophy, Cultural Studies, Media Studies and the Ethical Listening Subject," *International Journal of Listening* 23, 1 (2009): 7–20.

PART 3: CAPTAIN NEWFOUNDLAND & LABRADOR

For Victory, 1918 postcard. A postcard from the Oilette Connoisseur series "Victory & freedom." Image shows a Newfoundland infantryman in field dress standing in front of an unfurled Red Ensign containing the Great Seal of Newfoundland. (Source: Provincial Archives)

Newfoundland and Labrador has a history of being governed by charismatic premiers whose force of personality dominates all facets of the province's politics. This section demands we examine our knee-jerk idolatry of charisma and broaden our thinking to encapsulate a variety of forms of leadership. Youth, everyday citizens, senior public servants, and ministers are just some of the many people who are part of the democratic process, sometimes working behind the scenes.

Contributors explore different forms of leadership. What would public policy and laws look like if kids were in charge? What can we learn from leaders of the distant past? How has the patriarchal and aggression-driven narrative of the comic book "action hero" infiltrated our notions of powerful leadership? In contrast, what does artful leadership look like? Are political parties appropriate institutions for recruiting leaders? Should interim leaders be allowed to seek the position on a permanent basis? Who briefs the ministers? Contributors Paula Graham, Marica Cassis, Joel Deshaye, Ian Sutherland, Des Sullivan, Kelly Blidook, and Robert Thompson look at these issues in turn.

16 What If Kids Ran the Government?

Paula Graham

What if kids ran the government? What would kids cut to balance the budget? #cdnpoli #DemocraticReformNL

What if kids were city planners?
What would the speed limit be?
And would we grow gardens, not lawns?

What if a toddler was the Premier?
What colour would their campaign signs be?
And how much would they pay themselves?

Would they allow other Members of the House to be breastfed while in session?

What if children ran the Ministry of Finance?
What would they cut to balance the budget?
And would they hire a male secretary?

Would kids measure GDP, or would they survey love?

If your child was in charge today, would they change the voting age?
And would your kid be in favour of progressive taxation?

If babies held a public budget consultation, would it be on a bus route?
Would it be wheelchair accessible, and would all the facilitators be white?

What if an infant was Minister of the Environment?
Would they mind getting dirty?
Would they sell off land that wasn't theirs?
Would they read astrology and gaze at a full moon?

How many jobs would babies think justified spoiling an ecosystem?

What if kids ran the Ministry of Health?
What would they say to the grownups with no health insurance?
And if grownups got sick from pollution, how much compensation would kids think is fair?

What if your baby was a provincial court judge?
What formula would they use to calculate jail terms, and would reputation be one of the variables?

If children were treated as credible witnesses, would they report domestic violence?

Would kids put sick people in jail?
Would they befriend refugees, or would they be suspicious of immigrants?

What if toddlers told grown-ups "there's nothing we can do, it's the economy"?
And what if the grown-ups grew down thinking that this is the way things *have* to be?

If children ran the government, would they put their offices high on a hill?
And would they build doors big enough for the grown-ups to fit through? ★

About the Author

Paula Graham (Sociology, Memorial University of Newfoundland) is an activist, artist, and Ph.D. candidate in Sociology at MUN. Paula uses independent media writing, direct action, and artistic interventions to denounce capitalism, disrupt the patriarchal order, and support environmental sustainability. Paula grew up in Ottawa, Ontario, and now lives in Nova Scotia.

17 What a Byzantine Historian Can Contribute to a Discussion on Newfoundland and Labrador Governance

Marica Cassis

We're ancient history: @MaricaCassisexplains what the NL government can learn from the Byzantines. #NLpoli #DemocraticReformNL

In the sixth century AD, Procopius, historian of the Byzantine court, wrote a wickedly funny satire about the Emperor Justinian (AD 527–565). The *Anecdota*, more commonly known today as *The Secret History*, provides a scathing condemnation of an emperor he saw as corrupt, controlling, and ignorant. It also provides a fascinating look at the medieval civilization that followed the Roman Empire.[1] Although he had written other lengthy histories for Justinian, Procopius handily undoes all of his own "official" history with the *Anecdota*, saying:

> And yet in the end I was moved to write the history of these deeds by the following consideration, namely that it would also be made perfectly clear to future tyrants that punishment was almost certainly going to befall them on account of their wickedness, just as it did in my narrative. In addition, their deeds and characters would be publicized in writing for all time, which might give some pause to their illegalities.[2]

The text provides a cautionary tale for future leaders, an account of corruption, and an example of the damage possible at the hands of a smart person with a pen and a critical mind.[3]

Did Justinian deserve his bad press? Until the *Anecdota* surfaced in the seventeenth century, he seemed like a leader who encountered some bad luck.[4] The first half of Justinian's rule was characterized by an attempt to apply order to the crumbling Roman world — he wanted to reconquer Europe and he wanted to establish order in the heresy-plagued Christian church. He went so far as to send prefabricated "flat-pack" churches that were easy to erect to try to get uniformity in religion in different places.[5] He spoke under the authority of *romanitas*, an ancient parallel to nationalism, and he came to the throne when the coffers were full.

By the middle of his rule, however, the empire was plagued by earthquakes, plagues, environmental disasters, invasions, and migrations. The theologically-minded blamed these events on God, believing Him to be angry at the population or at Justinian himself. Justinian responded with violence and bigotry, particularly against anyone who did not believe in his form of Christianity or did not buy into his narrative of the reconquered Roman Empire.[6] By the time he died, Justinian left an empire in disrepair, overextended financially and militarily, wracked with religious division.

So what changed? When times were good at the beginning of his rule, the narrative of pseudo-nationalism and religious unity worked with people. However, little thought went into his actions, and Justinian was saved many times by his wife, Theodora, who was a mistress of the critically thought-out response. When she died, Justinian was left without his best weapon — and he was unable to respond to the problems in his empire in any kind of creative way. The old patterns continued to repeat themselves because *he allowed them to.* Procopius's account, although based in classical images of tyranny, was really a stunning exposé of Justinian's ignorance.

Such concern for good governance is a constant theme in ancient literature. In Mesopotamia, the Epic of Gilgamesh focuses on the redemption of a terrible king who learns that immortality only comes through decent leadership. Rulers in Middle Kingdom Egypt, a bleak world, worried over moral leadership, expressed most clearly in the *Instructions to King Merikare.*[7] And classical Greece, as Thucydides tells us, struggled through oligarchy and tyranny before it rested on democracy. Every society struggled with how to make governance fair and inclusive (even when their norms of inclusive did not include whole groups of people like, say, women. I'm looking at you, ancient Greeks!). If history teaches us one thing, it is that everything we face in the modern world has been seen before: environmental crisis, political instability, migration, refugees, economic collapse. Societies that survived did so through an aptitude for adaptation and resilience.

So, where am I going with this? Good governance begins with an investment in education, one that teaches students at all levels to think critically about the past, present, and future. In these times of cutbacks and fiscal control, education is a soft target, particularly in relation to the arts and humanities. We'll put more kids in the class, we'll cut libraries, we won't worry about innovative curriculum reform, and we won't worry about giving teachers the resources and the autonomy they need to teach people to become critical members of society. But it is precisely in these difficult times that these things are most needed. As the world becomes more interconnected, and as our environmental, political, and economic problems get worse, we need students who can think beyond localized, nationalistic information; rather, we need students who have been taught to apply critical thought to any problem and who understand past mistakes. We also need to train students to be critical of their leaders — and leaders who can take that criticism. After all, Procopius brought down the memory of an emperor with a pen and an education. Let's give our students that same ability. We'll all be better for it. ★

About the Author

Marica Cassis (History, Memorial University of Newfoundland) is a Byzantine historian and archaeologist. She is the director of the medieval field project at Cadır Höyük, a large multi-period archaeological project in Turkey. She teaches late antique and medieval Middle Eastern history.

Notes

1. Peter Sarris, *Byzantium: A Very Short Introduction* (Oxford: Oxford University Press, 2015).
2. Anthony Kaldellis, ed. and trans., *Prokopios, The Secret History* (Indianapolis: Hackett Publishing, 2010), 4.
3. Anthony Kaldellis, *Procopius of Caesarea: Tyranny, History, and Philosophy at the End of Antiquity* (Philadelphia: University of Pennsylvania Press, 2004).
4. Anthony, ed. and trans., *Prokopios, The Secret History*, viii–x.
5. Nick Clark, "Byzantine 'Flat-pack' Church to Be Reconstructed in Oxford after Spending 1,000 years on the Seabed," *The Independent*, 12 Nov. 2015, at: http://www.independent.co.uk/arts-entertainment/art/news/byzantine-flat-pack-church-to-be-reconstructed-in-oxford-after-spending-1000-years-on-the-seabed-a6732376.html.
6. J.A.S. Evans, *The Age of Justinian: The Circumstances of Imperial Power* (London: Routledge, 1996).

7. Miriam Lichtheim and Antonio Loprieno, *Ancient Egyptian Literature. Volume I, The Old and Middle Kingdoms* (Berkeley: University of California Press, 2006), 97–109.

18 The Hero's Energy in Newfoundland and Labrador

Joel Deshaye

Enough Comic Book Charisma and Superheroes! Time for new metaphors in NL leadership. #NLpoli #DemocraticReformNL

To change our politics of energy, we have to change the attitudes involved in creating energy. Instead of thinking "heroic," can we think "humble"?

Politics in Newfoundland and Labrador, like politics almost anywhere in North America and Europe, suffers from a hero complex. In literature, a hero is often a male soldier who fights against all odds to win a major battle or contest. He is the model Olympian and a distant relative of all politicians. Although he might win fame and glory, he seeks primarily to stabilize his corner of the world and is therefore a political figure.[1]

In politics, the leaders who are sometimes described as heroes evidently imagine governance and even democracy as a battle or contest. Listen for martial metaphors in politics — attack ads, war rooms, strategic planning — and you will hear them everywhere, sometimes as a sports/war metaphor that encourages fans to be receptive to war as a game and to male domination.[2] They appear, too, in business and can be "barriers to effective organizational change"[3] when change might help more women to reach executive positions not only in corporations but also in organizations and governments. These metaphors are one example of evidence of a heroic mindset that is only rarely progressive.[4]

In history and in myth, heroes were actual warriors such as Beowulf and Leonidas, and in the United States and other countries the highest leader often gains respect for having served in the army, navy, or other forces. As myths evolved, and as the scope of political and military power increased, heroes became superheroes: Superman, Iron Man, Batman, Spider-Man, and so many more. These four, some of the most prominent in contemporary comics and movies, almost always battle their enemies physically and with great power. Their enemies often become threatening when they find the source of that power and either steal or compromise it.

Energy is often the heart of the matter, and how we use it offers insight into our democracy. Iron Man's "heart" is his power supply. Superman's energy is solar. Batman's is money, a sign of (energy) consumption. Spider-Man's is radioactive (i.e., nuclear) in the classic comics and genetic in the movies. In Newfoundland and Labrador, hydroelectricity and oil are central in narratives of boom and bust. Joey Smallwood's Churchill Falls hydroelectric project and Brian Peckford's focus on development through natural resources have both been described in the media and in political circles as heroic. Peckford might be described as the "selfless superhero" fighting against the legacy of Smallwood the "devil,"[5] but in fact they can both be interpreted as "superheroes" or "supervillains," depending on your point of view. We might add Danny Williams and his "fight" for offshore oil,[6] and Kathy Dunderdale of Muskrat Falls. They are all public figures whose major focus on energy has been a power play to create economic stability (that hallmark of heroism) through economic growth.

In focusing every generation or so on a single new source of energy, however, these leaders and the mass media have fostered a with-us-or-against-us relationship between other politicians and the public. Megaprojects overshadow smaller projects and their contributions to the economy. And the polarizing of opinion that comes with megaprojects involves suspicion. A key difference between classic heroes and modern superheroes is that, today, superheroes usually have a secret identity or a mask. If the public senses that politicians want to be heroes (e.g., through a legacy project), they expect them to wear masks. They expect deceit. When public confidence in politicians is low, legitimate government is difficult to maintain.

Co-operation between heroes is not the answer because, according to the narratives of the Avengers and the Justice League, teaming up only widens the scope of the damage. In these recent superhero movies, the public momentarily turns against the superheroes partly because of the damage they cause in defeating their enemies. The "team" is just a sign of escalation in the war.

The metaphors related to heroism could be replaced with non-heroic metaphors of interdependence. Dispersed and local but connected power generation could be not only more reliable but also more innovative and greener. Our province has wind and waves that could contribute more significantly to our network of energies. Diversity can help to ease the historical reliance on a few sources of energy and revenue (e.g., hydro or oil and cod).

Questioning the hero as a figure (that is, as a public figure *and* as a product of figurative language) and seeking non-heroic leaders might help, too. Coalition governments based on non-partisan co-operation might be an outcome. Another result might be more women in city councils and legislatures. More people — not only women — who do not usually think of themselves as potential leaders might participate if the ideal were humbler, less heroic. When politicians are superheroes, people sometimes learn helplessness, and the almost inevitable electoral failure of any politician can lead to apathy rather than engagement. ★

About the Author

Joel Deshaye (English, Memorial University of Newfoundland) has published on superheroes and on metaphor, which come together in this contribution through war metaphors and notions of heroism in politics. One of his most recent publications is "Tom King's John Wayne: The Western in *Green Grass, Running Water*" in the journal *Canadian Literature*. He is the author of *The Metaphor of Celebrity: Canadian Poetry and the Public, 1955–1980* (University of Toronto Press, 2013).

Notes

1. Brian Murdoch, *The Germanic Hero: Politics and Pragmatism in Early Medieval Poetry.* (London: Hambledon, 1996), 4–5.
2. Sue Curry Jansen and Don Sabo, "The Sport/War Metaphor: Hegemonic Masculinity, the Persian Gulf War, and the New World Order," *Sociology of Sport Journal* 11, 1/2 (1994): 14.
3. José Luis Felício dos Santos de Carvalho and Sergio Proença Leitão, "Violence and Change in Organizations: A Critique of the Business-as-War Metaphor," *Revista de Administração Pública* 35, 2 (2001): 39.
4. Frank J. Williams, *Lincoln as Hero* (Carbondale: Southern Illinois University Press, 2012), 81.
5. James Overton, "Progressive Conservatism? A Critical Look at Politics, Culture and Development in Newfoundland," *Ethnicity in Atlantic Canada* 5 (1985): 86, 87.

6. Philip Demont, "Williams' Hebron Victory: A Long Time Coming," CBC News, 20 Aug. 2008, at: http://www.cbc.ca/news/business/williams-hebron-victory-a-long-time-coming-1.759516.

19 Artful Leadership

Ian Sutherland

Let's think about new approaches to political leadership. #DemocraticReformNL

Leadership, inherent in democracies, politics, and governance, needs development. Yet, it has become a buzzword, a hopeful panacea for problems faced, conceptualized as a thing that exists a priori. How often do we hear the call for more leadership? These calls are typically devoid of reflection on what we mean by leadership and our desires for it. In fact, it would seem there are as many beliefs and theories about leadership as there are people who have created them. A cursory reflection on many of them uncovers a subtext of self-interest and ambition, rather than service to society. To be clear, I am not calling for more leaders. I am calling for developing leadership and doing so differently — artistically.

Unfortunately, "leadership development" has become as much buzz and noise as "leadership." As you read this, billions of dollars are churning through its industry. These labours, and their fruits, are not without critics,[1] myself included.[2] Yet, we critics are quick to add that we really do need leadership development. It just needs to be done differently, to develop leadership as a practice.

Plato would agree, or so I like to think. As any reader of *The Republic* knows, he imagined one ideal state — Kallipolis.[3] This state was to be governed and led by philosopher queens or kings to whom alone, "when perfected by years and education," the state would be entrusted. While the idea of toga-sporting wisdom lovers sitting in government is not what

I am advocating (there are many problems with Plato's conceptualizing, particularly rampant inequality), what strikes me most is Plato's focus on development. His ideal governors needed to be developed a lot. He knew they would not appear fully formed from wombs or elections.

Would Plato be satisfied with today's landscape? A brief glance at contemporary headlines and political speak suggests a different base assumption:

[X] is "running for leadership"
[X] is a "candidate for leader"
[X] "has won the leadership race"

In contrast to the imaginary citizens of Kallipolis, we believe leadership is a prize to be chased or a race to be won — not something to be developed.

This is wrong. Leadership is a practice. Through practice, it develops. It's akin to how artists and musicians develop. It takes a lifetime of practice and development. If we want healthier democracies, politics, and governance, we must develop leadership. It's not a prize. It's a practice.

Let me follow this artistic motif I've introduced. Leadership development, despite big promises, has not delivered much (at least according to many). We need to do it differently. Critics decry an amorality, or a self-aggrandizing tendency, in leadership development. We have come to conceptualize leadership as an end goal rather than a means. This creates insular leadership and ultimately leadership that exists to serve its own goals.

Yet, great leadership is not insular. It serves the needs of the many — the citizens. It is a lived phenomenon in the world, occurring in social interaction, in tune with the complexities and contradictions that characterize the nature of human experience. It is steeped in creative approaches and innovative solutions, much like great music and art.

In fact, if we can accept the need to focus on leadership as something to be developed rather than attained, the arts provide fertile ground for new understandings. How do artists develop? They develop through practice, through mentorship, and through constructive critique. These are all mobilized through self-reflection and a yearning to do better.

Let me offer a story that weaves these strains together. A few years ago I worked with Sarah, CEO of a large financial services firm, in a leadership development workshop involving a choir. Though not a musician, Sarah volunteered to try conducting the choir. Nervously, she stood before the organization, made some apologetic remarks about not being musical, then closed her eyes. She breathed, opened her eyes, and began to wave her arms. Slowly the choir sang. Awkward at first, but a connection developed. The music happened. Then, tears began rolling down Sarah's face. After she finished, I invited Sarah to reflect on this experience.

Her response was telling. She described a life in leadership, but only realizing then what leadership could really be: "It's not about me, it's not even about them, it's about what we are trying to do together." Over several months I helped Sarah bring critical reflection to her leadership practice. Gradually things changed. Much like my assertions above, Sarah had viewed leadership as something to be won or gained; the ultimate goal was to be a leader. It took an artistic, musical experience for her to realize that leadership is practice. It's not a thing. It is a means, not an end.

More than this, her experience through music cultivated a yearning to do better. She worked on listening, connectivity, empathy, and creativity. As she developed new understandings of leading, she began mentoring others. Over time I saw her organization become more democratic, more empowering, and more engaged.

That did not happen because there was a focus on leadership. It did not happen through calls for more leadership. It happened through a commitment to developing leadership differently and artistically.

If we want healthier democracies, politics, and governance, let us focus not on leadership. Let us focus on its practice and develop artful leadership. ★

About the Author

Ian Sutherland (Music, Memorial University of Newfoundland) is a leading international expert within the arts, business, and leadership nexus. He has published widely on the topics of leadership development and leadership practice as well as organizational creativity and innovation. In particular, articles appear in *Academy of Management Learning & Education* (Outstanding Article of the Year 2016), *Management Learning*, and *Academy of Management Review*. As a speaker, facilitator, and consultant he has worked in more than 40 countries.

Notes

1. L. Crevani, M. Lindgren, and J. Packendorff, "Leadership, Not Leaders: On the Study of Leadership as Practices and Interactions," *Scandinavian Journal of Management* 26, 1 (2010): 77–86; B. Carroll, L. Levy, and D. Richmond, "Leadership in Practice: Challenging the Competency Paradigm," *Leadership* 4, 4 (2008): 363–79; E. Guthey, T. Clark, and B. Jackson, *Demystifying Business Celebrity* (London: Routledge, 2009).

2. I. Sutherland, "Arts-based Methods in Leadership Development: Affording Aesthetic Workspaces, Reflexivity and Memories with Momentum," *Management Learning* 44, 1 (2013): 25–43; I. Sutherland, J. Gosling, and J. Jelinek, "Aesthetics of Power: Why Teaching about Power Is Easier Than Learning for Power, and What Business Schools Could Do about It," *Academy of Management Learning & Education* 14, 4 (2015): 607–24.
3. Allan Bloom, *The Republic of Plato* (New York: Basic Books, 1968).

20 Political Parties as an Essential Link to Better Governance Process

Des Sullivan

#NLpoli political parties must reform candidate selection processes, says @DesSullivan. #DemocraticReformNL

The strengthening of governance systems is a frequent preoccupation of democratic politics, including in this province. One approach is to enhance the role of elected members. On the surface this seems a sensible option, except that our elected politicians as a group, governing or in opposition, are already under-qualified. The problem needs remedy. This article proposes a modified district nomination system, one more broadly focused on securing the right mix of Members of the House of Assembly (MHAs) and skill sets.

Governing parties are frequently challenged by MHAs' inability to assess public policies and to engage in governance and oversight roles. A "more sophisticated and professional approach"[1] will both screen candidates and advance gender balance — a goal of modern society that is substantially unfulfilled. There is ample evidence to justify such a reform.

In this province, an incomplete and impermanent governance system has evolved in both the legislative and executive branches. During the Joey Smallwood era no institutional framework grew to permit detailed legislative review by dedicated parliamentarians. Similarly, economic, resource, and social programs underwent no structured involvement at the executive level until they reached the cabinet table.

Following the Smallwood years, and possibly as a reaction to that time, all-member committees appeared in both branches in the early 1970s. In the legislature, the system was functionally weak and remains that way. Within the executive branch, policy and planning committees became a distinct and important source of review and analysis by ministers. It also enabled a collective style of leadership — likely because it had the backing of successive premiers of different political stripes, a formalized structure, and strong bureaucratic support. By the early 2000s even this governance mechanism began to fray. What seemed an essential model, albeit with tenuous roots, proved not to be embedded at all. The reasons for this breakdown are clearer than any precise remedy. One is that collective leadership threatens to diminish the power of the premier. Then, too, ours is a society that favours strong and charismatic leadership. A collective style of government is not a demand of democratic outcomes. Parliamentarians are not valued as policy wonks or as legislators. Proof is the limited use of the legislature except to vote supply and to amend statutes. More pervasive is the view that they are procurers of a share of the fiscal "pie."

In contrast to this assessment, politicians should be viewed as people possessing good judgment, capable of evaluating public needs and mediating policy conflicts. When public policy is thought to be the creation only of the premier or of bureaucrats, essential connections to an important skill set and to benchmarks of performance are lost.

Lopsided election victories also affect critical mass and diminish the effectiveness of legislative committees. The reduction in the number of electoral districts from 52 to 40 since 1975 threatens to exacerbate this problem. One might suggest grossly uneven electoral results make more talent available to the executive branch. A numerical advantage alone offers no such assurance.

All societies want to be governed better. Yet it seems foolish that we should expect, from a relatively small legislature, the diversity of talent and intellectual heft afforded by a large one — unless we have a better plan. The portal to the House of Assembly is through the political party system. Parties consistently promise to supply politicians who inspire good government and good governance processes. But it is an empty gesture, notwithstanding an earnest commitment to serve, if their ideas remain concepts and parties fail to match political exigencies with essential human resources and political leadership.

The idea of a pre-selection process assumes that political parties will establish criteria for what constitutes "qualification" and that they will form resourced and ethical committees to conduct the screening process. Active recruitment should be followed by candidate interviews and possibly other means of assessment. Screening implies some potential candidates will be disallowed. The most optimistic outcome is that the enlarged process will result in both gender and skills balance across each party's slate. One might reasonably expect a well-balanced slate to serve as a counterweight to authoritarian leadership.

This proposal is not a substitute as much as it is an enhancement to the current party nomination system — one that some believe favours not the best, but the best-funded candidates and those advantaged by name recognition. Its success can be judged by how well the goals of skill and gender balance are met.

Naturally, any pre-selection system will incite worries over favouritism and elitism. Indeed, large democracies, like those of Great Britain[2] and Australia[3], which have used pre-selection systems for decades, are encouraging their parties to adopt more inclusive practices. Still, pre-selection remains an integral part of their political systems.

Jurisdictions with relatively small populations, like ours, need to innovate. The status quo is not working. It is costing us more than we realize. Governance systems have implications both fiscally and for our quality of life. Parties don't need to mirror each other's pre-selection practices. But they do need to understand that their raison d'être is inseparable from the institutions they serve. ★

About the Author

Des Sullivan (Sullivan Capital Corporation) is a businessman living in St. John's. He was executive assistant to Premier Frank D. Moores from 1975 to 1979 and to Premier Brian Peckford from 1979 to 1985. Des writes a blog called Uncle Gnarley (unclegnarley.blogspot.ca) that promises "opinions on Newfoundland politics that bite."

Notes

1. Margaret Reynolds, "Women, Pre-selection, and Merit: Who Decides?" Parliament of Australia, Papers on Parliament No. 27, Mar. 1996, at: http://www.aph.gov.au/About_Parliament/Senate/Research_and_Education/pops/~/link.aspx?_id=DB87E15C703242179906EACC1253891C&_z=z.
2. Susan Scarrow, "Candidate Selection for the 2015 Election: A Comparative Perspective," 11 Jan. 2015, at: http://britishpoliticsgroup.blogspot.ca/2015/01/candidate-selection-for-2015-election.html; Rhys Williams and Akash Paum, "Party People: How Do — and How Should — British Political Parties Select Their Parliamentary Candidates?" Institute for Government (2011), at: http://www.instituteforgovernment.org.uk/sites/default/files/

publications/Party%20People.pdf.

3. Library Council of New South Wales, "Information about the Law in New South Wales" (2016), at: http://www.legalanswers.sl.nsw.gov.au/guides/hot_topics/voting_and_elections/who_can_stand/choosing_candidates.html.

21 Levelling the Field for Potential Party Leaders

Kelly Blidook

Here's Your Hat, What's Your Hurry: Interim Leaders Can't Stay On by @kblidook #DemocraticReformNL

Interim leaders of political parties play an important and unique role in the democratic process. They are typically highly respected members of their caucuses who fill a significant though temporary role during transition periods. In some cases, they also fill the role of premier or leader of the official opposition. Nevertheless, despite the fact that interim leaders often have excellent leadership skills and might be desirable as permanent leaders (an observation made in recent years about both Bob Rae and Rona Ambrose in their respective federal parties), some parties in Canada disallow someone who holds the interim position to run in the subsequent leadership election, while other parties follow this standard as an unwritten rule. A formal rule of this nature would be appropriate in Newfoundland and Labrador.

There are common violations of this standard in cases where a rule is absent. In 2014, for example, Manitoba Premier Greg Selinger requested a leadership convention following a large exodus of ministers from his cabinet. He nevertheless maintained his position as premier and interim leader of his New Democratic Party. A *Globe and Mail* editorial called on Selinger to allow a neutral leader to replace him while he competed for the job, which Selinger did not do.[1] He subsequently won the vote to remain leader in 2015.

There are important reasons why a rule of limiting interim leaders to the interim alone should be standardized and followed by political parties in Newfoundland and Labrador. This province has seen its two most recent elected premiers secure the leadership of their respective political parties in a similar manner to that of Selinger, though neither is an exact parallel. In the first case (Progressive Conservative Kathy Dunderdale), the interim leadership was secured alongside a pledge to not seek the permanent leadership. The pledge was not maintained.[2] In the latter case (Liberal Dwight Ball), the interim leadership was held for 18 months alongside a pledge to seek the permanent leadership, with the position being relinquished three months before the leadership vote.

Such cases present a problem because interim leaders are bestowed with all the formal powers of the party leader. In a case where the leader is also premier — an extremely powerful position[3] — this means that policies and spending priorities can be fashioned after her/his preferences. Further, the interim leader chooses other positions of leadership within the legislative caucus, such as ministers and parliamentary secretaries for government, or critics for opposition. The interim leader can determine which members will be given opportunities to ask questions during Question Period, who will have the opportunity to move a given motion in the House, and who will fill specific committee appointments. Any of these decisions can be used to buy support or reward supporters. They can also be used to punish or diminish would-be challengers.

Whether by using the power of the position, or simply by the ability to exercise it, interim leaders are given a significant advantage over potential competitors. As some degree of loyalty is necessary for the caucus to function in the legislature and to present a united party, other caucus members are less likely to enter the race and potentially be seen to be undermining the party's current leader. Indeed, those who have benefited under the leader will often prefer maintaining that leader and may provide support. The interim leader becomes the public face of the party, gaining additional media exposure and opportunities to present her/himself in capacities not afforded to any other competitors. In a case where the interim leader is also the premier, a potential competitor from inside the caucus risks upsetting the status quo among the most powerful actors in the government, and perhaps giving up a cabinet position to do so.

Ideally, political parties would see the potential danger that lurks in allowing interim leaders to use their office to benefit themselves for the longer term, and they would make the necessary changes to their constitutions to avoid this (the wording used in the Conservative Party of

Canada's constitution, section 10.9.1, is a good example).[4] An alternative to be considered by the elected legislative members, and which would serve both their collective interests and those who elect them, would be to include language in Newfoundland and Labrador's Elections Act, or House of Assembly Act, imposing the same measure. As these statutes refer to — but do not regulate — party leadership, an added section would need to stipulate that holding the position of interim leader disqualifies one from the subsequent leadership contest for that party.

If our democratic goal is to ensure that all qualified persons can compete for any office without any one person holding an undue advantage, then implementation of regulations forbidding interim leaders from seeking permanent leadership must be part of achieving that goal. ★

About the Author

Kelly Blidook (Political Science, Memorial University of Newfoundland) primarily researches Canadian Parliament. He is author of *Constituency Influence in Parliament: Countering the Centre* (University of British Columbia Press, 2012) and co-author of *Canadian Politics: Critical Approaches* (Nelson, 2016). His next co-authored book, *Representation in Action*, will come out in 2018.

Notes

1. "Play Levelly, Mr. Selinger," *Globe and Mail*, 14 Nov. 2014, A16.
2. James McLeod, *Turmoil as Usual* (St. John's: Creative Publishers, 2016).
3. Graham White, *Cabinets and First Ministers* (Vancouver: University of British Columbia Press, 2005).
4. Conservative Party of Canada Constitution, 2013, at: http://www.conservative.ca/media/documents/constitution-en.pdf.

22 The Role of Public Service Executives

Robert Thompson

Public service executives play an essential role in translating the government's mandate into action. Read more. @IPAC #cdnpoli #DemocraticReformNL

Scenario: A Member of the House of Assembly has just been appointed as a cabinet minister. The Clerk of the Executive Council, who is head of the public service and Secretary to Cabinet, visits the Minister to provide a briefing.

Clerk: Good morning, Minister. Congratulations on your appointment. I trust you are settling in and you've met your deputy minister.

Minister: Yes, but this world of governing is new to me. I know how caucus works, and the House of Assembly, but the inner workings of government are somewhat mysterious.

Clerk: Well, that is why I am visiting you. I meet with each minister after their appointment to cabinet to explain the procedures around cabinet decision-making and the expectations we have for senior public servants, who are the executive team of your department.

Minister: Excellent! Take me through it.

Clerk: There are two essential ministerial roles. You are accountable to the House of Assembly for the activities of your department, and you are the sponsor of proposals to the cabinet from your department. In both roles the deputy minister and senior staff will provide support. They will aid you in pursuing the mandate provided by the premier, and they will help you manage your democratic responsibilities.

Minister: The deputy minister and other senior staff seem quite capable, but they were appointed under previous governments. Can I trust them?

Clerk: Minister, our system of government includes the expectation that all public servants are appointed on merit and serve in a non-partisan manner. Most have served governments of both political stripes. Their promotion to senior levels is based on demonstrated ability to deliver the mandate of the elected government of the day.

Minister: But we have a "change" agenda. How can they switch perspective so quickly?

Clerk: Their performance is judged on turning the government's mandate into reality. They will provide you with advice, including alternatives on how to implement your mandate. Their advice will bring out both the challenges and the opportunities with each alternative. The results are always better if you work as a team.

Minister: Is my whole senior team made up of career public servants? Is that a wise thing?

Clerk: While it is true that most public service executives are promoted from within government, we do hire from other sectors as well. Some are subject experts and some have private-sector management experience. All appointments are ultimately made by the premier. The key is that your departmental senior team can quickly establish your trust and use their experience and networks to start implementing the government's agenda

Minister: How do I get my proposals turned into cabinet decisions?

Clerk: Cabinet decisions start with a ministerial memorandum to cabinet. This memorandum is prepared by your senior staff under your direction, with a prescribed standard for the analysis and recommendations. Once submitted it is analyzed by the Cabinet Secretariat staff and placed on a cabinet committee agenda where you will discuss it with your colleagues.

Then it proceeds to full cabinet where the premier will ask you to defend your recommendations. Your executive team can help you to be well prepared to argue your case. Some members of your team have also served in other departments and central agencies, so they can help you manoeuvre through the system.

Minister: What about the House of Assembly?

Clerk: You represent the government in the House when it is sitting, and you will have the support of your deputy minister and staff. This includes Question Period and the sponsorship of legislation. Your senior staff will brief you about departmental activities that could arise during Question Period, and they will prepare notes on legislation to help you defend the provisions of a bill.

Minister: For Question Period, can they advise me on political questions?

Clerk: There is a dividing line that is sometimes hard to define, but you and your DM will find that line without a problem. Essentially it is your political responsibility to assess how to respond to partisan questions. But to the extent that such responses include information about departmental activities, your public service staff will provide briefings as required.

Minister: Why aren't all these things written down somewhere? You would expect clear rules about senior public servants that we'd all know before being appointed to cabinet.

Clerk: Good observation. Some parts of government operate by norms rather than rules. I wish everyone had a better appreciation of non-partisan public service executives. This institution facilitates democratic government. It's a bedrock of stability and continuity when governments change. Senior bureaucrats are duty-bound to implement the agenda of the new government. Sometimes there are initial doubts about loyalty and trust, but the ministers usually value the experience of the executive team and appreciate the headaches avoided through good advice. The role of the senior public servants at the juncture of the political world and the public service world is critical, and the norms under which they operate should be protected and reinforced. Too often they work in the shadows. A better understanding of these norms will make for a better democratic system. ★

About the Author

Robert Thompson (Newfoundland and Labrador Medical Association) is currently the executive director of the NLMA, the voice of organized medicine in Newfoundland and Labrador. He spent 31 years as a public servant in the Government of Newfoundland and Labrador, including seven years as Clerk of the Executive Council and Secretary to Cabinet, as well as serving as deputy minister in three departments.

PART 4: COMMUNICATION

Printing the Aglait Illumatik, Labrador newspaper, circa 1910. Interior view of Moravian print shop. Man (left) setting type; man (right) working portable printing press. The printing press was brought to Nain, Labrador, in 1900 by the Moravians. (Source: Provincial Archives)

Vibrant news media are essential to the delivery of democracy. Fast and radical changes in the modes of news dissemination are occurring as regional media markets shrink and local organs struggle to provide cogent arguments. At the same time as investigative journalism disappears — along with the downsizing of smaller media outlets that make local stories available — grassroots organizations, politicians, and individuals have turned to the immediacy, ubiquity, and heat of social media networks to make viral the concerns of communities and people who might otherwise be denied an opportunity to voice political concerns as they arise.

Contributors in this section discuss the ways in which the mechanisms of communication are susceptible to cracks, flaws, and manufactured "noise" between the government and its constituency. Ramona Dearing starts off by lamenting the "planted" partisan caller on radio call-in shows devoted to political discussion. Erwin Warkentin sounds the alarm on the demise of local media outlets. A summary of the little-known history of the press gallery in the House of Assembly is presented by Michael Connors. This gives way to Sonja Boon's discussion about the dumbing down inherent in the echo chambers of Facebook and Twitter, as well as the risks of becoming prey to anonymous trolls in the often shallow and hostile arena of social media. Opportunities to put digital communications technology to good use by government are suggested by Peter Trnka. Finally, Scott Matthews argues that a society whose interpretation of information conveyed by the media needs to be grounded in a solid understanding of public opinion surveys. Collectively, these authors explore how various modes of communication can be fine-tuned to ensure the appropriate dissemination of information and to facilitate the opportunity for debate among a diversity of voices.

23 Hogging Call-In Show Lines

Ramona Dearing

What, politicos manipulate call-in show phone lines?? @RamonaDearing of @CBCNL calls 'em out. #NLpoli #DemocraticReformNL

Dear politicians:

Please stop manipulating the phone lines by filling them with your supporters on call-in radio shows. We all know that it happens. For instance, you'll find evidence in Steven Bartlett's 2013 article in *The Telegram* called "Message Managers." The subtitle does a nice job of summing it up: "Leaked exchanges prove government pads web polls, phone-in shows." Memorial University professors have also commented on the practice and analyzed related tactics.[1]

Let me share what I've experienced as a call-in show host on the CBC. Say we're in the middle of a provincial election campaign. The show invites each leader of each party to come on, separately, on different dates, to answer questions from across the province. We want to give our audience an opportunity to get to know the leaders and become familiar with their policies. In fact, we feel it's our obligation as a public broadcaster.

Invariably we do indeed get calls from lots of places across Newfoundland and Labrador. However, many of those people appear to be reading scripts, and those scripts have a distinct pattern. They can be in full rah-rah support of the politician who happens to be on the air, or they can criticize the leader of another party. I've heard the same script on the same phone-in from two different callers. Other times it's slightly more nuanced. For instance, the caller in support of the on-air politician will say, "I've got a little bone to pick with you about such and such but overall I think you're doing a great job." The thing is, I've heard several callers in one particular show use this same approach.

I'll admit to being fond of the people who place those calls: the "stackers," as one former open-line radio host calls them. I am intrigued by their sense of party loyalty. Occasionally they speak with passion. Occasionally they sound miserable, as if they just want to get the call over fast.

But here's the thing: whether the individual call comes across on air as flat or ardent, the manipulation of phone lines sounds ridiculous. Stilted and forced. I'll see instant public backlash on social media; listeners understand exactly what's going on.

I've done many interviews over the years about low voter turnout; about the need for political parties to drum up younger, more diverse candidates; about the need to convince bright minds of any age that it's really not such a bad thing being a politician; or about the importance of exercising the franchise to vote.

In what way do phone lines that are very obviously manipulated by the parties give anyone the sense that our political system is open and fair and sexy? This is such a serious issue that my bosses have considered not doing any more phone-ins with politicians. They feel that the manipulation comes extremely close to making those shows a waste of listeners' time.

So how to fix the problem? On our end, we could indeed stop inviting politicians to go on air as call-in show guests. That would be sad and odd. On your end, there must be a way, a simple way, to stop the time-old ritual of political parties in Newfoundland and Labrador stacking the phone lines. Notifications to that effect going out on the mobile phones of party faithfuls? I'm kidding.

Could it be as uncomplicated as a letter of agreement to stop the practice, a letter that is signed by all party leaders (and subsequent leaders) and distributed to members and supporters? I'm guessing the parties themselves would be efficient at policing any perceived breaches. To take a wider view, would a House of Assembly media liaison committee be helpful? Members could include MHAs from all parties and media representatives from all local outlets. The committee would allow for discussion about resolving issues such as this one. If it proved helpful for those journalists who cover the legislature, the existing Press Gallery Association could be folded into a media liaison committee.

But really, I can't tell the parties what to do. And let's be realistic — it seems an extreme, overly grand notion, doesn't it, a call for a formal process to end the manipulation of lines on call-in shows? I can't quite see it myself. No laws are being broken and of course parties attempt to grab perceived advantages wherever possible. Besides, there are lots of pressing issues that need your attention and ours.

Much as I'd like to, I can't picture a day when political operatives will stop trying to mess with the phone lines. It's like the problem of litter here in Newfoundland and Labrador: icky, unnecessary, and perpetual. A problem that could be readily solved in that we all know the solution lies in not tossing crud onto the ground, and yet not at all easily dealt with in terms of changing habits and attitudes. However, individual responsibility still comes into play, doesn't it? Each one of you has probably gone out of your way to pick up unsightly trash, for the betterment of this place. A sincere thank you for doing the right thing. ★

About the Author

Ramona Dearing (CBC NL) studied at York University. She's worked for CBC in St. John's, Vancouver, and Happy Valley-Goose Bay in a wide variety of roles including as a news reporter and the host of *CrossTalk*, a phone-in show on CBC Radio. She's the author of the short story collection, *So Beautiful* (Porcupine's Quill, 2004).

Note

1. Steve Bartlett, "Message Managers," *The Telegram*, 17 Feb. 2013; Matthew Kerby and Alex Marland, "Media Management in a Small Polity: Political Elites' Synchronized Calls to Regional Talk Radio and Attempted Manipulation of Public Opinion Polls," *Political Communication* 32, 3 (2015): 356–76. See also "Radio Gaga" (editorial), *The Telegram*, 17 July 2014; Pam Frampton, "Mocking the Vote," *The Telegram*, 23 Feb. 2013.

24 The Media as a Cornerstone of Shared Power in Newfoundland and Labrador

Erwin Warkentin

What's the buzz? Tell me what's happening: a call for more confidence in the media. #cdnmedia #DemocraticReformNL

Democracy in Newfoundland and Labrador is not immune to our now interconnected global culture. In fact, it is most likely the case that Newfoundland and Labrador's information media are more susceptible to disruption than many others due the province's small market. Daily paid newspaper circulation in Newfoundland and Labrador has dropped significantly since 2010. *The Western Star* in Corner Brook is down 34.7 per cent and *The Telegram* in St. John's is down 43.5 per cent.[1] Moreover, local radio and television broadcasters are also noting significant drops in revenue, viewership, and listenership.[2] Revenues reported by the Canadian broadcasting sector decreased by 1.6 per cent in 2014. Within the context of an inflation rate of 0.97 per cent for the year, the decrease is more in the range of 2.6 per cent. There is no indication that the trend will reverse itself; most likely it will accelerate.

Newfoundlanders and Labradorians, like other Canadians, are turning away from traditional media. While some recent Canadian data on news source access exist, the provenance of the data and their analysis cannot be reliably ascertained and the sources are not without potential conflicts of interest. While it would be best to use Canadian data, a recent analysis from the American Pew Research Center,[3] based on surveys taken between 12 January and 8 February 2016, is instructive. In the past, US data related to this topic have revealed few statistically significant differences from Canadian figures. This study found that Americans still preferred to receive their news via television (57 per cent). Online sources were next at 38 per cent, with radio at 25 per cent and print newspapers at 20 per cent. In addition, those who in the past had received their news via print overwhelmingly had migrated to online sources. The statistics identify a further age-related trend. As the subjects interviewed become younger, they are more apt to choose an online news source, with those aged 18–49 having an almost 50 per cent preference for online news sources. Older Canadian data indicate that those aged 18–49 were moving towards receiving their news via smart devices. Why do the changing modes of news delivery matter in a discussion on improving democracy in Newfoundland and Labrador? The traditional fourth estate of governance has yet to find its place online. For the most part, newspapers are not weathering the migration to an online format particularly well. Those that appear to have been successful already have considerable readership and are now able to expand nationally, supplanting regional and local news. For example, amid falling readership of local and regional daily papers, a 2015 report by the *Globe and Mail* suggests that its readership nationally has increased to over seven million.[4]

While the principles of journalism continue to function, the business model of delivering information to the citizen has been disrupted.[5] What will eventually happen in Newfoundland and Labrador is what is already happening in other cities where the local coverage is being pared back in favour of more national and international news, which is more economical to deliver.[6] The Internet delivery system in Newfoundland and Labrador may inform readers of national issues, but the local and regional issues are under-reported. Though some local newspapers have tried to maintain an online presence, they simply do not have the resources to be successful.

A cornerstone of our democracy is our media because it shapes how we think of those with whom we share power as individuals and collectively. It lies at the very heart of democracy and, indeed, without it, a democracy cannot function. It moulds how we share power by building trust in our fellow citizens and in the mechanisms we have created to live together as civilized people. If most people are not sufficiently educated in the practices of civil society by our media, power cannot truly be shared.

To ensure a healthy fourth estate, the Newfoundland and Labrador government should lobby the federal government, specifically the Canadian Radio-television and Telecommunications Commission (CRTC), to institute a levy on Internet services to provide financial assistance to newspapers in small markets that would assist the development of online news services and the training of staff. The goal would be to ensure that the ethic of the existing newspapers be carried over into this new delivery format and that journalists take advantage of the communications possibilities offered by computer-mediated networks.

Establishing such a fund would not be without precedent. In 2008, the CRTC established the Local Programming Improvement Fund to mitigate falling advertising revenue at small television broadcasters. The surcharge was phased out by August 2014 when the CRTC was satisfied that the approximately $100 million per year collected by the cable providers had indeed stabilized local television productions as ad revenue recovered. It makes sense to lobby the CRTC because they govern Internet service providers (ISPs). Since what we think of as traditional paper-based news is being read online, and the ISPs are now the delivery mechanism for that news, it makes sense to ask the CRTC to establish a fund similar to the Local Programming Improvement Fund in order to ensure that local news continues to inform citizens on provincial and local issues, even if that print is now electronic. ★

About the Author

Erwin Warkentin (Modern Languages, Literatures and Cultures, Memorial University of Newfoundland) has published widely in the area of information control and has been a commentator on crisis communications. His recent publication, *American Information Control in Occupied Germany 1944–1949: The Past Imperfect* (Cambridge Scholars Press, 2016), deals with the relationship between the media and the development of democratic principles in British- and American-occupied Germany.

Notes

1. Newspapers Canada, "Circulation Report: Daily Newspapers 2015" (2016), at: http://newspaperscanada.ca/about-newspapers/circulation/daily-newspapers/.
2. Canadian Radio-television and Telecommunications Commission (CRTC), "Communications Monitoring Report 2015: Broadcasting Sector Overview" (2015), at: http://www.crtc.gc.ca/eng/publications/reports/PolicyMonitoring/2015/cmr.pdf.
3. James Bradshaw, "Globe and Mail Leading Canadian Newspaper Readership, Study Says." *The Globe and Mail*, 22 Oct. 2015, at: http://www.theglobeandmail.com/report-on-business/globe-and-mail-leading-

canadian-newspaper-readership-study-says/article26941782/.

4. Amy Mitchell, Jeffrey Gottfried, Michael Barthel, and Elisa Shearer, "The Modern News Consumer: News Attitudes and Practices in the Digital Era," Pew Research Center, 7 July 2016, at: http://www.journalism.org/files/2016/07/PJ_2016.07.07_Modern-News-Consumer_FINAL.pdf.
5. Jesse Drew, *A Social History of Contemporary Democratic Media* (New York: Routledge, 2013).
6. Beatrice Britneff, "Postmedia Reducing Percentage of Local Stories in Ottawa Papers," *iPolitics*, 3 Nov. 2016, at: http://ipolitics.ca/2016/11/03/postmedia-reducing-percentage-of-local-stories-in-ottawa-papers/.

25 Conflicts of Dependence and Independence in the Press Gallery

Michael Connors

NTV's @MikeConnors tells a cautionary tale from the NL press gallery's history. #cdnmedia #DemocraticReformNL

"It is clear that no solution will satisfy all stakeholders," Heather Boyd summarized in her 2016 report on press galleries. Boyd, a retired journalist, was commissioned by Alberta's NDP government to review accreditation practices across Canada after it barred a correspondent for a right-wing website, *The Rebel*, from covering two events.[1]

Boyd concluded journalists, not governments, should decide who can access press galleries. But that makes the issue no less thorny, because press gallery associations by their nature are trapped within contradictions of dependence and independence. When an association wields its collective authority against members who assert individual autonomy, the results can be catastrophic. The history of the Newfoundland and Labrador Press Gallery Association provides a cautionary tale on this point.

Administrative control over the parliamentary precinct — the legislative chamber and its associated offices — rests with the Speaker. The Speaker's authority is rooted in parliamentary privilege, which the Supreme Court of Canada has ruled is a constitutional power that cannot be overridden by the Charter of Rights and Freedoms.[2]

In most Canadian legislatures, the Speaker delegates custodial authority over the press gallery to the Press Gallery Association. Many of these associations have constitutions that define what kinds of journalists can get access. Most constitutions limit membership to professional journalists whose "principal occupation" is legislative reporting.[3]

The Newfoundland and Labrador Press Gallery Association is much less formal. It has not had a constitution since the 1990s. Instead, it elects a single president to act as a liaison with the Speaker's office. But it wasn't always that way.

The association was founded in 1969 with the sanction of Speaker George Clarke, who favoured an organized body that could speak for all members on matters of "protocol and ethics."[4] That principle was written into the press gallery's first constitution, which gave the association authority to discipline and expel members for "unethical conduct," but did not define what was unethical.[5]

That put the press gallery in the awkward position of regulating the behaviour of members who did not recognize its authority to do so. Conflict broke out in 1985 during a strike at Q Radio. The station hired a replacement worker and assigned him to the press gallery. A majority of press gallery members thought being a "scab" qualified as "unethical conduct" and voted to expel the reporter. Q Radio rejected the expulsion, leading to a physical standoff in the press room while the House was in session.[6]

The press gallery asked Speaker Patrick McNicholas to enforce the expulsion, but he refused, allowing the reporter to stay while he conducted a review. In early 1986, McNicholas presented a somewhat contradictory ruling. On one hand, he stated he would not intervene in the dispute, but on the other hand he invalidated the association's constitution. Poor institutional memory was partly to blame. McNicholas was given the wrong version of the constitution (a 1975 draft rather than a more recent 1980 amendment). Nobody could verify the provenance of the document, so McNicholas determined he could not trace its origin and advised the press gallery to write a new, less ambiguous constitution.[7]

Q Radio then declared it would continue to staff the press gallery without being a member of the association. It refused to pay membership fees until the gallery wrote a new constitution recognizing the Speaker's ultimate authority.[8]

The press gallery was cut off at the knees. It accepted the Speaker's recommendation and wrote a new constitution in 1989, but the restart was short-lived. Determining why it fell apart is difficult as the association stopped keeping written records after 1994, but I've spoken to some former members about it. It seems everybody was busy with their jobs and nobody had time to keep up with the administrative work. The gallery simply stopped collecting fees, stopped electing executive committees, and stopped following the provisions of its constitution. All authority reverted to the Speaker's office.

Should the press gallery write a new constitution and rebuild the structure it lost? A third constitutional regime could work, or it could end the same way the first two did: either the association destroys itself in an internal conflict or the small membership forgets its history and lets the structure atrophy.

There have been no recorded battles over access on the scale of that of Q Radio since the demise of the last constitution. Accreditation requests currently go through the Speaker's office, which then consults the gallery president. Flipping the onus so requests go through the press gallery first, as Heather Boyd suggests, would theoretically increase the independence of the association.

But the Press Gallery Association would still be vulnerable to clashes of dependence and independence. Expanding its mandate means regulating members who reject regulation, defining a profession that rejects definition, and limiting access for people who reject limitation. Nothing can override parliamentary privilege, so internal conflicts would still be settled by the action, or inaction, of the Speaker. Whether it's McNicholas's approach to Q Radio or Boyd's approach to Rebel Media, no solution will satisfy all stakeholders. ★

About the Author

Michael Connors (NTV News) is the legislative reporter for NTV News and has covered the House of Assembly since 2005. He was elected president of the Newfoundland and Labrador Press Gallery Association in 2016. He has a Bachelor of Arts from Memorial University of Newfoundland and a Master's degree in Journalism from Carleton University in Ottawa. He recently presented a detailed account of the press gallery's history to the legislative library at the House of Assembly.

Notes

1. Heather Boyd, "Accreditation and Access in a Changing Media Landscape," submitted to the Government of Alberta, 17 Mar. 2016.
2. *New Brunswick Broadcasting Co. v. Nova Scotia (Speaker of the House of Assembly)*, 1 SCR 319, 1993, CanLII 153 (SCC), at: http://www.canlii.org/en/ca/scc/doc/1993/1993canlii153/1993canlii153.html.
3. Boyd, "Accreditation and Access."
4. "Legislature Newsmen to Form Association," *Daily News*, 4 Mar. 1968.

5. Constitution, Newfoundland Legislative Press Gallery Association, approved 18 Mar. 1969.
6. "Speaker to Rule after Q Reporters Refuse Order to Leave Press Gallery," *Evening Telegram*, 7 Dec. 1985.
7. P.J. McNicholas, letter to Q Radio news director, 1 Feb. 1986.
8. Q Radio, news release, 6 Feb. 1986.

26 Governing in the Twitter Era

Sonja Boon

We need to take responsibility for ensuring a respectful approach to social media, says @storied_selves. #DemocraticReformNL

Social media have become a key component of electoral politics. Political campaigns rely heavily on virtual networks to advance their messages. Governments, too, increasingly rely on online forums, not only to advance their messages but also to invite community engagement. Indeed, social media are ubiquitous to contemporary communications. And yet, it is clear from a number of cases reported by Newfoundland and Labrador news media over the past few years — the shutting down of PC Premier Kathy Dunderdale's Twitter account after it was discovered she was following an x-rated porn site (2013), the reprimanding of NDP MHA Gerry Rogers (2013) in relation to comments made by others on a Facebook group of which she was a member, the removal of a volunteer provincial advisory board member after penis-related political commentary on a Facebook post (2010), the online bullying experienced by Liberal Finance Minister Cathy Bennett (2016) — that the architecture of virtual social networks and their role in relation to governance are poorly understood and cross party lines.

It is evident that individuals and groups have been able to harness the power of social media in productive ways, drawing on the possibility and potential of "going viral" to bring socially and politically relevant issues to the fore, to open a space for debate, and to spread ideas across a wide geographic reach. In this regard, these media perform a vital communications function, making visible and amplifying the needs and concerns of communities who might otherwise not have direct access to the halls of power.

In addition to this, as Conley[1] has observed, hashtags are themselves "political actors" that can enable marginalized groups to write "counterstories"; that is, a hashtag can allow for the possibility of telling stories from new perspectives. So, too, can hashtags promote affective engagement with social issues, in this way encouraging citizen engagement at the level of emotions.[2] Furthermore, the immediacy of virtual social networks has made possible highly responsive social justice organizing that moves fluidly between virtual and real worlds.

And yet, as ubiquitous as virtual networks are to contemporary communications, and as liberating as their political potential might be, it is clear that they are not always politically productive spaces; indeed, social media can be unsafe, hostile, threatening environments that undermine citizen engagement rather than supporting it. Thus, while the immediacy of the virtual network can enable rapid, co-ordinated responses to issues of social and political concern, it can also serve as a space for heated and abusive responses; an ever-growing body of research points to the pervasiveness of cyberbullying and, further, to the ways in which certain communities (among them racialized, LGBTQ+, and women) are particularly targeted in this way. The CBC's recent decision to close comment boards on articles dealing with Indigenous issues offers just one indication of the limitations of social media as a venue for civil discourse. Virtual social networks are not necessarily safe or generous spaces; rather, they can easily — and rapidly — descend into chaotic and profoundly dysfunctional spaces in which only the loudest and most abusive voices remain.[3] In such environments, engaging in virtual debates becomes an endeavour fraught with risk. It is worth recalling, in this regard, internationally recognized feminist writer, columnist, and blogger Jessica Valenti's decision to leave social media for an extended period of time after rape and death threats were directed against her young daughter.[4] More locally, the continuing discussion about the Donald Dunphy case[5] raises questions about free speech, surveillance, and safety.

How, then, might a responsive government, committed to community engagement, act? How might governments productively engage with social media? How might they effectively harness virtual social networks not for brand management, but rather as tools for community and citizen engagement? How might they do this while also recognizing the inherent limitations of this venue for political participation? And finally, how can governments contribute to developing not only a positive and thoughtful social media presence but also an emancipatory one that allows for the active participation of all members of society?

At issue here is a politics of stepping up and stepping back. That is, for social media to succeed as forces for social good, rather than forces of evil, they need to be (re)imagined as open, generous, and generative spaces where listening, rather than speaking, is the foundational value.

While the government's Communications Branch, Executive Council has released a document entitled, "Social Media Policy and Guidelines," this document is concerned only with marketing and brand management; it is not a tool for critical social media awareness. But such awareness is integral to effective and ethical online engagement. Critical social media training can educate political leaders, parties, and governments about the architecture of virtual social networks and the assumptions embedded into their design. So, too, can it elucidate the politics of social media participation — bringing to the fore the idea of the hashtag as a political actor, for example, while also working through the documented limitations of social networks as venues for participatory politics. Through this process, which could be facilitated through the Communications Branch, political leaders, parties, and governments can learn to model alternative forms of social media engagement that are attentive not to "shouting the loudest" — which has become a default response — but rather, to taking time, making space, and listening actively. A politics of stepping up and stepping back requires governments to take active responsibility for the virtual spaces they create, and further, to ensure that those spaces — through their active commitment to listening — are truly respectful and responsive. ★

About the Author

Sonja Boon (Gender Studies, Memorial University of Newfoundland) has research interests in the body and embodiment, feminist theory, life writing, and autoethnography. She has also published and taught on the topic of social media, including a 2015 article on online lactivism and breastfeeding selfies, which appeared in the *International Journal of Communication*. Her most recent book, on life writing, citizenship, and the body, was published in 2015.

Notes

1. Tara L. Conley, "From #RenishaMcBride to #RememberRenisha: Locating Our Stories and Finding Justice," *Feminist Media Studies* 14, 6 (2014): 1111–13.
2. Shenila Khoja-Moolji, "Becoming an 'Intimate Publics': Exploring the

Affective Intensities of Hashtag Feminism," *Feminist Media Studies* 15, 2 (2015): 347–50.

3. K.K. Cole, "'It's Like She's Eager to Be Verbally Abused': Twitter, Trolls, and (En)Gendering Disciplinary Rhetoric," *Feminist Media Studies* 15, 2 (2015): 356–58.
4. Jessica Chasner, "Guardian Columnist Quits Twitter over 'Rape and Death Threat' against 5-year-old Daughter," *Washington Times*, 14 Oct. 2016, at: http://www.washingtontimes.com/news/2016/jul/27/jessica-valenti-guardian-columnist-quits-twitter-o/. See also Alison M. Novak and Emad Khazree, "The Stealthy Protestor: Risk and the Female Body in Online Social Movements," *Feminist Media Studies* 14, 6 (2014): 1094–95.
5. See, for example, Sue Bailey, "Inquiry to Ask: Why Did Newfoundland Police Officer Shoot Don Dunphy?" CTV News, 8 Jan. 2017, at: http://www.ctvnew.ca/canada/inquiry-to-ask-why-did-newfoundland-police-officer-shoot-don-dunphy-1.3232174.

27 Real-Time Virtual Democracy

Peter Trnka

Democracy Fitbit Bracelets on Sale Now! Apps for Action!
by Peter Trnka #DemocraticReformNL

A major problem with our democratic form of government is apathy, alienation, and distrust of the very form of democracy. If this is true, I propose the idea of "virtual democracy" to find solutions, both theoretical (in terms of the meaning of democracy) and practical (as immediate ways to improve our democratic habits). The idea of virtual democracy promises to raise suspicion that democracy is not (fully) real; to encourage the sense that democracy is a matter of degree, of more or less (a struggle rather than a guarantee); to promote a sense of democracy broader than representatives and elections; and to explore new institutions of democratic culture and conversation by means of the Internet and telecommunications technologies.

Virtual democracy, in short, pushes us to question basic assumptions and to create structures and institutions for democratic expression. By doing so, we may edge away from representational democracy altogether to a fuller, direct, participatory democracy.[1]

Our contemporary situation lacks democratic habits at the social and cultural level. As Raymond Williams argued: "the real power of institutions . . . [is] they actively teach particular ways of feeling, and it is at once evident that we have not nearly enough institutions which practically teach democracy."[2] The challenge of virtual democracy is how to construct new institutions, new structures of feeling, and new habits of expression and communication.

What prospects do the Internet and telecommunications technologies hold for practising democracy? In general terms, there are two major promises: mediating (or bridging) distances across space and across time. The outcome will be bringing distant communities together (or creating new communities) and allowing real-time experience of distant events.[3] Both promises appear to target the deficiencies of a representative system.

In specific terms, I distinguish between two kinds of virtual systems (or applications): one-way, and two-way or interactive. Each type of system has positives and negatives: the issue is not choosing between them but maximizing the democratic potential of each.

One-way systems do exactly what the name suggests, i.e., construct one-way flows of information. Three such systems deserve mention.[4] First is the provision of government services electronically or online. This is a traditional notion of e-governance in which the information flows from the top down. Second is electronic voting, in terms of elections as well as referendums. Here the flow goes from bottom up but is also one-way only. The third such virtual system is the live streaming of events, both governmental events such as debates in the House as well as people's events such as marches and demonstrations. Each of these virtual extensions of representational democracy is to some extent actualized. The challenge is to extend and intensify them.

What is of more interest than the one-way systems are the two-way/interactive models. It is here that something like a democratic conversation or a democratic community might be formed, but it is also here that we find the very opposite: that is, the anonymity and distance of the World Wide Web encourage stalking, bullying, and other "troll-like" behaviours. I distinguish between two forms of interactive virtual communication. Choosing between these forms is a choice for more or less democracy.

The first form is reactive and personal. We find it on Twitter and Facebook. The norm is something like this: a government event angers or annoys someone who then goes to the web to gripe. Unlike the other forms of virtual democracy, this type seems to encourage alienation and distrust. It seems, also, to make little use of the capacities of the virtual world.

In contrast to the reactive and personal uses of the web, I propose that we develop active and impersonal applications to promote democratic conversation. In terms of Twitter and Facebook, providing structure and timing to conversations, akin to the Reddit format, would be a step forward. Such improvements of existing practices are to some extent already out there.[5]

What is not really out there is anything like the mass data aggregation that we find in relation to consumer behaviour. An application of the web to individual (and group) democratic preferences is lacking. As a health app informs me of my steps walked each day, I envisage a democracy app into which I may input my opinions, and these may then be aggregated (across municipality, province, nation, etc.).

Real-time provision of democratic opinion, in response to government initiatives and in advance of these initiatives, would be a material advance in democratic culture. There are various risks with virtual democracy, but the promise of being able to point to what the people actually say they want, as opposed to trusting what representatives say people want, would be a big step.

The range of options for the virtual extension of democracy is broad. I recommend that the All-Party Committee direct Newfoundland and Labrador's Office of Public Engagement (now part of the Communications and Public Engagement Branch) to explore the various options and make recommendations concerning implementation. The costs of many of the virtual options are either negligible or could be met by repurposing funds from existing budget envelopes. For the development of software apps, public competitions would be best, as has been done in the United States. ★

About the Author

Peter Trnka (Philosophy, Memorial University of Newfoundland) is a political philosopher who works on radicalism, revolutionary theory, and subaltern resistance. His recent work is focused on the nature of groups and associations and features a collaboration with the Gwich'in Tribal Council. He was co-editor of the special issue on Aboriginal citizenship for *Northern Public Affairs* (August 2015).

Notes

1. For representative versus direct/participatory democracy, as well as relevant history and etymology, see Raymond Williams, *Keywords: A Vocabulary of Culture and Society* (London: Fontana, 1976), 93–98. See also Raymond Williams, *The Long Revolution* (New York: Harper & Row, 1961), for an argument concerning the interlinks between the democratic, industrial, and communication revolutions.
2. Williams, *The Long Revolution*, 312.
3. One visionary account of how such new communities are forming is Roy Ascott, *Telematic Embrace: Visionary Theories of Art, Technology, and Consciousness*, ed. Edward A. Shanken (Berkeley: University of California Press, 2003).
4. Each is discussed in relation to contemporary examples in Evika

Karamagioli, "Transparency in the Open Government Era: Friends or Foes?" in Christina Akrivopoulou and Nicolas Garipidis, eds., *Digital Democracy and the Impact of Technology on Governance and Politics: New Globalized Practices* (Hershey, Penn.: IGI Global, 2013), 1–9. For specific focus on Canada and the direct democratic practices of Switzerland, see "E-Government and E-Democracy in Switzerland and Canada: Using Online Tools to Improve Civic Participation," *Public Policy Forum*, 8 Apr. 2011, at: Ppforum.ca. See also Elena Murru, "E-Government: From Real to Virtual Democracy" (2003), at: Workspace.unpan.org.

5. For a broad assessment of the positive and negative consequences of virtual democracy, see Vincent Mosco, "Approaching Digital Democracy," *New Media and Society* 11, 8 (2009): 1394–1400.

28 Towards a Poll-Savvy Citizenry

Scott Matthews

What place, if any, should public opinion polls have in #NLpoli? @jsmatthews99 explains. #DemocraticReformNL

The news media are commonly censured by politicians, political observers, and even concerned citizens for their outsize focus on surveys of voter intention, or horserace polls, both during and outside of election periods. One worry is that poll-focused coverage squeezes out more substantive political reporting on the social conditions and policy controversies that ought to inform citizens' political judgments. Another concern is that polls are an irrational and conformist influence on voter decision-making, a threat captured in the notion of the bandwagon effect. Further, a host of technical challenges confronting professional pollsters in recent years has raised concerns about the quality of the polls themselves and their value as indicators of collective preferences. These technical worries are in addition to any troublesome effects polls may exert on the media or voters.[1]

What should we make of these various concerns and how might we respond to them as we consider democratic reform in Newfoundland and Labrador? First, it must be observed that some of the concerns are better founded than others. There is no question that journalists, especially at election time, commonly interpret political affairs through the prism of the horserace — portraying politics in terms of winners and losers, tactics and strategies, attack and counterattack. Equally, pollsters are much less able to conduct polls that adhere closely to the strictures of scientific survey research (especially regarding the use of random sampling to recruit samples) than they were as recently as two decades ago.

On the other hand, the magnitude and the meaning of polls' influence on voters are much less clear. While systematic research finds that exposure to polls has, on average, a modest effect — pushing the exposed in the direction of the leading alternative in the poll[2] — the effects of polls can vary greatly. In many settings, in fact, we would expect polls to have little to no effect. When polls do have effects, it is often unclear whether they reflect an undesirable pressure to conform or, more optimistically, individuals' beliefs that there is wisdom in the crowd, i.e., that a strong majority implies a correct (or at least reasonable) opinion. Also, whatever the methodological complications of scientific polling these days, there is a bright line to be drawn between such polls and "media straw polls" wherein a media outlet invites its audience to answer (online or on the phone) a question concerning a current social or political topic. Participation in such polls is entirely self-selected and may be subject to considerable bias and potentially skewed not only by audience characteristics, but by partisan manipulation and repeat participation.[3]

As sanguine as the above take on the media's taste for scientific polling sounds, there is a caveat to note for citizens of small polities such as ours: the influence of a poll, for good or ill, is likely to increase to the extent that it presents new or unique information about collective preferences.[4] In Newfoundland and Labrador, where few polls of provincial voter intention are conducted, any given poll is likely to attract considerable attention from the media, surely, but also from voters. The effects of polls in this province, thus, are likely to be uniquely powerful, relative to polls' effects in larger provinces and at the national level.

What does this view of polls and their effects imply for democratic reform? Certainly there is no straightforward case to be made that polls, or the reporting thereof, present serious complications for our democracy, such that they are deserving of regulatory attention. Indeed, we should be reluctant, in general, to encroach on the operation of the free press, especially when the benefits of doing so are ambiguous.

At the same time, there are opportunities to improve the level of understanding around polls. One key lesson — especially in our small, relatively poll-deprived polity — is that a single poll ought to be taken with a grain of salt. There is always some probability that the poll may be a statistical outlier, or it may reflect questionable methodological choices (e.g., regarding question wording or sampling). More interestingly, it may reflect transient political currents: indeed, one thing we know about public opinion is that it can change quickly in response to circumstances, especially outside of elections. For instance, a poll conducted during a week of bad news for the government may suggest an eye-popping shift in voters' opinions, but that shift may dissipate as quickly as the bad news leaves the headlines. The poll-savvy voter, or journalist, ought to weigh the importance of any given poll in light of this fitful aspect of public opinion.

None of this is to suggest that polls are not an important source of information about public attitudes. Indeed, for learning about collective preferences, they are as good as it gets. But a suitably skeptical attitude towards polls is complementary to informed citizenship in a democracy. It is an attitude, moreover, that those who produce, disseminate, and analyze poll information ought to consciously foster. ★

About the Author

Scott Matthews (Political Science, Memorial University of Newfoundland) specializes in the study of elections in Canada and the United States. In 2012, he published (with M. Pickup and F. Cutler), "The Mediated Horserace: Campaign Polls and Poll Reporting," *Canadian Journal of Political Science* 45, 2: 261–87.

Notes

1. J. Scott Matthews, "Horserace Journalism under Stress?" in Alex Marland and Thierry Giasson, eds., *Canadian Election Analysis: Communication, Strategy and Democracy* (Vancouver: University of British Columbia Press, 2015).
2. Sibylle Hardmeier, "The Effects of Published Polls on Citizens," in Wolfgang Donsbach and Michael Traugott, eds., *The SAGE Handbook of Public Opinion Research* (London: Sage, 2008).
3. Matthew Kerby and Alex Marland, "Media Management in a Small Polity: Political Elites' Synchronized Calls to Regional Talk Radio and Attempted Manipulation of Public Opinion Polls," *Political Communication* 32, 3 (2015): 356–76.
4. Neil Malhotra, Jon A. Krosnick, and Randall K. Thomas, "The Effect of Public Opinion Polls on Closeness Assessments: Evidence on Belief Updating," presented at the annual conference of the American Political Science Association, Philadelphia, 2006.

PART 5: ENGAGEMENT

A Work Committee in the Ballroom at Government House (1915). The Director of the Work Committee was Mrs. Henrietta [John] Harvey. The mandate of the Committee was to prepare the work, work rooms, and materials and to arrange work parties. Note that some of the women are sewing by hand and machine; others are knitting. For more information relating to the committees of the Women's Patriotic Association, please refer to the article by Margaret Davidson, "The Women's Patriotic Association of Newfoundland" (*Among the Deep Sea Fishers*, Jan. 1916). (Source: Provincial Archives)

Encouraging democratic participation is challenging at the best of times. Clear lines of communication are needed between constituents and leaders, and civic literacy must be promoted at all levels of society. Using the school system to educate current and future voters about governance, initiating community consultations, and encouraging voter turnout are among a myriad of considerations here.

This section addresses ways to refine the practices of public consultation to ensure that citizens are heard and to foster an informed citizenry. Amelia Curran begins on a reflective and poetic note. Mechanisms to encourage turnout in elections are identified by Nahid Masoudi. Educating young people about government institutions and processes is urged by James Bickerton, Raymond Blake, John Hoben, and Simon Lono. Meaningful consultations among people on the margins of political power are advocated by Ailsa Craig, Rose Ricciardelli, and Anne Graham.

We are left with a sense that a healthy democracy doesn't just happen — it requires effort and opportunity.

29 Youth Vote

Amelia Curran

Youth Vote: a creative essay by Juno Award-winning @Amelia_Curran #cdnpoli #DemocraticReformNL

vote is a paper crane. Cast by the millions. Stolen by the sneakiest puff of hot air and littered somewhere far off.

I folded my cranes to the left. Sharp shiny corners drawing blood. Tucked into the belly and it always bothered me there were no eyes in the end. Expressionless thing of cold hope.

In grade school we would tie their heads to strings and hang them from the ceiling with push pins or just tuck an inch of twine under the chalky tile and it holds, asbestos dust and last year's erasers making the weight.

The ones nearest the exit rustling with every swift slam of the door. Three or four of them twisted together from the brief disturbances, wings all akimbo, heads smashed.

They hung there most of the first term and we grew accustomed to the polkadot effect after a day and forgot they were there in a week.

We had an election that year, three Grade 4 classes shouted and pointed and squealed for two days and wrestled out a capital between them. It was Monkeys versus Robots in the end. I can't recall the third contender. Maybe a crocodile. Something with a thick skin made friendly with a backwards ball cap.

Every class voted for itself save a few bleeding hearts urged to display an early development of pathos. An against-the-grain distaste for winning.

"Their song was better," said the double crossers. "It's stupid," said the losers. "It doesn't count."

The winners got a pizza party.

We conjugated French verbs, en masse, ad nauseam. One afternoon we turned the lights off and got to watch a Hollywood movie, *Look Who's Talking*, and the most Catholic of the parents got mad because John Travolta touches Kirstie Alley's thigh in a suggestive manner, and so there were no more Hollywood movies after that.

Before Christmas break we cleaned out our desks. Abandoned granola bars and brown bags made soft as baby leather. The tallest kids on chairs to rip down the paper cranes, but they are careless in their job and leave pushpins hidden and hungry for vulnerable feet.

The Monkeys and the Robots and the Maybe-A-Crocodile are forgotten and within a year the reminder of it is embarrassing and we move on to more serious elections like class treasurer.

I took a paper crane home and drew eyes on it but it had a carnivorous effect so I threw it away in the end but not before trying to make it fit in. Put it on a shelf between a koala bear and a cabbage patch doll and the crane looked like it was going to eat them when I wasn't looking. Or when I *was* looking, which was too terrifying to let pass.

I was a year shy of being able to vote in the Quebec Referendum, which made the idea of a vote very serious and precious to my generation. A cold hope of singular responsibility. Our first legal vote was the 1997 federal election. "Their song was better," said the double crossers. "It's stupid," said the losers. "It doesn't count."

It's like that every time. Grow mystified on the short walk home from the polls, back to where you belong, wondering what you've done, if anything. Draw the eyes on it in the hopes of uncovering its humanity. Try and make it fit and pretend the carnivores don't see you.

Those paper cranes were a nice idea though. Creased and tidy busy work. ★

About the Author

Amelia Curran (musician) is a Juno Award-winning songwriter from St. John's who is celebrated for her complex and poetic lyricism that delivers powerful imagery in song. Amelia's political and humanitarian work has seen her raise awareness about mental health issues through community initiatives and documentary work. As a speaker and author, she has brought these discussions to schools and music conferences across Canada.

30 Motivating Voter Turnout

Nahid Masoudi

We can get people interested in voting. Here's how. #cdnpoli #DemocraticReformNL

Voting is the foremost right of citizens in a democracy. However, many — including about 35 per cent of eligible voters in Newfoundland and Labrador — do not exercise this right. The voter turnout rate in Newfoundland and Labrador for the 2015 federal election was only 67 per cent of registered voters. Although this was 9 per cent higher than in the 2011 election, the province still has the lowest voter turnout in the country.[1] Historically, Newfoundland and Labrador has among the lowest turnouts at the federal level and its turnout is chronically low at the provincial, municipal, and even school board levels.

Low turnout is often considered undesirable since a basic feature of democracy is the capacity of all voters to participate freely and fully in society and to have an equal say in law-making. Also, non-voters can eventually lose interest in other areas like civic rights. In fact, voter turnout is frequently used as a measure of a democracy's health.

Social scientists have done significant research in various fields on why citizens decide to vote or not and on factors to help increase turnouts. The low turnout has been attributed to a wide array of economic, demographic, cultural, technological, and institutional factors. The main conclusion is that there is no perfect solution: a mix of strategies should be used with each having an incremental effect. The main justifications given by Newfoundlanders and Labradorians for not voting in 2015 federal elections are: everyday life or health reasons (48 per cent, i.e., too busy, 18 per cent; out of town, 19 per cent; illness or disability, 11 per cent); political reasons (36 per cent); and electoral process-related reasons (6 per cent).[2]

The main suggestion for overcoming "everyday life or health" reasons is to create multiple voting opportunities, e.g., advance polls, vote-by-mail options, and even electronic voting systems. The City of St. John's uses vote-by-mail, which at least theoretically should reduce these obstacles. However, more study is needed on the real impact of vote-by-mail systems as some research finds the benefits fairly minimal and others find it counterproductive. For example, Kousser and Mullin observed that voters assigned to vote by mail turn out at lower rates than those sent to a polling place.[3]

The most common reason, given by 32 per cent of Newfoundland and Labrador non-voters in the October 2015 federal election, is "not being interested in politics." Studies typically focus on informing people about the importance of their vote in electing a government that works for them, and convincing them that their vote is pivotal. Theoretically, if voters feel that not many people will vote, they will have more incentive to vote. It is clear that if no one else votes, then the probability that a single vote will be pivotal is significant, creating an incentive to vote. The underlying assumption is that voters only care about influencing the election. In line with that, Ledyard[4] showed that when the two candidates take distinct positions, it provides incentive for voters to vote. This reasoning has been followed in most elections. However, these theories haven't been sufficiently successful in convincing people to cast their votes.

In the decision-theoretic approach, economists have suggested that voters derive "a consumption benefit" from the act of voting, for example, a "payout" from fulfilling their civic obligation to vote.[5] Behavioural scientists provide a neat explanation about what this benefit is and what affects it. They say the environment in which we make decisions can fundamentally alter them. Whether or not we cast our vote is affected by what we think others are doing, how voting makes us feel about ourselves, and what we need to do to vote. Here is a list of the main factors suggested by behavioural science to increase turnout:[6]

1. Making concrete plans helps people translate goals into actions. Voter records show there is a greater chance people will vote if they are asked about their plans (when, where, and how they will vote).
2. Desire to conform to the social norm is important. We are more likely to do what most people are doing. This goes against the logic of

convincing people that not many will vote. However, researchers[7] have observed that when potential voters receive direct mail saying that they and their neighbours will be advised after the election of who voted, more than an 8 per cent increase in turnout is achieved. Publicizing voting records may therefore increase the salience of this social obligation, possibly by shaming non-voters.

3. Be a voter. When people recognize their identity as voters or upstanding citizens, there is a better chance they will act on it and vote. Studies[8] showed a considerable increase (more than 10 per cent) increase in turnout among people who participated in a pre-election survey on "How important is it to you to be a voter?"

These points suggest that a very effective way to increase turnout is to remind citizens of their responsibility to vote and help them have a step-by-step plan of how and when they will vote. A combination of all these suggestions could have a massive impact. ★

About the Author

Nahid Masoudi (Economics, Memorial University of Newfoundland) is an economist and game theorist interested in behaviour and the strategic interactions of individuals. She has used game theory to study issues in environmental and natural resource management and has published in *Resource and Energy Economics*, *Environmental and Resource Economics*, *Environment and Development Economics*, and *Automatica*.

Notes

1. Statistics Canada, "Reasons for Not Voting in the Federal Election, October 19, 2015," *The Daily*, 22 Feb. 2016, at: http://www.statcan.gc.ca/daily-quotidien/160222/dq160222a-eng.htm (accessed 6 Sept. 2016).
2. Ibid.
3. T. Kousser and M. Mullin, "Does Voting by Mail Increase Participation? Using Matching to Analyze a Natural Experiment," *Political Analysis* 15 (2007): 428–45.
4. J. Ledyard, "The Pure Theory of Large Two-Candidate Elections," *Public Choice* 44, 1 (1984): 7–41.
5. T. Feddersen, "Rational Choice Theory and the Paradox of Not Voting," *American Economic Association* 18, 1 (2004): 99–112.
6. S. Syal and D. Ariely, "How Science Can Help Get Out the Vote," *Scientific American* (Sept. 2016), at: http://www.scientificamerican.com/article/how-science-can-help-get-out-the-vote/.

7. See A.S. Gerber, D.P. Green, and C.W. Larimer, "Social Pressure and Voter Turnout: Evidence from a Large- scale Field Experiment," *American Political Science Review* 102, 1 (2008): 33–48.
8. See C.J. Bryan, G.M. Walton, T. Rogers, and C.S. Dweck, "Motivating Voter Turnout by Invoking the Self," *Proceedings, National Academy of Science* 108 (2011): 12653–56.

31 Enhancing Democratic Engagement through Electoral Reform and Civic Literacy

James Bickerton

#NLpoli and @NLElections need a new voting system and higher levels of youth engagement, argues StFX professor. #DemocraticReformNL

Common in many political systems today, within Canada and beyond, is a long-term erosion in democratic engagement. This takes the form of both declining political participation and declining levels of knowledge about politics. The fall-off is particularly acute among younger citizens, and especially those with lower levels of education; studies show that age and education are the primary determinants of political engagement. As for Newfoundland and Labrador, voter turnout in federal elections has been the lowest in the country for decades; more recently, turnout has fallen off dramatically in provincial elections as well.[1] These are indicators of a systemic problem, often referred to as a "democratic deficit," and it seems to be getting worse.

Research into political disengagement, including decreasing levels of trust and rising levels of voter cynicism, falling party membership, and declining voter turnout, suggests that the causes are multiple. Political institutions, especially the intertwined electoral and party systems, have been identified as a primary cause. A generational shift associated with cultural and technological changes in communication media is another primary cause.[2]

The defects of the first-past-the-post (FPTP) electoral system have been well documented. It regularly produces results in seats that are disproportionate to party share of the vote, giving super majorities to the governing party while stripping seats from other parties, sometimes reducing them to ineffectiveness as an organized opposition. It also tends to suppress both diverse voices in the legislature *and* overall voter turnout due to the predictability of electoral outcomes in many constituencies. By producing one-party majority governments, it exaggerates the bias towards executive dominance over the legislature that already exists within our Westminster-style parliamentary democracy. This "winner-take-all" approach creates and feeds a pathological pattern of politics that stokes adversarial politics while disincentivizing cross-party co-operation.[3] While there is no ideal electoral system, the defects of FPTP are clearly detrimental in their long-term impact on both democratic engagement and the functionality and legitimacy of Canada's representative democracy. It is arguably the chief culprit in a democratic deficit that has emerged in tandem with the changing expectations of an increasingly diverse and more highly educated population, who are less disposed to a grudging acceptance of "politics as usual." Ignoring the need to reform this outdated system seems increasingly difficult to justify, especially now that the fundamental principles that should guide any proposed alternative are fairly clear and agreed upon. In this connection, note the five principles for electoral reform in the motion establishing the House of Commons Special Committee on Electoral Reform — namely, effectiveness and legitimacy, engagement, accessibility and inclusiveness, integrity, and local representation.[4]

The technical questions surrounding how best to incorporate these principles into a viable alternative voting system have been addressed elsewhere through a range of innovations and modifications to the standard voting systems on offer. These include hybrid systems such as mixed-member proportional that seek to combine the benefits of FPTP and proportional representation; the use of vote thresholds (a minimum percentage of the vote in order to be awarded seats) that eliminates fringe and extremist parties; open lists that allow voters to choose between competing candidates within the same party; ranked ballots to ensure that winning candidates in single-member constituencies win a majority (50 per cent plus one) of the votes; and differential treatment for very large rural or remote ridings.

So it can be said that electoral system reform is perhaps the most straightforward way of increasing societal levels of political engagement (by changing the incentive structure for party behaviour, removing the vote-suppression effects of FPTP, etc.). The provincial legislature could begin this process, as others have done, with a special commission on electoral reform that could include a referendum after raising public consciousness and providing information about alternatives.

An even more vexing problem, though, is the political disengagement of youth. The current problem of non-participation in politics is rooted in the cultural and technological changes of the past quarter-century. Research suggests that non-participation among youth is particularly problematic, and contrary to expectations, it is not related to political alienation from, or a rejection of, democratic processes. Rather, it is primarily associated with a lack of political knowledge and interest.[5] Proposed solutions have tended to focus on raising the "civic literacy" of youth through various means of promoting a politically knowledgeable citizenry. It appears that many young adults, especially those with low levels of educational attainment, lack the habits and skills needed for media attentiveness to politics. Widespread access to the Internet, the multi-channel universe of cable television, and the pervasiveness of social media has not helped to raise overall levels of civic literacy in society. On the contrary, it has contributed to a decline in political knowledge for many "by discriminating ever more strongly between uninformed and informed voters in their choice of online content." This is reinforced by social inequalities in online political participation that are related to income and education.[6] It seems the ever-expanding supply and variety of digital sources of information have not politically re-engaged the majority of youth. Comparative research suggests that the best chance for governments, legislatures, and civil society organizations to improve this situation is through determined efforts at "finding ways to use digital technologies for the purpose of civic education," especially in the schools and through enhanced programs of adult education.[7] The provincial legislature and government could begin to address this systemic problem by establishing a task force to first canvass the efforts of other jurisdictions, with a mandate to recommend a set of initiatives targeting youth political engagement, tailored to provincial circumstances. If the legislature were to establish a broader Commission on Democratic Renewal, both electoral reform and youth political engagement could be included in its mandate. ★

About the Author

James Bickerton (Political Science, St. Francis Xavier University) is co-author of *Ties That Bind: Parties and Voters in Canada* (Oxford University Press, 1999) and co-editor of *Canadian Politics*, 6th ed. (University of Toronto Press, 2014) and *Governing: Essays in Honour of Donald J. Savoie* (McGill-Queen's University Press, 2013). His research interests are in the areas of federalism, regionalism, and party politics.

Notes

1. Luke Flanagan and Alex Marland, "Newfoundland and Labrador," in J. Wesley, ed., *Big Worlds: Politics and Elections in the Canadian Provinces and Territories* (Toronto: University of Toronto Press, 2016), 1–18.
2. A. Brian Tanguay, "The Limits of Democratic Reform," in J. Bickerton and A.G. Gagnon, eds., *Canadian Politics*, 6th ed. (Toronto: University of Toronto Press, 2014), 281–308.
3. Alan Cairns, "The Electoral System and the Party System in Canada, 1921–1968," *Canadian Journal of Political Science* 1, 1 (1968): 55–80; Roger Gibbins, "Early Warning, No Response: Alan Cairns and Electoral Reform," in G. Kernerman and P. Resnick, eds., *Insiders and Outsiders: Alan Cairns and the Reshaping of Canadian Citizenship* (Vancouver: University of British Columbia Press, 2005), 39-50.
4. Francis Scarpaleggia, "Strengthening Democracy in Canada: Principles, Process and Public Engagement for Electoral Reform," Report of the Special Committee on Electoral Reform, 42nd Parliament, 1st session, 2016, at: http://www.parl.gc.ca/content/hoc/Committee/421/ERRE/Reports/RP8655791/errerp03/errerp03-e.pdf.
5. Paul Howe, *Citizens Adrift: The Democratic Disengagement of Young Canadians* (Vancouver: University of British Columbia Press, 2010).
6. Henry Milner, "Participation, Mobilization, and the Political Engagement of the Internet Generation," in A.G. Gagnon and A.B. Tanguay, eds., *Canadian Parties in Transition*, 4th ed. (Toronto: University of Toronto Press, 2016), 414, 416.
7. Ibid., 409.

32 Literacy, Democratic Governance, and Political Citizenship

Raymond Blake

Lower levels of education and literacy give rise to populism in #NLpoli and inhibit healthy democracy, says Univ. of Regina prof. #DemocraticReformNL

For much of its history, Newfoundland and Labrador has struggled. Its reputation for underdevelopment, high unemployment, low per capita incomes, and a disproportionate share of family incomes coming from state transfers has been largely deserved. Yet, its economic fate cannot be attributed to resource weakness or elite control and government mismanagement. Its political culture has created a political system that has seen the province led by several premiers who have enjoyed almost cult-like devotion for much of the time since the return of responsible government in 1949. Each of those premiers has claimed to be defending the province against outsiders (corporations, other governments) that simply did not understand the province. Such political rhetoric has been eagerly accepted by voters.[1] Sluggish economic growth may have fostered uncritical populism that permitted charismatic leaders to build up deep popular loyalty by pandering, which meant confirming biases and conventional wisdoms and avoiding innovative policies based on research and complex analyses.

Historian David Alexander was turning his attention to the linkages between literacy and economic development before his untimely death. He recognized a linkage between the extent of illiteracy in Newfoundland and the quality of public life and public decision-making. Low educational levels, he suggested, led to deference among citizens towards the political and governing elites: low literacy levels bred "a sluggish intellectual life and an unimaginative and inefficient debate about the goals of the society and how they might best be realized."[2] Low levels of educational attainment and low literacy rates contribute to a political culture that gives durability to populist politics. They also foster a political culture that fails to produce a vibrant and effective democracy. Civil and social engagement, including political knowledge, political engagement, and voter turnout, are impacted by education and literacy levels.

Few would dispute that an educated population enhances social and economic well-being. Education contributes greatly to economic prosperity; educated people not only enjoy higher incomes but they also foster innovation and economic development as well as contribute to a vibrant social environment and the general enrichment of society. Positive health outcomes and improved social conditions, ranging from less crime to better playgrounds, are more likely in educated societies. Civic and political participation also increases with the educational level of citizens.

We have to wonder, too, if a populist political pattern induces governments to decline to plan for consistent economic growth. Economies do not flourish in policy vacuums. Strong economic performance and strong economic development depend on good economic public policy. Government must know when intervention is needed; what intervention is needed; and when natural, inherent, or structural conditions require withdrawal from intervention. Economic management cannot be on the basis of fortuitous factors and complacency. Governments have to decide what fundamental conditions are necessary for solid economic growth, and they must include policies on effective early childhood development and solid investment in effective education. Educational attainment is crucial.

Educational outcomes and literacy levels in Newfoundland and Labrador are among the lowest of any in Canada. A 2016 study of literacy ranks Newfoundland and Labrador, with nearly 60 per cent of its adults having inadequate literacy skills, among the lowest of the provinces.[3] In the 2012 Programme for International Student Assessment (PISA) for 15-year-olds, Newfoundland and Labrador ranked eighth among the 10 provinces even as Canada's performance generally was trending downward.[4] Yet, in the decade beginning in 2002, school enrolments in Newfoundland declined by more than 17 per cent while spending increased from $653 million to $868 million. One might have thought learning outcomes would have improved. They did not.[5]

Given that literacy and educational achievements impact economic performance, social well-being, and political engagement, there is a pressing need for government and the educational system (school boards and schools) to rethink how children are taught and how literacy and numeracy are promoted among adults. Attempts at education reform in the 1990s focused on the denominational system of delivery, not on learning outcomes and student achievement. Reforms in the education system are necessary, and the provincial government and the trustees of local school boards must implement a learning environment that adequately equips young people to live successfully and participate as engaged and excited adults in all aspects of their world. Let's start with a provincial curriculum that requires all students to complete a rich program in the social sciences and humanities, sciences and math, and one that encourages participation in the volunteer sector, in community and civic engagement. Students are not passive learners and must be engaged as critical thinkers and active citizens. Civics courses are long gone, but democratic education is being embraced elsewhere, and it is a model to consider as part of a revamped system of public education. Schools are not institutions but communities where students must experience democracy in action. If young people experience democracy and are taught to fully appreciate and participate in the democratic process in their curriculum, in the process of education, in governing their schools, and even in youth councils to advise legislators as part of the policy process, it will lay the pathway to economic and social well-being for the province. It will also improve democratic governance. ★

About the Author

Raymond Blake (History, University of Regina) has published widely on Canadian history. His recent books include *Lions or Jellyfish: Newfoundland–Ottawa Relations Since 1957* (University of Toronto Press, 2015) and *Conflict and Compromise: Post-Confederation Canada* (University of Toronto Press, 2017). He is now researching the history of citizenship in twentieth-century Newfoundland and the role of Canada's prime ministers in creating national identity.

Notes

1. Alex Marland, "Masters of Our Own Destiny: The Nationalist Evolution of Newfoundland Premier Danny Williams," *International Journal of Canadian Studies* 42 (2010): 175.
2. David Alexander, "Literacy and Economic Development in Nineteenth Century Newfoundland," in Eric Sager et al., *Atlantic Canada and Confederation: Essays in Canadian Political Economy* (Toronto: University of

Toronto Press, 1983), 137.

3. Conference Board of Canada, *How Canada Performs: Provincial and Territorial Ranking, Education and Skills, 2016*, at: http://www.conferenceboard.ca/hcp/provincial/education.aspx.
4. Pierre Brochu et al., *Measuring Up: Canadian Results of the OECD PISA Study. The Performance of Canada's Youth in Mathematics, Reading and Science, 2012* (Toronto: Council of Ministers of Education Canada, 2013).
5. Deani Van Pelt, *Education in Newfoundland and Labrador: Fewer Students, More Spending, Poorer Results* (Vancouver: Fraser Institute, 2016).

33 Educating Tomorrow's Citizens in Today's University

John Hoben

Is it time for a summer school for #NLyouth in democracy @MemorialU? #DemocraticReformNL

Democracy doesn't just happen. There is nothing natural or inevitable about it. Rather, it requires continuous renewal through shared commitment to the simple notion that the people are entitled to make and learn from their own mistakes. When we think of democracy, we immediately think of free and open elections, majority rule, minority rights — the usual litany of lofty ideals that are so hard to take seriously in the wake of the latest political scandal.

Newfoundland has a rich history of populist movements, political satire, and socially conscious art.[1] Yet, somehow colonialism, sparse employment, powerful religious organizations, geographical isolation, elite interests, and nationalism's seductive appeal have combined to create a culture that has stigmatized the practice of civic dissent. This is disconcerting since open public debate is vital to ensuring government accountability and a strong rights culture. Indeed, democracy requires a citizenry that understands that commitment to a particular party, or even a strong regional identity, should not take precedence over fundamental democratic principles like the rule of law, popular sovereignty, and the protection of minority rights.

Education is so important because without an understanding of basic democratic freedoms, citizens cannot meaningfully contribute to the political process.[2] It can also help us to recognize that democracy entails much more than periodic participation in the electoral process.[3] Teachers and policy-makers need to recognize that an active public sphere can only arise from a critical citizenry who are secure enough to express a broader concern for the integrity of the political system and any abuse of public political office. Rather than seeing vocal minorities as troublemakers, we all have a moral duty to support the right of our fellow citizens to dissent — not because we necessarily agree with the particular content of what is said, but because we recognize the value of the principle itself.

If we are to ensure that tomorrow's citizens are critically literate, educators must move away from the simplistic but all too commonplace idea of education as the transmission of pre-packaged content. Instead, all levels of citizenship programming must offer enhanced opportunities for experiential learning and community engagement through a problem-solving curriculum that uses interdisciplinary frameworks to develop students' critical thinking skills. These lessons relate to political, legal, scientific, and historical forms of knowledge and the everyday functioning of representative political institutions embedded within concrete social and political networks.

Accordingly, citizenship educators need to develop inquiry-based integrative programming that allows students to develop their ingenuity and confidence by grappling with some of the province's most pressing political and socio-economic issues. One such initiative might be a summer school in democracy and social justice for transitioning secondary school students and undergraduate university students interested in democratic governance. Here tomorrow's leaders and citizens can push our collective thinking on how our society defines democracy at the same time as they learn to find their own critical voice.

Such an initiative could use existing staff and facilities at Memorial University, such as the Leslie Harris Centre of Regional Policy and Development, or the Collaborative Applied Research in Economics (CARE) initiative, as well as other experts in policy, governance, and social justice. The aim is to provide a broader citizenship focus that includes politics, economics, and environmental and civic participation by drawing on faculty and community volunteers. This program would fall squarely within the Harris Centre's governance and policy mandate by focusing on the educational needs of young citizens and disseminating essential knowledge and skills for enhanced democratic governance. It would also expand the mandate of CARE to include a broader emphasis on civic participation and the legal, cultural, and educational aspects of citizenship education.

Programs like the First Year Success program,[4] Memorial's Experiential

Learning Centre, and the Faculty of Education also provide important pedagogical expertise that could be used to further this initiative. In addition, Memorial's Teaching Chairs and the University's Teaching Framework with its emphasis on community engagement and applied learning also provide a broader institutional context for garnering interest and planning a summer school in democracy.

Of course, the scope of democracy and its problems extends far beyond the ivory tower into every corner of daily life. For this reason, greater community engagement will also help to embed citizenship education throughout the post-secondary curriculum by encouraging problem-based learning, by using applied internships, and by drawing on the invaluable insights of Indigenous leaders, academics, journalists, community-based organizations, managers of non-profits, politicians, and social justice activists. This will also require involving people with a sense of the power of social media and digital technology, as well as of the more conventional media of talk radio and print, as tools that can be used to further democratic debate.

A broader collaborative project might include an institute for democracy and social justice whose main goal is to promote research and public engagement on issues related to policy-making and governance. By supporting intellectuals and activists, such an institute could help to explore policy options such as alternative energy co-operatives, micro-energy production, sovereign wealth funds, civil rights associations, improved conflict-of-interest legislation, green energy Crown corporations, and carbon reduction initiatives. Here scientists, activists, and scholars could promote new forms of environmental literacy by exploring sustainability initiatives that effectively respond to a rapidly changing energy economy and new digital technologies.

First and foremost, however, the effectiveness of a summer school in democracy or a democracy institute requires us to think about a different form of intellectual work that is more public, open, and community-oriented as a means of building inclusive institutional structures that will ensure that politics becomes more open and deliberative rather than being seen as a zero-sum game played by our province's elites at the people's expense. Loss is a hard taskmaster but it inevitably teaches us not to be waylaid once again by a simplistic story of rogues and heroes that gives the people permission to become nothing more than the disgruntled spectators of today's political events. There are lessons in hardship for us to learn yet, and perhaps a steady courage that comes from moving past resignation and resentment to take measured hope in hand. Both conscience and necessity demand it. ★

About the Author

John Hoben (Education, Memorial University of Newfoundland) holds an LLB from the University of Western Ontario and a Ph.D. from Memorial University. A non-practising lawyer, in 2007 he was awarded a SSHRC Canada Graduate Scholarship (Doctoral) to conduct a study of teacher free speech, which formed the basis for his recent book on teacher speech in Canada and the United States. John's areas of expertise include post-secondary education, fundamental rights and freedoms, the sociology of law, and democratic education.

Notes

1. R. Guy, *That Far Greater Bay* (Portugal Cove, NL: Breakwater Books, 1976).
2. P.R. Carr, *Does Your Vote Count? Critical Pedagogy and Democracy* (New York: Peter Lang, 2011); P.L. Thomas, ed., *Becoming and Being a Teacher: Confronting Traditional Norms to Create New Democratic Realities* (New York: Peter Lang, 2013); J. Dewey, *Democracy and Education: An Introduction to the Philosophy of Education* (New York: Macmillan, 2013).
3. Carr, *Does Your Vote Count?*; Thomas, ed., *Becoming and Being a Teacher*.
4. See V. Burton et al., *Making Memorial Student-Ready: Reflections on the First Year Success Experience* (St. John's: Memorial University of Newfoundland, 2016), at: http://onesearch.library.mun.ca/01MUN:Everything:Eprints-MUN12143.

34 Empowering Young Newfoundlanders and Labradorians for Future Political Engagement

Simon Lono

How can we get #NLyouth involved in #NLpoli? By empowering them. #DemocraticReformNL

If we accept that a core issue for democracy is the quality and level of public engagement in grappling with and understanding public issues, then we must target the youth for education. On a practical level, it's hard to expect a high quality of public engagement if the general public has minimal understanding of public policy or legislative process, and starting that process as adults is too late. When government decision-making is a black box, the results are alienation from democracy, inability to fully participate in the public decision-making process, confusion, frustration, and a growing lack of political agency.

I am always shocked when I encounter profound gaps in awareness of basic principles of responsible government. Yet the ability to distinguish among, for example, the legislature, the executive (cabinet) branch, and an independent judiciary opens the possibility of more meaningful input properly directed from an informed general population. In the classic *How Canadians Govern Themselves,*[1] one finds a clear and elegant description of the Canadian system of responsible government designed for a general student audience. Yet even when available at no cost, try to find a school classroom in this province in which this material is used.

Modifying legislative and/or electoral processes might eventually lead to improved democratic processes, but such change will not necessarily lead to more and better-quality public engagement. In other words, are we swapping alienation from one system for alienation from another?

I contend that imposing legislative/electoral reforms onto the existing provincial system will make little practical difference unless and until we educate more of our population — at an early level of education — in how to evaluate public issues and how to interact with government. We combat political alienation with education that promotes political understanding and political agency.

From time to time there have been calls to include a "civics" course as part of our education system, but we need much more than a stand-alone course to be endured and forgotten. Instead, the solution lies in more active education, integrated with the social studies curriculum, in public policy and legislative process from a younger age.

Specifically, the curriculum should include a broader set of activities featuring public policy debating and youth parliaments. Public policy debating is an activity that mimics the process used by decision-makers to reach policy conclusions. Combining advocacy, reasoning, and research in history, economics, and other social studies, students learn to explore ideas on how to best use limited public resources to achieve public policy ends.[2] The process of learning and practising debate offers profound and lasting benefits for individuals and for society. With its emphasis on critical thinking within a context of public policy, effective communication, independent research, and teamwork, debate teaches skills that serve individuals well in school, in the workplace, in public life, and in fulfilling their responsibilities as citizens of democratic societies. Once students have learned how to debate, they are better able to critically examine the pronouncements of their political representatives, make informed judgments about crucial issues, and take appropriate actions to make their views known.

Familiarizing the next generation of the electorate with our system of government is the other part of this process. While public policy debate provides the content for political engagement, youth parliaments provide direct and active education in legislative principles to ensure that students understand the form and processes of government. Through interaction in an environment that mimics the legislative process, debate, deliberation in a committee structure, and passage of bills and resolutions, students learn and internalize the fundamental principles of responsible parliamentary government.

Most importantly, these activities encourage political agency over political passivity and alienation. I have seen these effects first-hand among numerous young people over 30 years of teaching, coaching, and participation in debate and parliamentary activities.

Both youth parliaments and public policy debating have long histories in Newfoundland and Labrador in producing political leadership and in airing public issues when few other outlets could be found, particularly during the period of Commission of Government. Public debating societies, most notably the Methodist College Literary Institute (MCLI), originated in the 1860s and survived well into the 1960s. As a training ground shaping the likes of Joseph Smallwood and other provincial government leadership, their regular public debates were considered news by the media of the time.[3] Youth parliaments in Newfoundland and Labrador reportedly date back to at least 1960.[4]

There is no perfect governing system. In fact, many very successful political societies use very different governing formats than ours, so we will find no magic bullet in changing the format. Once you get beyond the basic common features of a democratic society (open and free elections, free media, rule of law, transparent economies, etc.), successful political societies have one characteristic in common: a popular sense that people can engage with the political process in a meaningful way and thus have political agency.

If we want to improve democracy in our province, we need a deliberate program to educate youth to illuminate the content and form of the black box of government, thus creating a public empowered, and equipped with the skills, to engage in democratic discourse. ★

About the Author

Simon Lono (entrepreneur) has more than 25 years of experience in practical politics working as a political and policy aide to premiers, ministers, MHAs, and MPs. During this time he has developed expertise in the training and education of young Newfoundlanders and Labradorians in the theory and practice of policy debate, parliamentary procedures, and process.

Notes

1. Eugene Alfred Forsey and Joseph Schull, *How Canadians Govern Themselves* (Ottawa: Public Information Office, House of Commons, 1991).
2. Joseph P. Zompetti and David Cratis Williams, "Democratic Civic Engagement and Pedagogical Pursuits: Using Argumentation and Debate to Energize Concerned Citizens," *Conference Proceedings to the NCA/AFA Alta Conference on Argumentation* (2007).

3. Joseph R. Smallwood, *The Book of Newfoundland*, vol. 5 (St. John's: Newfoundland Book Publishers, 1967), 400.
4. "Newfoundland and Labrador Youth Parliament," *Wikipedia* (accessed 17 Nov. 2016).

35 "Following Up and Following Through" with Community Consultations

Ailsa Craig

It's time to turn government consultation into ethical conversation. Here's how. #DemocraticReformNL

Democracy relies on consultation. If governance is to be democratic, there must be ongoing opportunity for those of us outside government to participate. It is not enough that we vote for those we feel are best suited to represent us. Those elected officials and their offices must then ensure ongoing communication with constituents, and engage with those who are directly affected and therefore well positioned to give feedback on effective policy, successful programs, and community needs.

Government knows this — it knows there must be consultation. But the ways consultation happens often seem to meet bureaucratic government requirements, without paying attention to the needs of constituents. I speak not as an expert on democratic governance but as one who is sometimes "consulted." This consultation has ranged from the broad-based work of being an invited participant in a day-long workshop on health and wellness in the province, to more focused requests for group presentations to select politicians on the realities and needs of LGBTQ citizens, to direct personal consultation, where MHAs have called on my expertise for input on LGBTQ issues for the province. In all of this experience, instead of consultation involving reciprocal engagement between government and "the rest of us," current practice has felt like being "harvested" to meet government need, and never being given a chance to cook or to eat. This is as true for developments like deliberative polling[1] as it is for traditional consultative processes where community groups or individuals provide feedback and information to aid politicians in their work.

Central to this problem is that, too often, those of us in marginalized groups are consulted, but it is unclear what happens with our thoughts, feedback, and opinion once we leave the room. Consultation processes, while they may tick off boxes for those performing them, therefore miss the opportunity to increase engaged democratic participation. Instead of fostering productive dialogue that would benefit all involved, well-intentioned consultations can alienate those they were meant to engage. How do we know you are listening? Was this a waste of my time? What are they going to do with what I said? Why did they ask us *that*? In addition to these frustrations, there can be the irritation of feeling we are being mollified — that after giving hours of time, we are agreed with, thanked profusely as we leave, and will never hear a word or see any action related to that about which we were "consulted." Even with online consultation (a process that aims to expand possibilities for engagement), there are no assurances that the efforts of citizens have any effect on government decisions.[2]

It is unrealistic to think people will work for free if we never see the results of the work we do. It is also unrealistic to think people will fully engage in a conversation if there is no evidence anyone is listening. This does not mean everyone must be paid (indeed, that would raise ethical problems), and it does not mean the government must put into action everything suggested in consultation. It does, however, mean that the consultation must be more accountable.

We can learn a lot from the disability rights movement slogan: "nothing about us, without us."[3] While the slogan is simple, the effects of taking it seriously are far-reaching. And if we take that challenge seriously, it can go a long way towards transforming community consultations into productive, collaborative conversation. But what might that look like, practically?

Transparency and accountability are key. This means that government needs to make clear what a consultation is for: Why are we being consulted at this time? What issue is being addressed? Is the consultation exploratory or evaluative? What is the intended use of the information gathered? It means taking the ethical stance of ensuring that all those in the room know why the consultation is happening, what problems it will contribute to solving, and what actions it can or cannot inform.

It also means asking those who are consulted if they have questions about the process and what they hope the outcomes will be. And finally, it means following up, and following through, with accountability. Which brings me to my central point and recommendation: It is insufficient to have the only point of contact be the point of consultation. Follow-up communication needs to happen with those consulted, reporting back on any outcomes and decisions, clearly stating how the information shared was used, and explaining the reasons for what actions were taken as well as those that were not.

By adding this point of contact into the process, the dynamics of community consultation can shift to foster active inclusion and help to make the transition from using marginalized people as policy fodder to including us as engaged collaborators. With transparency and accountability gained from "following up and following through," we can work together to move from empty consultation to a more engaged, collaborative, democratic community. We told you what we thought. Now tell us what you did. Show us the connections, and turn the consultation into conversation. ★

About the Author

Ailsa Craig (Sociology, Memorial University of Newfoundland) is a cultural sociologist interested in connections between mentorship, sustainable community, inequality, and activism. Ailsa's recent work includes a widely read *Gazette* op-ed on the shooting at Pulse, a gay nightclub in Orlando, Florida; asset mapping workshops with community organizations; and developing disability-centred and inclusive curricula.

Notes

1. J.S. Fishkin, *When the People Speak: Deliberative Democracy and Public Consultation* (Oxford: Oxford University Press, 2011).
2. S. Coleman and P.M. Shane, *Connecting Democracy: Online Consultation and the Flow of Political Communication* (Cambridge, Mass.: MIT Press, 2011).
3. J.I. Charlton, *Nothing About Us Without Us: Disability Oppression and Empowerment* (Berkeley: University of California Press, 2000).

36 A Democratic Process for Informing Public Safety and Justice

Rose Ricciardelli

Controversy in the justice system? How about a different process for informing change? #DemocraticReformNL

Penal populist agendas generally are supported and informed by public influence instead of penal experts.[1] In response, a politicization of crime policy is embedded in a "tough on crime" stance and evidenced in how controlling crime, and thus criminals, is a central topic of political debate.[2] In light of our democratic processes, the public, when voting for or against policy change, is often a largely "uninformed" yet influential party. Such "tough on crime" positioning, however, strives to "other" those who come into contact with the law and leaves many of the most vulnerable in society with limited opportunities (and hope) as law-abiding and contributing members of society.[3] This further negatively impacts society as correctional costs extend beyond the facilities, staff, and prisoners to include the longer-term economic losses tied to the reduced, often lifelong, labour force participation and the associated loss of taxation that prisoners might otherwise have contributed after their release.[4] Harsh sentences, or being tough on crime, satisfies the public's desire for retribution and complements the public's misinformation and fear of crime. Clearly, correctional expenditures in their current form are unlikely to help reduce the provincial deficit. Of course, this is before accounting for the millions of dollars in correctional officer overtime and sick leave our government spends annually: it is necessary given the work environments of officers and the fact that some work 24-hour shifts when necessary (32 back-to-back 24-hour shifts were worked in July 2016). But where is the provincial forum to discuss these practices?

Central to the idea of positive re-entry for prisoners and improved staff working conditions, which would reduce sick leaves and overtime, is to replace Her Majesty's Penitentiary (HMP), which dates back to 1859, with a new prison that isn't falling apart at the seams (i.e., with reliable hot water, room temperatures, and clean air). But where is this new prison? It was promised as a "top priority" under the Davis administration in 2014 after a riot; a contract was awarded and designs were said to be underway. It is now known that there will be no new prison — HMP will not be replaced any time in the near future — due to "financial constraints." But where is the democratic, open, transparent process with accountability that shapes provincial justice-related decision-making? When were discussions had and how were decisions made about correctional needs? Further, where were the voices of citizens, officers, experts, and prisoners?

Under the former premier, there was an Advisory Council on Crime and Community Safety with representation from local agencies and service providers (although lacking prisoners). The Council's findings were centralized in the public safety and justice expenditures articulated in the 2015 budget, but were then ignored in the more recent premier's release in March of 2016.[5] The budget speech of April 2016 did note two investments in Public Safety and Justice: one for family court expansion and the other for the office of the chief medical examiner.[6] How were such needs identified? Where are the transparency and the accountability of the government to *all* the people of the province? Where are the voices collected by the former premier's council and why are we not turning to people with expertise or experience to inform decision-making? Some of these issues were identified by the former premier's council. Others have emerged from the literature. Yet these have not been included in the budget.

In 2002, the Supreme Court of Canada ruled that federal prisoners have the constitutional right to vote and thus to have their voices heard.[7] Newfoundland and Labrador prisons are unique in that they also house federally sentenced prisoners. These voices should be accounted for both during and between elections. A renewed democracy in the province, within the contexts of our provincial governance, must look to include the voices and insights of all citizens, including the most marginalized. We need to bring these voices to the table alongside those of area experts, and these voices need to be heard. Including officers, prisoners, and experts in such decisions can also have positive impacts on cost-cutting measures by reducing what doesn't work and reforming spending to situate what works in areas that may not seem to be so transparent to someone outside the field. In corrections, we can do better with existing resources — the idea is to use the resources in ways that will do the most to facilitate positive re-entry. The populist provincial ideologies in regard to the penal system may negatively impact democratic processes as the already vulnerable persons in our society are further silenced. The current ministry is all about transparency and accountability — so let's see it come to light, starting with informed decision-making that includes all civilian participation. ★

About the Author

Rose Ricciardelli (Sociology, Memorial University of Newfoundland) has published in many academic journals, including *British Journal of Criminology, Sex Roles, and Theoretical Criminology*. In her first book, *Surviving Incarceration: Inside Canadian Prisons* (Wilfrid Laurier University Press, 2014), she explores the realities of penal living for federally incarcerated Canadian men. Her primary research interests include gender, vulnerabilities, risk, desistance, and experiences and issues within different facets of the criminal justice system.

Notes

1. J. Pratt, *Penal Populism* (New York: Taylor & Francis, 2007).
2. Ibid.
3. D. Garland, *The Culture of Control: Crime and Social Order in Contemporary Society* (Chicago: University of Chicago Press, 2001).
4. T. Colbourne, "Training Prisoners for the Real World: Prison Work Does Little for Prisoners' Employment Prospects," *Prison Service Journal* 134 (2001): 30–31.
5. F.F. Fagan, "Creating the Foundation for a Stronger Tomorrow," Speech from the Throne, news release, 8 Mar. 2016, Government of Newfoundland and Labrador, at: http://www.releases.gov.nl.ca/releases/2016/exec/0308n07.aspx.
6. C. Bennett, "Restoring Fiscal Confidence and Accountability, Budget Speech 2016, First Session of the 48th General Assembly of the House of Assembly, news release, 14 Apr. 2016, Government of Newfoundland and Labrador, at: http://www.releases.gov.nl.ca/releases/2016/fin/0414n05.aspx.
7. "Inmates Have Right to Vote, Supreme Court Rules," CBC News, 1 Nov. 2002, at: http://www.cbc.ca/news/canada/inmates-have-right-to-vote-supreme-court-rules-1.306843.

37 Learning from Public Consultation about the Proposed Closures of Libraries

Anne Graham

Here's what we can learn from whole @NLPubLibraries consultation debacle. #DemocraticReformNL

Six months after the provincial budget was released in April 2016, one budget issue was still being hotly debated: a $1 million reduction in the budget of Newfoundland and Labrador libraries, which was slated to close 54 of the province's 95 libraries. Reaction to the proposed library closures was swift and prolonged and it eventually prompted the Minister of Education and Early Childhood Development on 30 June 2016 to suspend the decision to close the libraries and to make a promise of an "organizational and service review" of the public library system, which included mention of public consultation.[1]

The initial public response to this reprieve on library closures was positive. However, the consultation process, which began on 5 October 2016, generated its own set of problems. Notably, many of the participants walked out of the meeting held in St. John's on 6 October due to frustration with the format of the meeting and the absence of elected officials at the meeting. The format of the meetings was reportedly "tweaked" since then.[2] While the library review is still ongoing at the time of writing, events related to the proposed library budget cuts can act as a useful case study on when and how to best incorporate public consultation in governance decisions in the future.

First, there has to be a determination of which kinds of decisions will warrant public consultation. The reaction to the announced library closures and to the library review processes demonstrate that *proactively* engaging the public in a decision will always be better received than doing so after a decision has been made and public outcry has forced the consultation. To be fair, the scale of budget cuts in April 2016 meant that it may have been particularly difficult for the government to assess which of the many important issues needed public engagement since it would not be feasible to consult on all of them. The province has a *Public Engagement Guide*, which provides a series of questions that can help determine when to use public engagement.[3] Two of these questions are particularly pertinent to this issue. (1) Is there a clearly defined question or concern? (2) Is the public interested in the issue or question at hand? The answer to the first question is a clear yes, while the second question requires discernment. However, since the issue of rural life in Newfoundland and Labrador has always been important to the cultural fabric of the province, it can be surmised that the closure of services in towns and smaller communities will generate more public concern than, for example, an increase in certain fees, which does not tap into an issue of socio-cultural importance.

The second issue concerns the proper mechanisms for public consultation. Reaction to the format of the meeting in St. John's can provide us with some useful information here. The complaints of the participants in St. John's concerned the lack of notice given for these meetings, the absence of elected officials at the meeting, and the hiring of an outside firm of consultants at a cost of $187,000. Further complaints concerned the ability of participants to express their views openly (the session was structured around predetermined questions) and access to the meetings, as some people were turned away at the door.[4]

Again, the province's *Public Engagement Guide* provides helpful information regarding some of these complaints, including guidelines regarding sufficient notification of the engagement activities and a process that is adaptive to the needs of participants. Reaction to the meeting in St. John's demonstrates that the government was not in touch with the level of public interest and anger related to the threat of library closures. Additionally, a claim by a government official that it was feared that the presence of elected officials at the consultations would have the effect of the public feeling less free to express their views "openly" demonstrates perhaps that the government is not in touch with the current level of political engagement of residents of the province.[5]

Governments everywhere are recognizing the increased need for public engagement and input into significant policy decisions as a result, in part, of a more educated and engaged electorate.[6] The province's *Public Engagement Guide* also mentions this need. Reflecting more fully on both the historically important issues of the province as well as the new level of political awareness and engagement of the citizenry should help the provincial government in the future to assess which kinds of decisions would benefit from public consultation and what public expectations are concerning the processes of this consultation. The government might also look to guides to public consultation created in other jurisdictions to further refine its own guidelines: the *Principles and Best Practices* guide created by the Office of the Auditor General of British Columbia is one such example.[7] ★

About the Author

Anne Graham (Modern Languages, Literatures and Cultures, Memorial University of Newfoundland) is a specialist of early modern French theatre. She has published in various Canadian and international journals. Her current projects include an article on the evolution in the representation of Sara in French medieval plays on Abraham and Isaac and a translation into modern English of the 1550 French tragedy, *Abraham sacrifiant*.

Notes

1. Education and Early Childhood Development, "Ensuring a Long-Term and Sustainable Library System," Government of Newfoundland and Labrador, news release, 30 June 2016, at http://www.releases.gov.nl.ca/releases/2016/edu/0630n04.aspx
2. Jonathan Parsons, "Province's Library Consultations Come to Clarenville," *The Packet*, 18 Oct. 2016, at: http://www.thepacket.ca/News/Local/2016-10-18/article-4666099/Province%26rsquo%3Bs-library-consultations-come-to-Clarenville/1.
3. Government of Newfoundland and Labrador, Office of Public Engagement, *Public Engagement Guide* (n.d.), at: http://ope.gov.nl.ca/publications/pdf/OPE_PEGuide.pdf.
4. Peter Cowan, "Dale Kirby Re-evaluating Library Sessions after Angry Walkout," CBC News, 7 Oct. 2016, at: http://www.cbc.ca/news/canada/newfoundland-labrador/minister-library-consultations-walkout-1.3796043; Hans Rollman, "Government's Library Review Implodes in Spectacular Fashion," *The Independent*, 7 Oct. 2016, at: http://theindependent.ca/2016/10/07/governments-library-review-implodes-in-spectacular-fashion/.
5. Cowan, "Dale Kirby Re-evaluating Library Sessions."

6. James Fishkin, *When the People Speak: Deliberative Democracy and Public Consultation* (Oxford: Oxford University Press, 2009).
7. Office of the Auditor General of British Columbia, *Public Participation: Principles and Best Practices for British Columbia* (2008), at: https://www.bcauditor.com/sites/default/files/publications/2008/report11/report/public-participation-principles-and-best-practices-british-columbia.pdf.

PART 6: POWER TO THE PEOPLE(S)

Parade truck, 1940s. Three men standing on truck decorated with flags. (Source: Provincial Archives)

How do we create a democracy that might be enacted in the daily lives of all constituents of the province? Authors in this section demand equal access to political debate, policy creation, and reform for the diverse voices of Newfoundland and Labrador.

Mary Dalton opens with the character of Alba, a recurring voice in Mary's poems, who here reflects on democracy through the ages. We are then introduced to different ways that power can be transferred from political elites to the citizenry. Jonathan Parsons suggests this can occur through mechanisms for citizen-initiated referendums, while Carol Lynne D'Arcangelis and Christina Doonan argue for institutional reforms to be more inclusive of Indigenous women and mothers, respectively. Newfoundland and Labrador society also needs to be more inclusive with immigrants and former mainland Canadians who are treated differently when they are branded as "come from aways," as Valérie Vézina, Tony Fang, and Kerry Neil explain. Sister Elizabeth Davis calls for a more compassionate society, maintaining that a democracy can only be inclusive with significant rethinking about the treatment of the most vulnerable and the Earth. Importantly, more must be done to include persons with disabilities in all areas of politics, as Aleksandra Stefanovic-Chafe and Mario Levesque observe.

38 Alba and The Old Woman

Mary Dalton

Alba scoffed at the notion of ghosts,
thought them a trick of the neurons,
a drift of the light, or a dream.

But the old woman's persistence
brought her up short —
that and the state of her:

ragged skirts, a gauze of grime
all about her: a clutch of fraying
papers in her thin mottled hands.

And her keening voice, a voice
that would wake the dead:
demos, cratos, demos, cratos —

her chant was relentless,
a litany laden with
the torment and twisting of ages.

Alba felt the chill
rippling all down along her neck,
felt the shiver, the hairs rise.

What did the old crone want,
this tottering
bundle of old clothes

and lament, her
visits more frequent,
her cries growing louder?

Now she seemed to be morphing
into some sort of demented clown,
juggling letters of a wooden alphabet;

up she'd pop, just when
Alba'd settled into *The Telegram,*
or sat drowsing over the late-night news.

She was shifty, full of stratagems:
this week it was placards,
cobbled together out of old campaign posters,

tilted aloft in those scrawny old arms.
What is a library? read one,
edged with a chain of interlinked hands.

What is a school? read another;
Who knows best? Can you spell despot?
She had Alba moithered.

And now the ghost was bringing her cronies along;
Alba caught glimpses of
Armine Gosling, Cleisthenes, and Nellie McClung.

The Toms: Douglas and Paine,
Pankhurst and Parnell,
Mandela, Havel. What a din.

One stormy evening the wraith
waltzed with Ray Guy round her room — the pair
moaning and cackling like demons in agony.

Alba's resigned now:
the old dame *will* have her say.
Next time she shows up

Alba'll be ready to set off at her side —
with questions, wry hope;
with a sharp pen, a history book;

with counterpoints and suggestions;
with commitment and queries;
and her best protest shoes. ★

About the Author

Mary Dalton (English, Memorial University of Newfoundland) is the author of five books of poetry; her most recent book is a prose collection, *Edge: Essays, Reviews, and Interviews* (Palimpsest Press, 2015). Newfoundland society and culture are one focus of Dalton's writing. Her latest work, a chapbook entitled *Waste Ground*, has just been released by Running the Goat Books.

39 Direct Democracy

Jonathan Parsons

Forms of direct democracy give #DemocraticReformNL teeth by @jwpnfld #NLpoli

The introduction of forms of direct democracy (even limited forms) allows citizens to be involved in the functioning of government beyond the act of voting. As it is now, government attempts to engage citizens through initiatives such as those from the Office of Public Engagement. However, citizen input has no teeth: input does not necessarily translate into policy. Forms of direct and participatory democracy would give government legitimacy and authenticity and produce better outcomes.

As the term is used here, direct democracy is a political system in which members of a polity have a direct say in the decisions affecting their lives. An oft-cited example of direct democracy is the ancient Greek democracy in Athens, in which citizens gathered on the Agora to debate and cast their votes on various issues. Forms of direct democracy also operated among Indigenous peoples of North America, for example, in the Six Nations Confederacy. Direct democracy can be contrasted with representative democracy, in which citizens nominate someone else to make decisions on their behalf. Representative democracy is the general form of democracy in Newfoundland and Labrador (NL) and in the Canadian federation.

To be clear, I am not in this instance suggesting that our provincial government should entirely overhaul the system and introduce a full-fledged direct democracy. Instead, I am suggesting that modest reforms such as introducing even limited elements of direct democracy would be a welcome change. For example, in the province's current representative democracy there is no established threshold for petitions to trigger plebiscites or referendums in the political system. Although referendums have previously been used in NL, such as the 1990s referendum on education reform, these have been "top-down" and initiated by the government rather than "bottom-up" and initiated by citizens. With respect to the current petitions to the provincial government, theoretically every citizen of the province could sign a petition asking the government to do or not do some specific act, and yet government is not obliged to comply or even to publicly acknowledge the petition. Interestingly, the preamble of official petitions to the NL government takes the form of a "prayer" through which subordinates humbly pray some higher power to do something on their behalf.

Compared with the NL example, British Columbia has clear legislation regarding petitions: once a threshold of signatures is met (10 per cent), a citizen initiative is brought forward to the legislative assembly.[1] Such citizen initiatives can then lead to creation or re-evaluation of specific legislation or to plebiscites or referendums. Furthermore, beyond such mechanisms of petition-oriented democratic processes, a number of other forms of direct democracy could be blended with our representative system. These include the "liquid democracy" practised by the Swedish political party Demoex, which hosts community meetings and facilitates online platforms that allow citizens to directly inform their representative how to vote on a particular bill or piece of legislation.[2] Liquid democracy is also interesting in that citizens not only get to directly participate in the vote on specific legislation, but also can actively promote issues and generate policy through the public meetings and online spaces. It is important to note that the use of online forums in liquid democracy is not "clicktivism," a term sometimes used to describe the many online petition websites that are not recognized by our government. Instead, such online forums are legitimate and function as part of the formal political process. These directly democratic elements of liquid democracy feed into the representative system, in that elected politicians cast their vote according to the outcome of the deliberations and not based on party platforms or party discipline. For example, Demoex does not have specific policies or a platform per se, other than its commitment to direct democracy. In this sense, Demoex politicians are better understood as facilitators of a decision-making process and not as decision-makers themselves.

In short, elements of direct democracy can function and be triggered within representative systems in a number of ways, such as through straightforward petitions that reach a particular threshold or through public forums specifically designed to facilitate citizen input for policy-making.

In fact, some of the mechanisms to incorporate directly democratic elements in NL's representative system already exist. Petitions can be read in the House of Assembly and submitted to the government, even as there is no clear threshold for action. In recent years, the NL provincial government created the Office of Public Engagement, which hosts community meetings and online crowdsourcing to solicit citizen input. The difference between these mechanisms and forms of direct democracy is that direct democracy has teeth. With clear legislation around directly democratic decision-making and initiatives, government would be obliged to do as it is directed by citizens, whereas in our present system there is no such obligation.

It seems to me the reason such reforms have never been made, and the biggest hurdle for such reforms, is that introducing even limited forms of direct democracy is perceived by governing parties as giving up a certain amount of power. Governing parties may also worry that citizen initiatives will be a way for their political foes to mobilize public support to bring down the government or to force changes to legislation. On the other hand, the reason the NL provincial government currently has an Office of Public Engagement is, I argue, to reap the benefits of being able to say that public opinion shapes policy and, thus, that the government is directly carrying out the will of the people. Government wants to be perceived as facilitating the will of the people, because doing so grants political legitimacy, but it does not want to create a binding decision-making mechanism so the will of the people can be expressed. Instead of granting legitimacy to government, the contradiction between the appearance and the actual practice of forms of direct democracy creates cynicism and distrust.

As I see it, the citizens of NL want a more robust democracy in which they can be directly involved in the day-to-day business of government. This is not to say that everyone needs to be, or wants to be, involved in all the minute decisions that keep the province running. Rather, people simply want the option to participate to be available to them and, moreover, want that participation to actually matter. There are many different forms of direct democracy that could easily be introduced or blended into our representative system. If done, I believe government would benefit immensely with respect to popular legitimacy. The NL provincial government is long past due to begin a serious process of democratic reform, of which forms of direct democracy may be only one aspect. What is necessary, when starting such a process, is a spark of creativity and a steadfast belief that the people of the province deserve more political agency and to be the authors of their own future. ★

About the Author

Jonathan Parsons (English, Memorial University of Newfoundland) is a Ph.D. candidate and a community organizer, researcher, and writer from St. John's. He is a former board member of Social Justice Cooperative NL and a columnist for *The Independent*.

Notes

1. British Columbia, Recall and Initiative Act (1996), at: http://www.bclaws.ca/EPLibraries/bclaws_new/document/ID/freeside/96398_00.
2. Demoex, "Information about Demoex," at: http://demoex.se/en/.

40 Enhancing Indigenous Women's Participation and Formal Representation

Carol Lynne D'Arcangelis

Indigenous women are raising their voices. Here's how. #Aboriginal #DemocraticReformNL

As in most provinces across Canada, Indigenous people in general and Indigenous women in particular have had limited participation in, access to, and influence over provincial and local politics in Newfoundland and Labrador, whether as members of governmental bodies or as constituents voicing concerns.

According to Statistics Canada,[1] Indigenous peoples — namely, the Qalipu Mi'kmaq, Miawpukek Mi'kmaq, Innu, Nunatsiavut Inuit, and Southern Inuit of NunatuKavut—constitute approximately 7.1 per cent of the population of Newfoundland and Labrador, with Indigenous women comprising just over half of that total — 3.6 per cent. Although holding political office is but one measure of any group's political participation, Indigenous women are under-represented at the provincial and municipal levels: one of 40 provincial MHAs is a self-identified Indigenous woman (2.5 per cent of the provincial parliament) and there are no available statistics on the number of Indigenous municipal councillors. However, since women in general hold roughly 33 per cent of municipal council seats, it is safe to assume that Indigenous women are under-represented as municipal councillors, as they would need to hold 12 per cent of the current seats held by women for their proportional representation to be achieved. (Notably, one of Newfoundland and Labrador's seven federal

Members of Parliament, Yvonne Jones, is Southern Inuit from NunatuKavut, Labrador.) This provincial and local under-representation is brought into stark relief by the contemporary political moment in which Indigenous women's issues are increasingly on the public's radar — not least thanks to the tireless organizing efforts of Indigenous "warrior women" and their allies.[2] That such a lack of representation of Indigenous women is allowed to exist runs counter to the spirit of both the final report of the federal Truth and Reconciliation Commission on Indian residential schools and also the Trudeau government's recent launching of the Inquiry into Missing and Murdered Indigenous Women and Girls.

This is not to suggest that Indigenous women in the province and beyond are not, or have not been, politically active. As mentioned above, if not for Indigenous women's decades-long work to call attention to the colonial violence that over-determines their lives, our collective concern around the topic, however insufficient, would not be what it is. Indeed, Indigenous women have historically been at the forefront of their nations' struggles for sovereignty and self-determination.[3] On this note, Idle No More readily comes to mind — an Indigenous resistance movement that emerged in late 2012 that was initiated by four women, three of whom are Indigenous.

Newfoundland and Labrador is no exception in this regard. A host of organizations and groups across the province — all with Indigenous women in leadership capacities — are dedicated to the well-being of Indigenous women, their families, communities, and nations. These movements include, but are not limited to, the Newfoundland Aboriginal Women's Network (NAWN); women's groups of the Miawpukek First Nation and Qalipu First Nation; the Pauktuutit Inuit Women of Canada; the Mokami Status of Women Council; the St. John's Native Friendship Centre; the Labrador Friendship Centre and Aboriginal Family Centre; and the Provincial Advisory Council on the Status of Women.

Clearly, Indigenous women are politically active. Why, then, are they not more visible in formal political processes? Simply put, Indigenous women have been disempowered in specifically gendered ways by the colonial process, in particular by the sexist discrimination of the Indian Act.[4] As a result, Indigenous women's leadership and organizing capacities have not held sway in formal Canadian governance structures, including in the colonially imposed band council system. (Granted, not all Indigenous peoples share an equal desire to participate in Canadian political processes. Their myriad reasons for this position are beyond the scope of this essay.) Given the disconnect between Indigenous women's participation in the diverse channels referenced above — in grassroots groups, community groups, non-governmental organizations, and government-affiliated women's groups — and their formal political participation, several steps can and should be taken to remedy the situation.

The onus should be on all government officials in the province (local, provincial, or federal) to initiate contact with Indigenous women's organizations in their regions, perhaps starting with the organizations I have listed here. I envision earnest conversations about how government could best serve the Indigenous women (and men) of the province, including by supporting Indigenous women-led initiatives that emerge out of particular knowledge systems. Political institutions at every level should foster "the conditions needed for indigenous women to succeed in exercising their own forms of collective action."[5] Opening (and widening) channels of communication would be a powerful step — a simple, yet profound signal to Indigenous women that all Newfoundlanders and Labradorians will do our part to fulfill Canada's reconciliation mandate on Indigenous terms. In this spirit, political officials should consult Indigenous women about a host of topics — not just "Indigenous women's issues" — on a regular basis. (Additionally, in line with Dimitrios Panagos's essay in this volume [#48], there could be designated seats for Indigenous women in governmental bodies to achieve gender and race parity.) With all that said, Indigenous women themselves should ultimately determine if and how to redress the systemic under-representation and disregard of their voices in Canadian democratic processes in their current form. ★

About the Author

Carol Lynne D'Arcangelis (Gender Studies, Memorial University of Newfoundland) researches solidarity efforts between Indigenous women and non-Indigenous women in a contemporary Canadian context. Since 2005, she has participated in solidarity work as a non-Indigenous feminist around the issue of murdered and missing Indigenous women, and co-organized an August 2016 forum in St. John's on the recently begun public inquiry.

Notes

1. Statistics Canada, *Census of Population, 2006*, at: http://www.statcan.gc.ca/pub/89-503-x/2010001/article/11442/tbl/tbl002-eng.htm; Statistics Canada, *National Household Survey, 2011*, at: https://www12.statcan.gc.ca/nhs-enm/2011/as-sa/99-011-x/2011001/tbl/tbl02-eng.cfm.
2. R. Bourgeois, "Warrior Women: Indigenous Women's Political Engagement

with the Canadian State" (Ph.D. dissertation, University of Toronto, 2014).

3. D. Million, *Therapeutic Nations: Healing in an Age of Indigenous Human Rights* (Tucson: University of Arizona Press, 2013).
4. P. Palmater, *Beyond Blood: Rethinking Indigenous Identity* (Saskatoon: Purich Publishing, 2011).
5. K.P. Whyte, "Indigenous Women, Climate Change Impacts, and Collective Action," *Hypatia* 29, 3 (2014): 612, at: doi: 10.1111/hypa.12089.

41 Breastfeeding in the House of Assembly

Christina Doonan

Allow people to feed their babies in the legislature. Family friendly, inclusive and enhances democracy. Retweet if you agree. #cdnpoli #NLpoli #DemocraticReformNL

For well over a decade, women from jurisdictions including Australia (2003), Argentina (2015), Britain (2015), Canada (2012), and the European Parliament (2016) have struggled for the right to breastfeed their infants in legislative chambers while performing their duties as elected officials. Notably, in February of 2016, the Australian House of Representatives changed its rules to allow women to breastfeed in Parliament.

Canadian federal MPs have found this issue pertinent in the last five years with younger cohorts of MPs taking office. In 2016, the Standing Committee on Procedure and House Affairs issued a report that acknowledged the House of Commons as a space that is not family-friendly, and noted the significant barriers posed by parliamentary protocol to work–life balance, particularly for parents of young children.[1] Among other family-friendly initiatives, this report recommended finding new ways to provide flexibility for new mothers. There are good reasons why the Government of Newfoundland and Labrador should pay attention to these trends that recognize the needs of parents of young children, especially breastfeeding mothers, who require proximity to their infants. The standing orders for the House of Assembly of Newfoundland and Labrador should be amended to explicitly permit and even support breastfeeding in the chamber.

The standing orders governing conduct in the Newfoundland and

Labrador House of Assembly make no clear provision for the presence of children or breastfed infants. In other regions, standing orders related to "strangers" have applied to the presence of children. Following historical parliamentary practice in the UK, many legislative chambers throughout the world refer to anyone who is not an elected official, or an officer of the legislative assembly, as a "stranger." Although the UK abandoned the terminology of strangers in favour of "visitors" in 2004,[2] the term is still used in the NL House of Assembly. Standing Order 22 of the House of Assembly states that "[i]f any Member takes notice that strangers are present, the Speaker, or the Chairperson (as the case may be), shall forthwith put the question that strangers be ordered to withdraw without permitting any debate or amendment." This provision against strangers has been used in the past to eject breastfeeding mothers and babies from other legislative chambers, most notoriously Australian MP Kirstie Marshall and her infant in 2003. It is desirable to prevent such a state of affairs in Newfoundland and Labrador.

Let us begin with what is probably the most compelling reason from the perspective of democratic governance. We may take as given that diversity in representation is desirable and a public good since it broadens the scope of our democracy. The more diversity among elected representatives, the more likely that a variety of perspectives and interests will be heard at high levels. Women currently account for 25 per cent (10 out of 40) of MHAs, suggesting that there is still a significant gender gap in representation. It is unclear exactly what role the family-unfriendly environment plays in preventing parents of young children from running for elected office, to say nothing of breastfeeding mothers. However, it was noted in the Australian context that rules on strangers might discourage parents of children from becoming MPs.[3] In this case, any small and affordable gesture to encourage the political participation of this demographic should be welcome.

Further, amending the standing orders to reflect a welcoming attitude to breastfeeding and the presence of children more generally (e.g., newborns and bottle-fed infants) acknowledges and respects the presence of elected officials who diverge from the typical Western model of the political actor for the past several hundred years — to wit, the able-bodied male who is not a primary caregiver within the home.[4] Indeed, the more traditional the parliament, the harder it is for women to work there, because parliamentary protocol has been shaped by norms and expectations that took the traditional male political actor as the norm. This traditional structure "disproportionately affects women MPs, making it hard for women to compete with men on a level-playing field, since they have to play by the rules of a game which were determined in the days when there were hardly any women MPs at all."[5] This returns us to our initial concern about diversity and its relationship to democracy. For this reason, the model for accommodating breastfeeding should be proactive, not reactive. It is not enough to merely wait until someone attempts to breastfeed in the House of Assembly and hope that they will be accommodated through an exception. Rather, changing the standing orders signals a dynamic approach and acts as an affirmation of parents who are MHAs. It also encourages the political participation of parents of young children who might otherwise deem it impossible to become an MHA. As citizens with a significant stake in health care, education, and property, and a keen investment in the future of the province, their voices are needed.

Finally, the province has a strong breastfeeding initiative through its Baby-Friendly Council of Newfoundland and Labrador, a committee with members from across the province devoted to increasing and sustaining breastfeeding rates. Through its support for Baby Friendly NL, the province has acknowledged the manifold health benefits to society that follow from breastfeeding and has made support for extended breastfeeding a part of provincial health policy. However, the research is also clear that the return to paid work can pose significant barriers to breastfeeding.[6] and professional work spaces must promote breastfeeding as suitable workplace behaviour if it is to be supported.[7] It therefore seems consistent to open up the House of Assembly as a workplace venue that models support for breastfeeding. ★

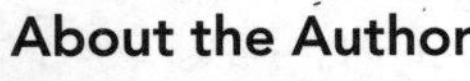

About the Author

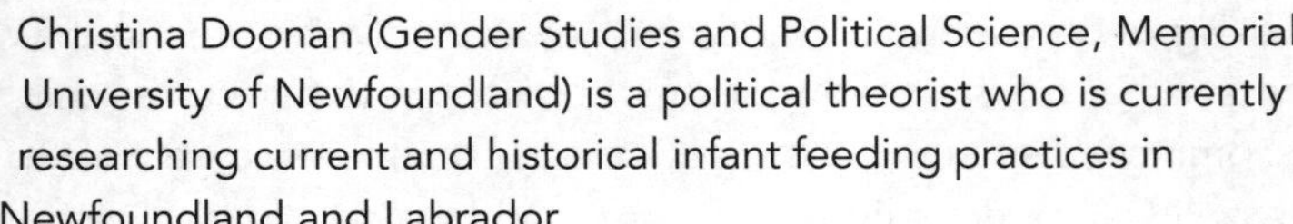

Christina Doonan (Gender Studies and Political Science, Memorial University of Newfoundland) is a political theorist who is currently researching current and historical infant feeding practices in Newfoundland and Labrador.

Notes

1. Standing Committee on Procedure and House Affairs, *Interim Report on Moving Toward a Modern, Efficient, Inclusive and Family-Friendly Parliament*, 42nd Parliament, 1st session (June 2016), at: http://www.parl.gc.ca/HousePublications/Publication.aspx?Language=e&Mode=1&Parl=42&Ses=1&DocId=8354291 (accessed 10 Oct. 2016).
2. Mark Rodrigues, *Children in the Parliamentary Chambers*, Parliament of Australia, Research Paper no. 9 2009–10 (2009), at: http://www.aph.gov.au/About_Parliament/Parliamentary_Departments/Parliamentary_Library/pubs/

rp/rp0910/10rp09 (accessed 15 Sept. 2016).

3. Ibid.
4. Bernice L. Hausman, "Things (Not) to Do with Breasts in Public: Maternal Embodiment and the Biocultural Politics of Infant Feeding," *New Literary History* 38, 3 (2007): 490–91.
5. Joanna McKay, "'Having it All?' Women MPs and Motherhood in Germany and the UK," *Parliamentary Affairs* 64, 4 (2011): 731.
6. Danielle Weber, Anneka Janson, Michelle Nolan, Li Ming Wen, and Chris Rissel, "Female Employees' Perceptions of Organisational Support for Breastfeeding at Work: Findings from an Australian Health Service Workplace," *International Breastfeeding Journal* 6, 1 (2011): doi: 10.1186/1746-4358-6-19.
7. Caroline Jane Gatrell, "Secrets and Lies: Breastfeeding and Professional Paid Work," *Social Science & Medicine* 65 (2007): 393–404.

42 When the "Other" Becomes a Proud Newfoundlander

Valérie Vézina

It's difficult for mainlanders to feel welcome in #NLpoli. Read more. #DemocraticReformNL

The pride that Newfoundlanders feel for their province and culture is evident in songs such as the "Anti-Confederate Song" and "The Islander." According to Statistics Canada,[1] 65 per cent of the residents of Newfoundland and Labrador are likely to have a strong sense of belonging to their province. Newfoundlanders and Labradorians consider themselves the "other distinct society" of Canada. This pride certainly needs to be celebrated. The long-separate political history of Newfoundland and Labrador should be on offer as an integral part of the education system. The province's shared narrative of resilience is often deployed against colonialist forces that threaten the unique culture here. This need to belong to a group, to a nation, as Guibernau[2] reminds us, is linked to the idea of maintaining social and psychological integrity and is a common feature of all nations.

Nevertheless, issues of nationalism and national identity in a small polity like Newfoundland and Labrador can sometimes lead to the rejection of "others" (those who are called mainlanders, or CFAs, an acronym for "Come From Aways"). How do we make those who "come from away" feel as though they belong? How can we assure the retention of newcomers who often end up just passing through?

First and foremost, as the Royal Commission on Renewing and Strengthening Our Place in Canada stipulated almost 15 years ago, the province needs to find its place within the Confederation.[3] Newfoundland and Labrador has mostly counted on powerful and "greater than nature" premiers to position the province within the nation. For example, under the Williams government, Newfoundland became known for being a fighting province. However, the previous PC administration was not the only administration to indulge in instances of Ottawa-bashing. Smallwood, Peckford, Wells, and others have also come out swinging against the federal government. Ottawa-bashing takes the form of a special kind of political nationalism that has fostered a sense of place for the province within the national framework by emphasizing Newfoundland and Labrador's unique economic, environmental, and societal conditions. This emphasis might also create the appearance of an unintentional isolationist attitude. Such forms of nationalism may be difficult to sustain in the long run and may hinder the ability to retain newcomers (mainlanders or migrants) who would be reminded daily that they are "not from here."

In order for the province to grow and be economically and culturally diverse and sustainable, it must be inclusive. It is important that CFAs feel part of the polity. Hence, part of the solution is to rethink the narrative of Newfoundland identity and resilience in the face of outside social and political influences. Instead of a pugilistic, top-down approach, where premiers are perceived as leading the way forward in direct opposition to the rest of the country, a bottom-up approach is required: a new approach that allows for citizens to take an active part in the national conversation as well as actively engaging with newcomers within the province.

The province should actively facilitate the integration of "others" through public forums and inclusive cultural events where Newfoundlanders and CFAs can share their respective histories through storytelling, in online and in-person visits to The Rooms (the provincial archives, museum, and gallery), and in the education curriculum at all levels. Local traditions of Newfoundlanders and newcomers can also be shared, for example, by pairing a Newfoundland family with a recent migrant family. Those encounters could foster a sense of uniqueness (through Jiggs' dinner, or perhaps a curry) while also being an opportunity to bond people together by sharing their experiences. Civic engagement could be fostered in public forums, where questions such as the following would be discussed: How do you imagine the Newfoundland and Labrador of the future? What would it take for you to settle for good in this place?

Cultural festivals might provide opportunities for sharing such things as culinary and musical traditions, dance, literature, film, and fine art. Education with an emphasis on the shared experience of the immigration process will help strengthen the links between residents of the province, no matter where they were originally from. The province has built itself through immigration and a back-and-forth process; it is important to be proud of the past (and the resilience of settlers and Indigenous groups) and to make links with the resilience of new Canadians as well as mainlanders who arrive with the hope building a new life with new opportunities and ideas. Through sharing experiences, the "other" can become an integral part of Newfoundland and Labrador and the sense of belonging and national identity will only be stronger. ★

About the Author

Valérie Vézina (Political Science, Memorial University of Newfoundland) is a visiting assistant professor who has studied nationalism in island settings. Her main focus has been Newfoundland where she has published in journals and edited books. She is currently working on a book entitled *Un île, une nation?* to be published by the Presses de l'Université du Québec.

Notes

1. Statistics Canada, "Sense of Belonging to Canada, the Province of Residence and the Local Community," 30 Nov. 2015, at: http://www.statcan.gc.ca/pub/89-652-x/89-652-x2015004-eng.htm.
2. M. Guibernau, *Nationalisms: The Nation-State and Nationalism in the Twentieth Century* (Cambridge: Polity Press, 1996); M. Guibernau, *The Identity of Nations* (Cambridge: Polity Press, 2007).
3. Government of Newfoundland and Labrador, *Our Place in Canada*. Main Report of the Royal Commission on Renewing and Strengthening Our Place in Canada (St. John's, 2003), at: http://www.exec.gov.nl.ca/royalcomm/finalreport/pdf/Final.pdf.

43 Building an Inclusive Democracy in Newfoundland and Labrador

Tony Fang and Kerri Neil

Why don't we have more diversity at the executive level? We'd have a more innovative economy if we did. #DemocraticReformNL

As a country whose population growth has been driven mainly by immigration, Canada is becoming increasingly diverse. Across the country, 19.1 per cent of the population identifies a visible minority and in large cities like Toronto and Vancouver this proportion rises to 47 per cent and 45.2 per cent, respectively.[1] Recognizing the importance of multiculturalism and employment equity has been a key cornerstone of the country, and much work has been done to ensure equal rights for all. Canada's Employment Equity Act legislates that every employer with 100 or more employees under federal jurisdiction must implement policies and longer-term goals in an effort to increase the representation of persons in designated groups.[2] Canada's diversity is an economic asset that drives innovation and creativity. To ensure our government makes the best possible decisions, it must reflect our population. This includes a representative executive leadership that is willing to challenge the status quo and provide perspectives and opinions that represent a wide range of social, economic, and cultural backgrounds.

Newfoundland and Labrador has a more homogeneous population than Canada as a whole, and arguably, this has weakened our ability to innovate. The province's history is marked by a series of large-scale projects that threatened to break the province's bank: the Newfoundland Railway, the Upper Churchill contract, the Sprung Greenhouse, and the current Muskrat Falls project are examples of attempts by our government to invest in projects that would improve the province's economy, but these initiatives lacked the forethought to innovate, to think long term, and to consider the ramifications of their decisions. While these examples go back a century, they all have one defining feature in common — these decisions were made under the leadership of homogeneous groups from the population. There is increasing evidence that homogeneous groups tend to reach a consensus easily, a phenomenon called "groupthink," which may preclude new ideas and various perspectives from a diverse population. Diverse groups, on the other hand, tend to bring forward more provocative thoughts, opinions, and perspectives on the very same issue.

Having a more diverse executive leadership, both at the minister and deputy minister levels, would provide much needed role models for those groups traditionally less represented in the public offices but who are otherwise interested in becoming more involved in government, such as young people, newcomers, visible minorities, Indigenous peoples, and people with disabilities. In the Public Service Commission's Mandate Letter, Premier Ball specified the promotion of gender diversity in leadership as a goal of the Commission, though ethnic diversity was not discussed.[3] Newfoundland and Labrador has a very low voter turnout at all elections, particularly in municipal elections, where some seats were not even filled. Changes at the top to fill positions with a range of citizens reflecting different backgrounds have the potential of creating role models for diverse groups of individuals to emulate and may encourage more people to get involved in democratic processes.[4]

Studies have found that social diversity has a positive influence on informational diversity. That is, being around people who have different backgrounds and experiences can result in more creative and innovative ideas, which facilitate positive economic growth. Deszo and Ross documented that having more women in top management positions improved a firm's growth if a firm's business strategy was focused on innovation.[5] Similarly, racial diversity in management could improve the performance of those firms with an innovation growth strategy, as Richard et al. concluded.[6]

Diverse leadership can also be a key asset in maximizing global economic opportunities by leveraging the international connections, cultural competencies, and language skills of those from different backgrounds. This is a key area for Newfoundland and Labrador, where examples of export-oriented businesses are generally limited to the oil and gas sector and the government has been slow to develop international trade relations with key trading partners such as China.

By having representative leadership in the public service, the government will be able to prove its commitment to gender equality and multiculturalism — policies to which all levels of government aspire but that have not been fully realized in our province. If the government is able to take concrete steps to become more representative, it has the potential to build trust and collaboration with groups that have been traditionally marginalized and have become apathetic to the democratic process.

Our province needs to shed its image as a homogeneous society and promote its diversity in order to become a real global player in the twenty-first century. To ensure our government makes the best decisions, it must reflect our population. Creating a representative government able to bring new and innovative ideas to the table would be pivotal. In order to build an inclusive democracy in Newfoundland and Labrador, we need an executive leadership willing to challenge the status quo and provide perspectives and opinions that represent a wide range of social, economic, and cultural backgrounds. ★

About the Authors

Tony Fang (Economics, Memorial University of Newfoundland) is Stephen Jarislowsky Chair in Economic and Cultural Transformation. He researches issues of immigration, diversity, and cultural changes, as well as high-performance workplace practices. Tony's most recent publications include "Vulnerable Groups in Canada and Labour Market Exclusion (*International Journal of Manpower*) and "Minimum Wages and Employment in China" (*IZA Journal of Labour Policy*).

Kerri Neil (Sociology, Memorial University of Newfoundland) is a Master of Arts candidate in Sociology. She holds a BA in Economics and Canadian Studies. Her research has focused on labour markets and issues of immigrant attraction and retention in Newfoundland and Labrador. Kerri has several publications through the Department of Economics Collaborative Applied Research in Economics (CARE) initiative, including "The Gender Wage Gap" and "NL's Human Capital Strategy."

Notes

1. Statistics Canada, *Visible Minority (15), Generation Status (4), Age Groups (10) and Sex (3) for the Population in Private Households of Canada, Provinces, Territories, Census Metropolitan Areas and Census*

Agglomerations, 2011 National Household Survey. Catalogue no. 99-010-X2011029 (Ottawa: Statistics Canada, 2011). In the calculations of Statistics Canada, Indigenous people are not considered to be among Canada's "visible minorities."

2. Department of Justice Canada, Employment Equity Act, 1995, C.44, at: http://laws-lois.justice.gc.ca/eng/acts/e-5.401/FullText.html.
3. D. Ball, "Public Service Commission Mandate Letter to Minister Bennett," Public Service Commission (2015), at: http://www.exec.gov.nl.ca/exec/cabinet/ministers/pdf/Minister_Bennett_Mandate.pdf.
4. T. Krywulak and A. Sisco, "The Value of Diverse Leadership," Conference Board of Canada (2008), at: http://diversecitytoronto.ca/wp-content/uploads/The_Value_of_Diverse_Leadership_CBC_final1.pdf (accessed 10 Nov. 2016).
5. C. Dezso and D. Ross, "Does Female Representation in Top Management Improve Firm Performance? A Panel Data Investigation," *Strategic Management Journal*: 33 (2012): 1072–89.
6. O. Richard, T. Barnett, S. Dwyer, and K. Chadwick, "Cultural Diversity in Management, Firm Performance, and the Moderating Role of Entrepreneurial Orientation Dimensions," *Academy of Management Journal* 47, 2 (2004): 255–66.

44 Reshaping an Inclusive Vision for Governance in Newfoundland and Labrador

Elizabeth Davis

It is time to take action to reduce poverty, get people involved in politics, and care for the environment. Retweet if you agree. #cdnpoli #DemocraticReformNL

Eating a nourishing meal; finding voice; caring for this place — these are simple phrases that challenge government to be more accountable for ensuring equity, inclusion, and participation and shaping the culture and environment citizens deserve. Government assumes responsibility for education, health, safety, and a robust private sector. However, it is not appropriately responsive to the needs of vulnerable citizens or care for the Earth.

Eating a nourishing meal symbolizes advantages most citizens enjoy; e.g., good meals, warm clothing, and access to a doctor. But many citizens are denied such advantages. Assessment of economic improvements shows that the poorest persons remain poor despite growing affluence. Newfoundland and Labrador's poverty reduction strategy states: "One area of concern highlighted by the Newfoundland and Labrador Market Basket Measure is that the number of people living in extreme low income has not decreased at the same rate as low income overall."[1] Government has not well integrated two realities into policy-making: (1) economic development is not a prerequisite for social development — economic and social development can only be achieved together with one making the other possible;[2] and (2) correlations among poverty, homelessness, mental illnesses, unemployment, imprisonment, and situations of abuse form intersections of vulnerability. The cause or consequence is not clear, but one visit to The Gathering Place, Stella's Circle, or Choices for Youth (community organizations in St. John's providing support for vulnerable persons) would confirm the correlations.

Democracy depends on *finding voice*, or citizen participation. Poor persons do not have the resources to be engaged; their everyday circumstances do not allow opportunity for civic action; and their limited engagement is provided primarily through organizations like Stella's Circle and The Gathering Place. Increasing evidence demonstrates that building the capacity of communities through social enterprises and community development is a viable, complementary alternative to the market-driven economy: an alternative that Canada and this province have been slow to develop.[3]

Caring for this place encompasses respect for Newfoundland and Labrador's land, sea, and air. While the provincial government is committed to creating a safe environment, there is limited recognition of its responsibility for the balance among health, environmental integrity, and ecological sustainability. An emerging ecological and economic order is exemplified by recent global agreements such as the Paris Agreement and the United Nations Sustainable Development Goals (SDGs). These global agreements integrate the pillars of sustainable development: economic, social, and environmental well-being. Success in implementing these agreements requires all levels of government to act.[4] Many SDGs relate to the intersections of vulnerability for which the provincial government has primary responsibility (i.e., Goals 1, 2, 5, 8, and 16). The Paris Agreement and SDGs 6, 7, 13, 14, and 15 relate to health, environment and sustainability considerations.

The provincial government must act to shape the new order. It must: (1) build an integrated social, environmental, and financial agenda; (2) implement the Paris Agreement and SDGs; (3) create circles of engagement for vulnerable citizens; (4) develop the social economy; and (5) commit to decent work for all.[5] Only then will Newfoundland and Labrador have the inclusive governance its citizens and land deserve. ★

About the Author

Elizabeth Davis (Sisters of Mercy of Newfoundland) is leader of the Congregation with responsibility for The Gathering Place, St. Patrick's Mercy Home, and the Mercy Centre for Ecology and Justice in St. John's. She has previous experience in health care as

Administrator of St. Clare's Mercy Hospital and as the first President and CEO of the Health Care Corporation of St. John's (now Eastern Health).

Notes

1. Government of Newfoundland and Labrador, "Empowering People, Engaging Community, Enabling Success," Newfoundland and Labrador Poverty Reduction Strategy Progress Report (June 2014), xi. On the global level, see David Woodward and Andrew Simms, "Growth Is Failing the Poor: The Unbalanced Distribution of the Benefits and Costs of Global Economic Growth," Working Paper No. 20, United Nations Department of Economic and Social Affairs, Mar. 2006, at: http://www.un.org/esa/desa/papers/2006/wp20_2006.pdf.
2. See the pivotal report, *Copenhagen Declaration on Social Development and Programme of Action of the World Summit for Social Development* (Copenhagen, 1995), at: http://www.un.org/esa/socdev/wssd/text-version/. The subsequent developments in the research are well summarized in United Nations Research Institute for Social Development, "Social Drivers of Sustainable Development," prepared by Esuna Dugarova and Peter Utting, UNRISD (2014), as an input to the Note by the Secretariat, *Emerging Issues: The Social Drivers of Sustainable Development* (E/CN.5/2014/8, 52nd session of the Commission for Social Development), at: http://www.unrisd.org/social-drivers-note. Research from Canada can be found from the Caledon Institute of Social Policy, at: http://www.caledoninst.org/.
3. See the websites of the Centre for Interdisciplinary Research and Information on Community Enterprises (http://www.ciriec.uqam.ca) and the Canadian Community Economic Development Network (https://ccednet-rcdec.ca/en).
4. See Canadian Council for International Co-operation, *Transforming Our World: Canadian Perspectives on the Sustainable Development Goals* (2016), at: http://www.ccic.ca/_files/en/what_we_do/jan2016_transforming_our_world-ccic-final.pdf.
5. Decent work has become a universal objective and has been included in major human rights declarations, UN resolutions, and outcome documents from major conferences, including Article 23 of the Universal Declaration of Human Rights (1948), the World Summit for Social Development (1995), World Summit Outcome Document (2005), the high-level segment of ECOSOC (2006), the Second United Nations Decade for the Eradication of Poverty (2008–2017), Conference on Sustainable Development (2011), and in the UN's 2030 Agenda for Sustainable Development (2015).

45 Disability and Civic Engagement in Newfoundland and Labrador

Aleksandra Stefanovic-Chafe

The NL government can do more for persons with disabilities. @NLCODNL @crwdp #DemocraticReformNL

Democracies pride themselves with giving voice to and protecting the rights of all the people they represent and our federal and provincial governments are no exception. However, when it comes to persons with disabilities, while progress has been made in advancing their rights in our province, their representation within government organizations is still unnecessarily limited. For a group that has been historically marginalized and discriminated against, it may seem particularly challenging to engage in what traditionally have been considered institutions that disadvantage those with disabilities. In addition, the national rates for both unemployment and poverty for persons with disabilities are considerably higher than those for persons without disabilities. When faced with the struggle to meet some of life's basic needs, this population group often feels politically apathetic and unwilling to participate in democratic processes, whether voicing opinions, advocating for their rights, voting, or joining a political party. This lack of participation keeps particular issues, concerns, and needs central to their lives at the margins of provincial policy–making.[1]

Disability is a complex phenomenon. Historically described in terms of an individual's deficit, the definition of disability has evolved to also reflect the interaction between persons with impairments and environmental and social barriers that hinder their full and effective participation in society.[2]

This social model of disability asserts that social organization and structure are among the main causes of disability and brings political empowerment to disability groups to demand inclusion and full citizenship.[3] However, more needs to be done to encourage better engagement of persons with disabilities in democratic processes, starting from the very early stages of their lives.

While we may lack data on political engagement for our province, let's look at what we know. Over 10 per cent of our province`s population is considered to live with a disability, and many of them are eligible voters. The act of voting is a right, and yet it has been a missed opportunity for many persons with disabilities for decades. In the recent past, significant improvements have been made in making voting accessible across the province. During the last elections in 2015, Elections NL and community disability organizations worked together to encourage voting and improve voting experiences of individuals with disabilities. This improvement was accomplished through accessible voting stations, instructional videos for persons with visual or hearing impairments, and information for election officers to provide appropriate support and assistance.[4] Persons with vision loss could place a tactile template over the ballot to vote independently, and others were provided special ballots that enabled them to vote outside a polling station. Online voting, while successfully used in many municipalities across the country, is yet to become a common practice in our province. In addition to making voting accessible, local disability organizations provided an opportunity for persons with disabilities to engage with the provincial leaders in a discussion regarding their party platforms and disability-related issues during the election campaign.

The activism and civic engagement of the province`s disability organizations are vibrant, meaningful, and strong. Agencies such as Coalition for Persons with Disabilities Newfoundland and Labrador and Empower continuously advocate for the rights of persons with disabilities. Along with enabling and encouraging them to vote, these organizations urge government to change election practices, strengthen and improve social policies related to disability, and work on reducing stigma and prejudice.

But encouraging voting and making it accessible is only one aspect of political and civic engagement. In order for citizens with disabilities to be inspired to vote, they need to see their issues discussed and put forward by individuals who could best represent them. There needs to be mirror representation of our diversity within political leadership. Persons with disabilities do not just make up a certain percentage of our voting population, but they also represent an untapped potential for leadership, for alternative perspectives and understanding of diverse ways to work, live, and contribute to our community. It is neither moral nor practical to hinder their opportunities for a chance to compete at the highest levels of decision-making.

It is unclear how many persons with disabilities are in senior positions in our provincial government. Research suggests that they are not seeking elected office in numbers that represent their place in the general population. Only about 1 per cent of the candidates who ran provincially across the country in the last three general elections were persons with disabilities.[5] In the three most recent provincial elections, Nova Scotia had seven candidates with disabilities seeking political office, British Columbia had five, and Newfoundland and Labrador has yet to elect a person who self-identifies as having a disability.[6] Similar to general employment issues, there are a number of systemic barriers for participation in elected politics, namely, lack of resources and supports for candidates with disability and existing prejudices and negative attitudes towards disability. Political parties should adopt more inclusive recruiting and nominating practices and take into consideration the diverse interests and experiences of all Canadians. Elected candidates should then be considered for cabinet appointments and key critic portfolios by premiers and oppositions leaders. The government also needs to ensure proper access to education for all persons with disabilities, continuous and co-ordinated services through all stages of life, early employment/internship opportunities, and supportive employment environments. Many of these changes and actions are attitudinal and would not require additional resources and funding. They do, however, require open communication lines and a strong commitment to advancing democratic processes in our province while giving voices to historically marginalized populations. ★

About the Author

Aleksandra Stefanovic-Chafe (Medicine, Memorial University of Newfoundland) is a Ph.D. candidate in the Faculty of Medicine's Division of Community Health and Humanities where she is researching disability and employment. Aleksandra holds B.A. and M.A. degrees in Political Science from MUN.

Notes

1. M.J. Prince, "The Electoral Participation of persons with Special Needs," Elections Canada (2007), at: http://elections.ca/res/rec/part/paper/special_

needs/special_needs_e.pdf.

2. World Health Organization, "Disabilities" (2016), at: http://www.who.int/topics/disabilities/en/.
3. T. Shakespeare, "The Social Model of Disability," *The Disability Studies Reader* 2 (2006): 197–204.
4. Elections Newfoundland and Labrador, "Accessible Info" (2016), at: http://www.elections.gov.nl.ca/elections/access/index.html.
5. S. Fletcher, J. Howard, M. Levesque, K. Murphy, and D. Onley, "Roundtable: Disability in Parliamentary Politics," *Canadian Parliamentary Review* 38, 1 (2015): 6–13
6. M. Levesque, "Searching for Persons with Disabilities in Canadian Provincial Office," *Canadian Journal of Disability Studies* 5, 1 (2016): 73–106.

46 Enabling the Political Participation of Persons with Disabilities

Mario Levesque

It's time to change campaign finance laws & provide incentives for parties to engage people with disabilities in #NLpoli. @NLCODNL #DemocraticReformNL

Persons with disabilities are significantly under-represented in elected office in Newfoundland and Labrador. Few have been elected at the municipal level while none have been elected provincially, based on what can be observed or has been declared by individuals.[1] This is despite the fact the province has a rate of disability of 14.1 per cent for people 15 years of age or greater, representing almost 60,000 people.[2]

The marginalization of persons with disabilities in Newfoundland and Labrador is significant and consistent with other Canadian provinces. For example, persons with disabilities represented less than 1 per cent of candidates in the last three provincial elections for *each* province.[3] This is noteworthy because there are symbolic and substantive benefits to having minority representation from persons with disabilities. Symbolic benefits include the fact that seeing those with similar characteristics to oneself in positions of power leads to more "buy in" or legitimacy. Substantively, the role played by disabled politicians is important, given that their inclusion may lead to greater consideration of disability in policy discussions, which can lead to better policy and the breaking down of stigma and discrimination.[4]

For Newfoundland and Labrador, the political participation of persons with disabilities is also consistent with existing government policy. For example, the province's Strategy for the Inclusion of Persons with Disabilities has been carefully crafted to align with the provisions of the Human Rights Act, the Canadian Charter of Rights and Freedoms, and the UN Convention on the Rights of Persons with Disabilities, which includes the political participation of persons with disabilities. Political participation is further elaborated in the 2015–2018 Action Plan for the Strategy, which proclaims that representation of persons with disabilities on government agencies, boards, and commissions is to be promoted. Yet, promotion needs to move beyond government agencies, boards, and commissions to elected office.

How to proceed? This is challenging because two main blockages prevent persons with disabilities from seeking elected office. First, provincial campaign finance laws are vague in relation to disability expenses in that they indicate that reasonable campaign expenses, including those related to transportation for election purposes, are excluded. What does reasonable mean? Is the use of specialized transit to attend community meetings, which can amount to thousands of dollars, excluded? Likewise, are the costs for an attendant to aid a blind person in going door to door or to translate speech for a deaf person excluded? Given their expense, would they be considered *reasonable* and therefore excluded? While candidates can have campaign expenses reimbursed, it is capped at one-third of eligible expenses provided they obtain at least 15 per cent of the vote, a high threshold. This leaves persons with disabilities in a precarious position when seeking elected office.

To remedy this, campaign finance laws need to be modified to ensure equal opportunity for disabled candidates. Specific language in campaign laws indicating that disability-related expenses do not count against campaign limits would be helpful. Also, disability-related expenses should be *fully* reimbursed provided candidates receive a certain portion of the vote. Manitoba, through its Manitoba Election Financing Act of 2013, has this provision with a candidate needing at least 10 per cent of the valid votes cast to be reimbursed. Yet, even this threshold is high and consideration is needed for reimbursement on a sliding scale, with the greater share of the vote a disabled candidate receives, the more he or she would be reimbursed. While not sufficient, this would at least make seeking elected office more attractive for persons with disabilities.

The second blockage for persons with disabilities seeking elected office relates to political parties that are not as inclusive as they could be. For example, none of the three main political parties in Newfoundland and Labrador has a disability wing, yet all have women's and youth wings. The Liberal Party goes further and also has Aboriginal and seniors' commissions.

Lastly, only the New Democrats have what can be called an "inclusion provision," whereby, among other things, they seek people of all "abilities." Other parties and their constitutions are silent on such issues. Why, especially considering the prevalence of disability in the province?

Making political parties more inclusive is hard to address. Mandated quotas are controversial and largely rejected by the disability community itself. A promising alternative is for the government to provide incentives for the nomination of minority candidates. This incentive can be in the form of reimbursing political parties additional monies should candidates be successful in being elected — up to an additional one-third or half of each disabled candidate's expenses. In addition, the provincial government can bypass political parties and create a fund that persons with disabilities could access to offset disability-related expenses, as the United Kingdom has recently done.[5] To offset these added costs, the reimbursement rate for non-disabled candidates can be reduced slightly.

Addressing campaign finance laws and providing incentives for political parties and disabled candidates to seek elected office would help persons with disabilities to be included in society. It is also consistent with the province's inclusion strategy and would contribute to breaking down stigma and discrimination while facilitating a vibrant Newfoundland and Labrador. ★

About the Author

Mario Levesque (Politics and International Relations, Mount Allison University) researches disability politics and policy in Canada related to political participation, leadership, accessible transit, and labour market programming. He is currently working on an SSHRC-funded study on disability leadership in Atlantic Canada and has published in various journals, including *Canadian Journal of Disability Studies*, *Canadian Public Policy*, and the *Canadian Journal of Nonprofit and Social Economy Research*.

Notes

1. Alex Marland, "Order, Please! The Newfoundland and Labrador House of Assembly," *Studies of Provincial and Territorial Legislatures*, Canadian Study of Parliament Group (2011): 1–48, at: http://cspg-gcep.ca/pdf/Newfoundland_Marland-e.pdf; Mario Levesque, "Searching for Persons with Disabilities in Canadian Provincial Office," *Canadian Journal of Disability Studies* 5, 1 (2016): 73–106.
2. Statistics Canada, "Canadian Survey on Disability 2012," at: http://www.statcan.gc.ca/pub/89-654-x/89-654-x2013001-eng.htm.

3. Levesque, "Searching for Persons with Disabilities."
4. Ingrid Guldvik, Ole Petter Askheim, and Vagard Johansen, "Political Citizenship and Local Political Participation for Disabled People," *Citizenship Studies* 17, 1 (2013): 76–91.
5. United Kingdom, "Disabled Peoples Elected Office Access Fund Extended" (n.d.), at: http://www.disabilityrightsuk.org/news/2014/february/disabled-peoples-elected-office-access-fund-extended.

PART 7: OH ME NERVES, THE OPPOSITION GOT ME DROVE

Members of the House of Assembly at their desks, circa 1909. (Source: Provincial Archives)

Two centuries ago, philosopher Joseph de Maistre wrote that "every nation gets the government it deserves." That is more likely to be true in democratic societies when steps are not taken to ensure a representative legislature as well as a robust opposition to keep the government on its toes.

The composition of the House of Assembly should roughly mirror society as a whole and its members should act as a check on the premier and cabinet. In this section, Nancy Peckford and Raylene Lang-Dion identify ways to get more women elected, and Dimitrios Panagos suggests that seats should be reserved for Indigenous citizens. No matter who is elected, there must be reasonable decorum during debate, as Taylor Stocks remarks. Paul Thomas maintains that there must be opportunities for MHAs to participate meaningfully in legislative committees that actively scrutinize government business. But this only works if there are a sizable numbers of MHAs from a variety of political parties, which is why James Feehan, Sean Fleming, and Glyn George call for electoral reform.

47 Electing Women to the House of Assembly

Nancy Peckford and Raylene Lang-Dion

C'mon Newfoundland and Labrador — let's do more to get more women elected! @EqualVoiceCA #NLpoli #DemocraticReformNL

The recent American presidential election between the Democratic Party's Hillary Clinton and the Republican Party's Donald Trump is a pernicious example of the yet-to-be-broken "glass ceiling" for women in the political life of the United States. However, it is only with deep political analysis and thorough academic discourse — as well as several formal investigations into the extent and impact of Russian meddling in the election — that we will truly understand what happened in this historic election where most pollsters were confident that the U.S. would elect its first female president. Instead, Donald Trump, not Hillary Clinton, succeeded President Barack Obama.

We are now faced with the daunting question of what this means for women in politics in the U.S., Canada, and beyond. Currently, Canada ranks 63rd on the Inter-Parliamentary Union's classification of women elected globally, which is an all-time low — with Rwanda, Bolivia, and Cuba electing the largest numbers of women to their respective legislatures. In Canada, on average, women comprise 25 per cent of those who are elected to political office. In Newfoundland and Labrador, the statistics tell the same tale. For example, currently there is one female municipal councillor out of a total of 11 for the City of St. John's. Ten women MHAs sit in the provincial legislature out of a total of 40, and three of the province's seven federal Members of Parliament are women.

Fundamental issues, including various systemic barriers, are numerous. However, for the purposes of this essay, our focus is on Equal Voice's initiative "livable legislatures," which seeks to shift the structural and cultural norms within politics so that the electoral arena is not only accessible for women, but a forum where they can thrive.

Equal Voice is Canada's only national, not-for-profit, multi-partisan, bilingual organization dedicated to promoting the election of more women to political office, addressing the barriers for women, and contributing to an improved discourse about women who seek to be elected and serve. Given that a Royal Commission nearly a half-century ago explored women's political participation and public life[1] and that countless papers, seminars, and conferences have addressed the subject, the time has come for the implementation of pragmatic solutions that borrow from innovations widely adopted by the public and corporate sectors. They include: the better use of technology for conducting business and meetings; sharing the workload by investing resources to cultivate a robust team to support the work of the legislator; and allowing for flexibility at critical periods of caregiving, such as after the birth/adoption of a child or, on the other end of the spectrum, the death of a loved one.[2]

Reviewing what has been proposed federally can provide some options for local legislative reforms in a practical, economical, and politically savvy manner. While none of these proposed reforms have been fully embraced in Canada's Parliament, they are being actively reviewed by a House of Commons committee, and House leaders are seeking to make federal political life more sustainable. Further, Equal Voice has called on decision-makers to ensure that the review of Canada's current electoral system fully recognizes the gendered effects of not only the first-past-the-post system, but also the cultural and political context in which individuals seek nomination within a political party.[3] Its submission to the Special Committee was authored by Dr. Grace Lore, Equal Voice's senior researcher, who conducted a comprehensive survey of gender and electoral systems in Europe and North America while at the University of British Columbia. She recommended: the evaluation of potential changes to the federal nomination process — not just the voting system — that might then be implemented; an ongoing review of retention issues and political culture to increase the representation of women in Canada; and consideration of the reasons for the relatively low numbers of women elected and what women can do to address issues that disproportionately affect them.

Structural changes can be implemented in myriad ways while taking into consideration a government's fiscal realities, the election cycle, the potential change of political representation and priorities, and the public's appetite for such structural changes. Nonetheless, despite these considerations, a strong movement exists for the election of more women in Canada and abroad, originating from a wide range of political influences inside and outside of the political process. By working together across political party lines, raising awareness of the importance of women having a voice at the political decision-making table, and through innovative and courageous ideas, the glass ceiling will be shattered once and for all. ★

About the Authors

Nancy Peckford (Equal Voice Canada) is the executive director of Equal Voice, a national multi-partisan organization dedicated to the election of more women to all levels of government in Canada. Nancy has worked with a variety of groups on issues critical to women's economic security, including the St. John's Women's Centre. Nancy remains very connected to her roots in Newfoundland and Labrador.

Raylene Lang-Dion (Equal Voice Ottawa) is past national chair of Equal Voice. She has worked in politics for over 15 years at the federal and provincial levels, including for two cabinet ministers and in two legislatures. She holds a Master's degree in Political Science, and completed her thesis on the topic of women and politics in her native Newfoundland and Labrador.

Notes

1. Florence Bird, *Report of the Royal Commission on the Status of Women in Canada* (Ottawa, 1970), at: http://epe.lac-bac.gc.ca/100/200/301/pco-bcp/commissions-ef/bird1970-eng/bird1970-eng.htm.
2. House of Commons, Standing Committee on Procedures and House Affairs, 19 Apr. 2016, 42nd Parliament, 1st session, presentation by Nancy Peckford and Grace Lore, at: http://www.parl.gc.ca/HousePublications/Publication.aspx?Language=e&Mode=1&Parl=42&Ses=1&DocId=8204546&File=0.
3. Equal Voice, "Equal Voice Calls on Electoral Reform Committee to Implement Gender-based Analysis as It Examines Electoral Systems and Democratic Engagement," news release, 13 Sept. 2016, at: https://www.equalvoice.ca/speaks_article.cfm?id=1089.

48 Reserving Seats in the House for Aboriginal MHAs

Dimitrios Panagos

How about we reserve some seats in the legislature for #Aboriginal representatives? #cdnpoli #DemocraticReformNL

One measure of the health of any liberal democracy is the degree to which its citizens participate in elections. It is now the case that, in both federal and provincial elections, Aboriginal Canadians consistently participate at lower levels than their non-Aboriginal counterparts.[1] Yet, there is very little in the academic literature on Aboriginal political behaviour. The work that does exist posits a number of possible reasons for this lower rate of participation: the most concerning is the different views held by Aboriginal and non-Aboriginal citizens on questions about the legitimacy of federal and provincial institutions of government.

From the point of view of Aboriginal Canadians, the legitimacy of these institutions is problematic in at least two ways. First, these institutions are "alien" in the sense that they were imposed on Aboriginal peoples as a result of settler-state colonialism. This form of colonialism led to the destruction of Aboriginal political authority and the creation of non-Aboriginal forms of government. Evidence illustrates that some Aboriginal Canadians stay away from the ballot box as a way of resisting the political authority of these "alien" governments.[2] Second, these institutions, which employ the first-past-the-post principle, create structural disadvantages for populations that are small and dispersed.[3] Given the fact that Aboriginal citizens constitute numerical minorities in many provinces and territories and the fact that these same citizens are, for the most part, dispersed throughout the country, the ability of Aboriginal citizens to shape the outcome of elections is generally limited. When minority voters are confronted with these sorts of structural problems, they arguably have good reason to skip the voting booth.

The House of Assembly in Newfoundland and Labrador, like all of its counterparts in Canada, is subject to these two legitimacy problems. A number of scholars have argued that changing existing electoral boundaries to recognize "communities of interest" is one way to address the latter legitimacy problem.[4] However, focusing on electoral boundaries will not address the former legitimacy problem stemming from the usurpation of Aboriginal political authority.

One possible way to address both of the problems of legitimacy, in a fashion that is reasonably cost-neutral, is to adopt the New Zealand model and create "reserved Aboriginal seats" in the legislature. These seats would be "reserved" in the sense that they would be elected solely by members of the Aboriginal population and only Aboriginal citizens could hold these seats. Creating reserved Aboriginal seats would require the creation of two different electoral rolls and providing Aboriginal Newfoundlanders and Labradorians with the choice of either registering on an Aboriginal electors' roll or a general electors' roll. Aboriginal voters on the former roll would elect the Aboriginal individuals who would hold the reserved Aboriginal seats and the other voters on the general roll would elect the remaining MHAs who would be either Aboriginal or non-Aboriginal citizens.

Reserved Aboriginal seats in the House of Assembly would address both types of legitimacy problems. In terms of the structural disadvantages that stem from the fact that the Aboriginal population is a numerical minority, the existence of these seats would offset some of the negative impacts of this factor. Since non-Aboriginal people could not vote for the reserved Aboriginal seats, the electoral results in these instances would be solely determined by Aboriginal voters.

In terms of the problems of legitimacy stemming from the usurpation of Aboriginal political authority, reserved Aboriginal seats are one way of highlighting the unique place of Aboriginal peoples in the province. These seats would guarantee that a certain number of Aboriginal citizens would be present in every legislative session. Aboriginal citizens could look at the composition of the House and see members of their community staring back at them. This representation is certainly of symbolic importance. Aboriginal presence in the House is, of course, also an effective way to bring attention to issues that are important to Aboriginal Newfoundlanders and

Labradorians and, potentially, to get these issues on the legislative agenda. Better legislation — legislation that addresses Aboriginal concerns — may go some way to mitigating this aspect of the legitimacy deficit.

The efficacy of such a scheme is certainly related to specifics not outlined here. Important questions remain. How many reserved Aboriginal seats would be appropriate? How would these seats be distributed? Should factors aside from Aboriginality (e.g., sex or community membership) impact the eligibility of those seeking to run for the reserved seats? The answers to these questions are best not determined without the active participation of the potentially affected Aboriginal parties. This is especially true given that an important part of the legitimacy problem outlined above resulted from the imposition of an alien political authority. Ideally, any changes to the electoral system must be the result of negotiations between Aboriginal peoples, the federal government, and the provincial government. ★

About the Author

Dimitrios Panagos (Political Science, Memorial University of Newfoundland) is a specialist in the study of contemporary political philosophy and Aboriginal rights, with research contributions combining both normative and empirical concerns. He has published work on aboriginality, rights, Aboriginal voting behaviour, and resource governance. He recently published a monograph entitled, *Uncertain Accommodation: Aboriginal Identity and Group Rights in the Supreme Court of Canada* (University of British Columbia Press, 2016).

Notes

1. A. Harell, Dimitrios Panagos, and J.S. Matthews, "Explaining Aboriginal Turnout in Federal Elections: Evidence from Alberta, Saskatchewan and Manitoba," in Jerry P. White, Julie Peters, Dan Beavon, and Peter Dinsdale, eds., *Exploring Voting, Governance and Research Methodology*, vol. 10 (Toronto: Thompson Education Publishing, 2011).
2. A. Harell and Dimitrios Panagos, "Locating the Aboriginal Gender Gap: The Political Preferences and Participation of Aboriginal Women in Canada," *Politics and Gender* 9, 4 (2013): 414–38.
3. Richard Johnston and Janet Ballantyne, "Geography and the Electoral System," *Canadian Journal of Political Science* 10, 4 (1977): 857–66.
4. Wayne Brown and Alain Pelletier, eds., *Electoral Insight*, vol. 4, no. 2 (Ottawa: Elections Canada, Oct. 2004).

49 The Downfalls of Debate

Taylor Stocks

Let's talk: An essay on Dialogue versus Debate in the legislature. #cdnpoli #DemocraticReformNL

Debate as a conversational form works best when its participants are relatively equal. Pairs should be similar in terms of their level of preparation and skill, their access to resources to interpret information on an issue, and their completion and strength of argument. High-level competitive debate can be beautiful to watch; formal styles bring debaters closer to parity, which allows for a clash of ideas and a rich exploration of topics. Debaters don't engage to convince their opponents. Rather, they aim to prove to the judges that their case is the most comprehensive and sound.

Within houses of government, including the House of Assembly in Newfoundland and Labrador, debate is the conversational mode that underpins policy formation. Ideally, the governing party would bring forward a policy to be debated. The opposing party would make a constructive case in contrast to what was offered, as well as refuting the arguments of government. The debate would be moderated by the Speaker of the House and we, as the citizenry to whom our politicians are beholden, would act as external judges, making the final call on whose case was strongest, and therefore whether or not a certain policy should move ahead.

But we don't live in this ideal world. Governing and opposition parties rarely have parity within the House of Assembly. This situation results in an imbalance of power and workload as the few members who are not within the governing party's caucus are expected to keep tabs not only on cabinet, but on all policy that the party creates. Populism, when fuelled by personalities such as former Premier Danny Williams, takes root regardless of supposed safeguards.[1] In addition, citizens do not get the chance to act as judges of quality, save for voting in elections every four years or so and those participating in smaller interest groups that can spend time and energy organizing around a particular issue. With majority governments, policy is passed regardless of opposition, circumventing the very form of conversation meant to bring rigour to the process.

As it functions in our systems of government, debate has harmful effects on policy formation. We have all grown tired with our politicians who rail against a policy when in opposition, only to adopt it wholeheartedly once in power, therefore undermining the trust that we have in our individuals and systems of decision-making. Debate insists that parties make themselves out to be right and the other to be wrong. This leads to entrenchment within party ideology and dissuades even internal questioning that could lead to more robust policy. Question Period, while an important accountability mechanism, contributes to the overplaying of partisanship and reduces what could have been quality debate to digestible sound bites.[2]

These features make long-term policy creation nearly impossible. Problems that will take 10, 20, or 50 years to solve never get the stable, enduring solutions they need. Once a new party gains power, part of their role is to show how wrong the other party was by undermining their policy directions and thus undoing policy that may actually be necessary for long-term change. This reinforces citizen bias towards short-term policy creation as long-term policy promises are not seen as credible.[3]

Innovation also suffers under government models of debate. Change requires a degree of comfort with the unknown, support in taking risks, and the opportunity to try something new and untested in the local context. Debate, especially within the House of Assembly, insists on having complete arguments, using unknowns against an opposing team, and wielding potential failure as proof of incompetence. This is not in line with recent change theory that instructs us to fail fast and learn quickly, where mechanisms like pilot projects allow for small-scale failure and therefore enable rapid local learning that can inform more high-cost initiatives.[4] It is no surprise that our House of Assembly has such a difficult time undertaking meaningful and long-lasting change.

This isn't to say that there is no place for debate in the creation of government policy. There are other conversational modes that, if integrated wisely, would produce more fruitful policy outcomes, allow governments to develop and maintain long-term policy, and foster change and growth within the institution. Dialogue is often juxtaposed with debate as a conversational form that privileges different kinds of behaviour and information. Dialogue encourages its participants to suspend judgment and entrenched party ideology and see the truth in other perspectives, even as we disagree with them. It fosters the co-creation of shared knowledge by blending research from multiple perspectives, i.e., what is true across party divides.[5] This process welcomes unfinished thought as an opportunity to explore new possibilities, which allows for risk-taking and innovation. Cross-party committees on issues are a good start but they will continue to embody principles of debate if conscious action is not taken to change the forms of listening, expression, and information-sharing within these spaces. Members of the House of Assembly must commit to holding dialogic cross-party spaces where admitting to incompleteness, or saying they do not know something, is seen as an opportunity to learn instead of chance to prove party incompetence.

In our society where problems are intractable without co-operation from all stakeholders, dialogic forms of policy formation are essential components to be integrated into government conversational models. Without dialogue to balance debate, our House of Assembly will inevitably follow in the tracks of previous generations. ★

About the Author

Taylor Stocks (Harris Centre of Regional Policy and Development, Memorial University of Newfoundland) is an institutional activist interested in facilitating long-term community change. With a background in emotional accountability of organizations, strategic systems change, and revolutionary politics, their current focus is on designing spaces where words connect vibrantly to action and where people can speak openly about how present power dynamics are affecting their capacity to act.

Notes

1. Margaret Canovan, "Trust the People! Populism and the Two Faces of Democracy," *Political Studies* 47, 2 (1999): 1–16.
2. Alison Loat and Michael MacMillan, *Tragedy in the Commons, Former Members of Parliament Speak Out about Canada's Failing Democracy* (Toronto: Random House Canada, 2014), 95–110.
3. Alan M. Jacobs and J.S. Matthews, "Why Do Citizens Discount the Future? Public Opinion and the Timing of Policy Consequences," *British Journal of*

Political Science 42, 4 (2012): 903–35, at: doi: http://dx.doi.org/10.1017/S0007123412000117.

4. Kakee Scott, Conny Baker, and Jaco Quist, "Designing Change by Living Change," *Design Studies* 33, 3 (2012): 279–97.
5. D. Yankelovich, *The Magic of Dialogue* (New York: Simon & Schuster, 1999), 35–46.

50 Democratizing the Legislative Branch

Paul Thomas

Empowering committees and extending sitting hours can help the legislature hold government to account. Retweet if you agree. #cdnpoli #DemocraticReformNL

The legislative branch of the Government of Newfoundland and Labrador is in trouble. As Canada's second smallest provincial legislature, the House of Assembly has long had difficulty scrutinizing government spending and proposed legislation.[1] The recent elimination of eight MHAs has only aggravated the situation. Cabinet members, parliamentary secretaries, and other government figures (i.e., the whip and caucus chair) now compose half of all Assembly members. If one also accounts for the Speaker, this leaves just 19 opposition members and government backbenchers to hold ministers to account. As shown in Table 50.1 (see page 240), the comparable figure for the New Brunswick legislature is 30 members, greatly increasing its scrutiny potential.

Yet legislative capacity is not solely a product of size but also varies with the procedures employed. Indeed, the 2015 motion passed by the House in support of the reduction in seats also noted that "modernizing procedures would allow for greater involvement of all MHAs in the legislative process," and called for reforms aimed at "enhancing the role of individual members."[2] However, no such changes were made. Instead, the Assembly continues to operate under standing orders that were last revised in 2005. Unless reforms are made now, the government's control over the House appears likely to grow further.

A recent study of Canada's provincial legislatures demonstrated that

Table 50.1: Membership Breakdown and Sitting Hours, Newfoundland & Labrador and New Brunswick

	Newfoundland & Labrador	**New Brunswick**
Member breakdown		
Ministers and parliamentary secretaries	18 (45%)	15 (31%)
Government whips and caucus chairs	2 (5%)	3 (6%)
Speaker	1 (2.5%)	1 (2%)
Government backbenchers and opposition	19 (47.5%)	30 (61%)
Total members	**40**	**49**
Sitting hours		
Average sitting days per year	51	61
Average sitting hours per week	15	21.5
Average sitting hours per year	191	327

smaller assemblies can use longer sittings and standing committees to enhance their ability to engage in scrutiny.[3] Longer sittings allow more members to participate in debates and improve the odds that bills will receive thorough review. They also increase the number of times that governments must face the opposition in Question Period. Standing committees allow legislatures to engage in parallel processing with different groups of legislators dealing with different issues simultaneously. The House of Assembly fared poorly on both fronts, having the second lowest average annual sitting hours of any provincial legislature and one of the least developed standing committee systems.[4]

Introducing longer sittings is a straightforward reform that would yield immediate benefits for scrutiny. However, procedural changes to reinvigorate the standing committees would have an even greater impact on the House of Assembly's capacity to connect with citizens and hold the government to account. In addition to allowing the legislature to focus on several issues at once, standing committees can also hear from witnesses, which allows citizens to engage directly with MHAs. Standing committee meetings also take place outside of the main chamber in a less confrontational atmosphere that can reduce partisanship and promote consensus.

Perhaps the most important reform would be to allow standing committees to undertake studies without a reference from the House. Given the Assembly's limited sitting days, standing committees should also be empowered to meet while the House is adjourned. These changes would enhance their autonomy and allow them to deal with topics the government might rather avoid. It also would make them more proactive, with the capacity to suggest new policies instead of waiting for an assignment from the House. Another major reform would be to require that bills be considered in standing committees rather than being reviewed in the Committee of the Whole House. This reform would greatly improve legislative review by allowing witnesses to speak to the measures proposed. It would also give members more incentive to specialize in particular policy areas. These initiatives would be further strengthened if legislators were appointed to committees for the duration of a legislature, which would prevent parties from removing members who are too independent.

The process of reinvigorating all standing committees simultaneously may seem daunting, but one straightforward reform would be for the Standing Committee on Government Services to conduct pre-budget hearings like those conducted by standing committees in British Columbia, Ontario, and the federal Parliament. At present, Newfoundland and Labrador's Minister of Finance holds consultations prior to releasing the budget. However, those meetings lack the non-partisan, deliberative dynamic possible in a legislative committee. A recent study of the pre-budget consultations by British Columbia's Standing Committee on Finance and Government Services found that they improve the legislature's role in both policy-making and in representing the views of citizens.[5] The key to the system is that the British Columbia government does not conduct its own parallel hearings, which leaves the Committee as the sole source of pre-budget recommendations. The Committee also releases its report well before the budget itself, which allows it to shape the government's agenda. Adopting a similar system would help to restore the House of Assembly as a focus of public attention and ensure that all parties have a voice in shaping budget priorities.

Extending the Assembly's sitting hours and reinvigorating the committee system may have marginal costs, such as those for committee transcripts. However, moving pre-budget consultations to the Standing Committee on Government Services would be revenue-neutral if the government followed British Columbia and ended its own consultations. The same is true if bills were considered in standing committees rather than the Committee of the Whole House. Moreover, reforms like those described here were supposed to have accompanied the seat reduction completed at the last election. As such, any marginal costs should be considered against the savings realized from that change. ★

About the Author

Paul Thomas (Political Science, Carleton University) is an SSHRC Postdoctoral Fellow who studies legislatures, parties, and the behaviour of elected officials in Canada and the United Kingdom. His recent publications include *Religion and Canadian Party Politics*, co-authored with David Rayside and Jerald Sabin (University of British Columbia Press, 2017), and "Evaluating Provincial and Territorial Legislatures," co-authored with Graham White, in C.J.C. Dunn, ed., *Provinces*, 3rd ed. (University of Toronto Press, 2015).

Notes

1. For a detailed analysis, see Alex Marland, "Order, Please! The Newfoundland and Labrador House of Assembly," *Studies of Provincial and Territorial Legislatures*, Canadian Study of Parliament Group (2011): 1–48, at: http://cspg-gcep.ca/pdf/Newfoundland_Marland-e.pdf.
2. Nick McGrath, Newfoundland and Labrador *House of Assembly Proceedings*. 29 Apr. 2015, 264.
3. Paul Thomas and Graham White, "Evaluating Provincial and Territorial Legislatures," in Christopher J.C. Dunn, ed., *Provinces: Canadian Provincial Politics*, 3rd ed. (Toronto: University of Toronto Press, 2015).
4. Ibid.
5. Geneviève Tellier, "Improving the Relevance of Parliamentary Institutions: An Examination of Legislative Pre-budget Consultations in British Columbia," *Journal of Legislative Studies* 21, 2 (2014): 192–212.

51 Institutionalizing a Strong Opposition through Electoral Reform

James Feehan

Here's an innovative type of electoral reform that is fairer for all parties. #cdnpoli #FairVote #DemocraticReformNL

One advantage of a first-past-the-post electoral system, which characterizes Canada's federal and provincial voting processes, is that elections generally produce majority governments. However, that system typically leaves the non-winning parties under-represented compared to their popular vote. That creates an argument for proportional representation, a system with its own problems such as unstable multi-party coalitions. Even the formation of a workable coalition can be elusive, as recent experience in Spain illustrates.[1] Mixed systems can be problematic and that may explain the persistence of the status quo in Canada, both federally and provincially, despite various reform proposals.[2]

If Newfoundlanders and Labradorians prefer a system that is likely to produce a majority government, then the challenge becomes how to ensure that the government's legislative agenda and policies are appropriately scrutinized and debated. That is the job of the opposition parties. However, at times their seat numbers have been demoralizingly low, making it nearly impossible to function effectively while facing overwhelming government majorities. In the 1966 general election, a Liberal sweep left the opposition with only 3 seats out of 42 in the House of Assembly; and in 2007 the Progressive Conservatives won 44 of 48 seats, leaving just 3 for the Liberals and 1 for the NDP. In these cases and in every other election where a party won a majority, the opposing parties' collective share of seats was much less than their share of the vote.[3] Similarly lopsided results have occurred elsewhere in Canada, especially at the provincial level, leaving opposition parties substantially under-represented.

A change in the process that leads to such under-representation is needed. Yet, most of the electorate probably does not want the minority governments that proportional representation would bring. On the other hand, a strong opposition in the legislature strengthens democracy. Therefore, a desirable electoral system is one that preserves the chances of a majority government but also guarantees that the losing parties will have enough seats to mount an effective opposition.

How might such a system be designed? For this province, one possibility is to maintain the current 40–district seat system, ideally with roughly equal numbers of eligible voters in each district, but add eight more seats for a total of 48. Call them "allotment seats." When a party wins 26 or more of the 40 districts seat then all 8 allotment seats would be awarded to the opposition parties according to their relative vote shares. This proposition preserves the winner's majority position but its magnitude is reduced. So, for example, if a party were to win all 40 seats, the opposition would have the 8 other seats, i.e., 17 per cent of all seats. Since opposition parties combined have never received less than 30 per cent of the popular vote in this province since 1949, this allotment is reasonable. More importantly, it ensures a meaningful number of opposition members.

If a party wins between 25 and 21 districts then the system would be majority-preserving by sharing the 8 seats. A winner with 25 district seats (the opposition having the 15 others) would receive 1 of the 8 allotment seats and the remaining 7 would go to the opposition. If it had won 24, the split would be 2 and 6 and so on, down to a 4 and 4 split at 22 as well as at 21. Table 51.1 (see page 245) summarizes these outcomes.

If the largest party wins 20 or fewer seats then the 8 seats would be allocated by popular vote shares across all parties, thus preserving the minority situation. To keep the system straightforward, the allotment could occur only following a general election and could not be subject to changes even if by-elections change the district counts. Members of the House in allotted seats would hold them at the pleasure of their respective parties. Here are some advantages of this type of system:

- The opposition would be less under-represented, relative to the popular vote.

Table 51.1: House of Assembly Configuration with Allotment Seats

Largest Party			Other Parties		
Districts Won	*Allotment*	*Total*	*Districts Won*	*Allotment*	*Total*
40	0	40	0	8	8
39	0	39	1	8	9
38	0	38	2	8	10
37	0	37	3	8	11
36	0	36	4	8	12
35	0	35	5	8	13
34	0	34	6	8	14
33	0	33	7	8	15
32	0	32	8	8	16
31	0	31	9	8	17
30	0	30	10	8	18
29	0	29	11	8	19
28	0	28	12	8	20
27	0	27	13	8	21
26	0	26	14	8	22
25	1	26	15	7	22
24	2	26	16	6	22
23	3	26	17	5	22
22	4	26	18	4	22
21	4	25	19	4	23

- The opposition would have sufficient numbers to effectively debate issues and to serve on legislative committees.
- It may encourage higher voter turnout because citizens who support a party with little chance of winning in a district would know that party could gain some of the allotted seats.
- It may encourage higher-quality candidates to stand for election, especially at times when one party is expected to win overwhelmingly, because a defeated candidate could be selected by her or his party to fill its allotment.
- Each opposition party and, where applicable, the governing party could select individuals to fill their share of the 8 seats according to expertise, demographics, region, gender, etc., which could address under-

representation concerns raised by White,[4] or the individuals could be elected from within party ranks.

This proposal adds eight more Members to the House of Assembly. Cost considerations are tiny relative to the sums spent by the government, but the argument holds for other configurations, e.g., 34:6, in which case the reform would be superficially cost-neutral. Variations on the proposed system are feasible as long as the total number of members is enough for the House to function and for legislative committees to operate.

Of course, sufficient opposition numbers is not enough to guarantee effectiveness. The opposition needs adequate resources as well. Also, political parties still have to attract quality candidates. The onus remains on them to do so, but this reform proposal would help. ★

About the Author

James Feehan (Economics, Memorial University of Newfoundland) has published scholarly works on public policy issues of particular relevance to Newfoundland and Labrador, notably on hydroelectric development, fiscal federalism, local government finance, offshore oil and gas, interprovincial trade, fisheries, and tax policy. In addition, he has published in international academic journals in economics and public policy. He is the editor of the journal *Newfoundland and Labrador Studies*.

Notes

1. "Spain's Uncertain Experiment with Minority Government," *The Ecomomist*, 8 Dec. 2016, at: http://www.economist.com/news/europe/21711525-mariano-rajoy-having-learn-negotiate-opposition-spains-uncertain-experiment.
2. For a review of various reform proposals, see A. Barnes, D. Lithwick, and E. Virgint, *Electoral Systems and Electoral Reform in Canada and Elsewhere: An Overview*. Background Paper, Publication No. 2016-06-E (Ottawa: Library of Parliament, 2016).
3. R. Koop, "Parties and Brokerage Politics in Newfoundland and Labrador," in A. Marland and M. Kerby, eds., *First Among Unequals: The Premier, Politics, and Policy in Newfoundland and Labrador* (Montreal and Kingston: McGill-Queen's University Press, 2014), 88.
4. G. White, "Comparing Provincial Legislatures," in C. Dunn, editor, *Provinces: Canadian Provincial Politics* (Peterborough, Ont.: Broadview Press, 1996), 209.

52 Strengthening the Opposition through Proportional Representation

Sean Fleming

Proportional representation would provide a more effective opposition and a more accountable government. #FairVote #cdnpoli #DemocraticReformNL

One of the most serious problems with democracy in Newfoundland and Labrador is the absence of an effective opposition. Provincial elections typically result in landslide majorities that leave the other parties too weak to keep the government in check. Although one-party dominance is due partly to Newfoundland and Labrador's culture of political bandwagoning, it is greatly exacerbated by the first-past-the-post voting system, which tends to award a disproportionate share of the seats to the winning party. Replacing first-past-the-post with a form of proportional representation would improve democracy in Newfoundland and Labrador by strengthening the opposition.

A healthy democracy requires competition for power. Even the most competent and honest governments are prone to groupthink and complacency, so it is necessary to have a strong opposition party that holds the government accountable and offers a credible alternative to voters. Newfoundland and Labrador has had many well-meaning governments that have made ill-considered and costly decisions. The weakness of the opposition creates the conditions for mismanagement and waste.

Ideally, first-past-the-post should produce a two-party system with a strong opposition party. In Newfoundland and Labrador, it produces alternating one-party dominance with "non-governing parties that are so dishevelled and partisan that there is often no credible opposition."[1] First-past-the-post magnifies one-party dominance by over-representing the government at the expense of the other parties (Table 52.1).

Table 52.1: Under-representation of the Opposition, 2003–2015

	Government		**Official Opposition**		**Third Party**	
	Seat %	*Vote %*	*Seat %*	*Vote %*	*Seat %*	*Vote %*
2003	70.8	58.6	25.0	33.1	4.2	6.8
2007	91.7	69.6	6.3	21.7	2.1	8.5
2011	77.1	56.1	12.5	19.1	10.4	24.6
2015	77.5	57.1	17.5	30.1	5.0	12.1

These exaggerated majorities leave the opposition with neither the personnel nor the resources to hold the government accountable. With so few opposition members, legislative committees are ineffective. The real decisions tend to be made in cabinet committees.[2] In addition, because research funding is allocated based on seat shares, the offices of the official opposition and the third party are underfunded.

What Newfoundland and Labrador needs is a voting system that awards the opposition a seat share approximating its vote share. One promising option is mixed-member proportional, which is used in Germany and New Zealand.[3] Voters in mixed-member systems cast two votes: one for a local candidate and another for a party. Some of the seats — say, two-thirds — are allocated to candidates based on their vote totals, as in first-past-the-post. The remaining seats, known as "list seats," are then allocated to parties so that their total seat shares are roughly equal to their vote shares. Mixed-member proportional is essentially a compromise between first-past-the-post and simple proportional representation.

For example, suppose that the 2007 general election was conducted using mixed-member proportional. There are 32 constituency seats and 16 list seats, and each party receives the same vote share and the same share of the constituency seats as it did under first-past-the-post. The distribution of constituency seats would be lopsided: 29 for the government, two for the opposition, and one for the third party. However, the distribution of list seats would balance out the result: four for the government, nine for the opposition, and three for the third party. The opposition and the third party would receive a combined total of 15 seats (31 per cent) instead of the four (8 per cent) that they received under first-past-the-post.

Mixed-member proportional would both mitigate one-party dominance and provide strong local representation. Newfoundlanders and Labradorians would get the opposition for which they vote, but they would still directly elect their local MHAs. It would even be possible to increase representation for remote areas of the province without adding constituencies. For instance, some list seats could be reserved for candidates from Labrador or the south coast of Newfoundland.

In the long run, mixed-member proportional would change the structure of the party system as well as the composition of the legislature. The case of New Zealand, which replaced first-past-the-post with mixed-member proportional in 1996, is instructive.[4] All 19 elections from 1938 through 1993 produced majority governments for either the National Party or the Labour Party, and other parties were all but shut out. However, none of the seven elections since 1996 has produced a single-party majority, and other parties currently hold about a quarter of the seats. The switch to mixed-member proportional did not result in chaos, as critics feared, and a healthy majority of New Zealanders voted to keep the system in 2011.

Mixed-member proportional would alter Newfoundland and Labrador's party system in similar ways. The NDP would become more competitive, the Labrador Party and the Green Party would likely win seats, and minority or coalition governments might eventually become the norm. The Liberal and Progressive Conservative parties would continue to win most of the seats, but they would often have to co-operate with other parties — sometimes even each other — in order to pass legislation. Newfoundlanders and Labradorians would get a more effective opposition, a more accountable government, and a political system much less prone to mistakes and mismanagement.

Even the Liberal Party and the Progressive Conservative Party would gain in the long run from replacing the first-past-the-post electoral system with mixed-member proportional. Although they would no longer win exaggerated landslides, they would no longer be decimated and humiliated when they lose. Never again would either party fall into disarray while its rival holds all of the power. ★

About the Author

Sean Fleming (Politics and International Studies, University of Cambridge) is a Ph.D. candidate and Rothermere Fellow at the University of Cambridge. His research has been published in the *European Journal of International Relations*. His interests include state responsibility, early modern political thought, and the politics of artificial intelligence. He is also a close observer of Newfoundland and Labrador politics.

Notes

1. Alex Marland, "Conclusion: Inferiority or Superiority Complex? Leadership and Public Policy in Newfoundland and Labrador," in Alex Marland and Matthew Kerby, eds., *First Among Unequals: The Premier, Politics, and Policy in Newfoundland and Labrador* (Montreal and Kingston: McGill-Queen's University Press, 2014), 265.
2. Christopher Dunn, "The Persistence of the Institutionalized Cabinet: The Central Executive in Newfoundland and Labrador," in Luc Bernier, Keith Brownsey, and Michael Howlett, eds., *Executive Styles in Canada* (Toronto: University of Toronto Press, 2005).
3. Matthew S. Shugart and Martin P. Wattenberg, eds., *Mixed-Member Electoral Systems: The Best of Both Worlds?* (Oxford: Oxford University Press, 2001).
4. Matthew S. Shugart and Andrew C. Tan, "Political Consequences of New Zealand's MMP System in Comparative Perspective," in Nathan F. Batto et al., eds., *Mixed-Member Proportional Systems in Constitutional Context: Taiwan, Japan, and Beyond* (Ann Arbor: University of Michigan Press, 2016); Jack Vowles, "New Zealand: The Consolidation of Reform?" in Michael Gallagher and Paul Mitchell, eds., *The Politics of Electoral Systems* (Oxford: Oxford University Press, 2005).

53 The Benefits of an Alternative Transferable Vote Electoral System

Glyn George

Alternative transferable vote would be a fairer voting system for #NLpoli elections. #DemocraticReformNL

Too many times in Canada, the U.S., and Britain, a party has taken power with an absolute majority of the seats but only a minority of the popular vote or, in some extreme instances, with even fewer votes than another party, which clearly denies the will of the voters. This happened in Newfoundland and Labrador in the general election of 1989, when the Liberal Party formed a majority government with 31 of the 52 seats, despite receiving fewer votes (47.0 per cent) than the PC Party (47.5 per cent).[1]

The present voting system of "first-past-the-post" must not continue: it encourages tactical (negative) voting instead of voting on positive principles and it leads to many wasted votes. Consider this example. Some electors support party "A" and are fiercely opposed to party "B" being elected. Opinion polls show that the election in that riding is between parties "B" and "C," with party "A" trailing badly. Under the present "first-past-the-post" system, votes by these electors for "A" are not only wasted on a third-place candidate but might also lead to the election of "B" with less than 40 per cent of the total vote. Switching to the second choice of "C" might provide enough votes for "C" to win and to prevent the election of "B."

The election of an MHA should follow this simple principle: in order to be elected, a candidate must have more votes than all other candidates combined. Balanced against that are (1) the need for as direct a link as possible between elected legislators and their constituents and (2) the desire for stable government.

The multi-member single transferable vote (STV) system has worked well in the Republic of Ireland for nearly all of its history.[2] In most general elections, one party or a coalition of two parties have been able to form a stable government. Each constituency elects up to five representatives and each party usually offers two or more candidates. Which of those candidates will be elected is controlled by the voters, not by the parties. However, the geography of this province rules STV out. Even now, some constituencies are geographically large and challenging. Under STV, constituencies would become far too large to be practicable.

The extreme of proportional representation is the closed-list system used in Israel: the entire country is one constituency, with seats allocated in proportion to votes cast for each party. But this system leads to unstable governments and destroys the link between an elected representative and the local electorate completely. The party machines control the ranking of candidates on their lists, not the voters.

The German hybrid system has many members elected directly by first-past-the-post, supplemented by additional members on a party list to bring the seats closer to proportionality with the votes gained by the parties. A modest threshold of 5 per cent of the votes keeps most fringe parties out. But it leads to two types of legislators: those chosen by the people and others who are not. The parties control ranking on the lists of additional members, not the voters.

The French system modifies first-past-the-post to hold a runoff ballot between the top two vote winners (except when a candidate is elected in the first round by receiving more votes than all other candidates combined). It draws out the election process unnecessarily and is too costly. It is far better to resolve the election in one alternative transferable vote ballot.

The alternative transferable vote (ATV) in the existing single-member constituencies would cause the least disruption to the way elections have been conducted in this province. ATV retains the existing links between elected representatives and their local electorates while ensuring that all elected persons enjoy the support of an absolute majority of the votes cast.

ATV and STV are very simple for the voter: just rank the candidates in order of preference. In an ATV ballot, a candidate is elected when that person has more votes than all other candidates combined. When no candidate has that majority, the candidate with the least number of first preferences is eliminated and the votes for the eliminated candidate are redistributed, according to the second preferences on those ballots, among the remaining candidates. If again none of the candidates has more than half of all the votes, then the candidate who now has the least number of votes is eliminated and those votes are redistributed, according to the highest preferences, among the other remaining candidates. The process continues until one candidate is elected with an absolute majority of the votes.

ATV is much simpler to count than STV. Many years ago I was a returning officer in an STV ballot for a small group, so I know how complicated the count can be. Recently I have conducted counts of ATV ballots for some small organizations. The counting effort was only slightly greater than for first-past-the-post; voters were able to vote positively in just one ballot and the results were much fairer. On its website, the Electoral Reform Society in the United Kingdom provides a good overview of these various voting systems, including their advantages and disadvantages.[3]

In my opinion, the alternative transferable vote should be used for all elections of Members of the House of Assembly and for other single-seat elections such as mayors and ward councillors. ★

About the Author

Glyn George (Electrical and Computer Engineering, Memorial University of Newfoundland) teaches mathematics. His volunteer work has included eight years as an elected school board member, 16 years as a community representative on two school councils in St. John's, and three years on the Executive of the Newfoundland and Labrador Federation of School Councils.

Notes

1. Government of Newfoundland and Labrador, *2015 Provincial General Election Report*, Elections Newfoundland and Labrador (2015), at: http://www.elections.gov.nl.ca/elections/ElectionReports/PDF/General.Elections/2015.GE.Report.FINAL.pdf, p. 399 (accessed 27 Oct. 2016).
2. Government of Ireland, Department of Housing, Planning, Community and Local Government, "Proportional Representation" (2016), at: http://www.citizensinformation.ie/en/government_in_ireland/elections_and_referenda/voting/proportional_representation.html (accessed 27 Oct. 2016).
3. Electoral Reform Society, "Voting Systems Made Simple" (2016), at: http://www.electoral-reform.org.uk/voting-systems (accessed 27 Oct. 2016).

PART 8: SCRUTINY

The Last Sitting of the House of Assembly (2 December 1933). Frederick Alderdice (1872–1936) was Prime Minister of Newfoundland from 1932 to 1934. Members of government are shown seated in the Colonial Building. This was the last government elected under the Dominion of Newfoundland. (Source: Provincial Archives)

The renowned American jurist Louis Brandeis once wrote that transparency is the best way to ensure good behaviour among those in positions of power. As he put it a century ago, "sunlight is said to be the best of disinfectants," a catchphrase that is used by all sorts of opposition parties seeking to form government. Once in power, however, all political leaders, and their policies, tend to become enveloped in secrecy, like a rolling fog.

Authors in this section envision transparency and scrutiny throughout all levels of political activity. All instruments and actors could work in tandem with people outside of government who draw on a modified access-to-information system, as suggested by Stephen Power. Stephen Wolinetz calls for the installation of a House of Assembly research bureau that would act as a think-tank. Alison Coffin explains the different tools available to bring financial data to the fore. These are data that a legislative budget officer would surely draw upon, a position that Jeffrey Collins feels is necessary. The auditor general could draw out even more data, particularly with respect to monitoring climate change responsibilities, argues Robert Sweeny. Jill Power suggests that efficiency committees be struck to identify ways to make better use of available resources. Concerns about government appointments are raised by Lynn Moore and Jeffrey Pittman. According to Gerald Galway, the province's school board system needs revitalizing. Evidently, Newfoundland and Labrador could do with a whole lot of sunlight.

54 Improving Newfoundland and Labrador's Access-to-Information System

Stephen Power

The access-to-information system can be streamlined in Newfoundland and Labrador. Here's how. #cdnmedia #DemocraticReformNL

Our province's government relies, to a large extent, on the private sector to function. Without businesses acting as vendors to government, it would have to make its own sandwiches, tires, MRI scanners, and most everything else it needs. By buying from the private sector, governments can in many cases take advantage of the efficiencies that businesses can create to procure goods and services at lower prices than had the government tried to produce them itself.

Government must therefore respect the privacy needs of the vendors it works with. The disclosure of confidential information could hurt the very vendors that government relies on for many goods and services. If vendors risked exposing their trade secrets or software codes to public disclosure every time they signed a contract with the government, fewer businesses might sign these contracts. This situation would make contracting with lower-cost options in the market potentially more difficult, and could force government in many possible cases to spend more for the same goods and services.

However, government also needs to ensure openness and transparency in all its operations. Beyond the ethical justification that backs the public's right to know what government is doing, this right to know is also premised on the idea that governments govern better when citizens have unimpeded access to this information. Good governance is promoted because the public can see how government is spending public funds, among other things.[1] This transparency identifies inefficiencies, discrepancies, and violations of the law related to public spending.[2] Mistakes can be corrected and learned from and wrongdoing can be discouraged,[3] which will hopefully result in a more efficient and trustworthy government.

Although not necessarily always opposed, these objectives — protecting privacy and maintaining an open government — must sometimes be balanced. This is the case if a requester of government information feels that the withholding of information from disclosure is not justified under Newfoundland and Labrador's Access to Information and Protection of Privacy Act (ATIPPA). Likewise, a vendor might seek to block the release of information it fears might give competitors an unfair advantage if that information were released to the public. Businesses often rely on keeping their plans and transactions secret, so as not to allow competitors to subvert their plans or steal proprietary information. However, this need must be balanced with the public's right to information on public institutions, particularly information on how these institutions spend public funds, if the principles underlying access-to-information systems are to be upheld. Such principles can also be extended to cover government information that touches on public safety, the environment, and other concerns.

Opposing claimants who want to appeal an access-to-information request will typically go through an appeals process. ATIPPA provides for the review of a request by an arm's-length agency,[4] but parties also have the option of pursuing an appeal through the courts. Such appeals can take years to resolve. One case involving a request for the disclosure of a contract signed between Memorial University of Newfoundland (MUN) and the office supplies company Staples in 2011 spent years in the courts before it was resolved four years later.[5] Although not all cases involving appeals will take this long to resolve, the MUN/Staples case is emblematic of the difficulties in trying to maintain an open government while protecting the legitimate business interests of vendors to government. Such work is ultimately costly, and lack of resources is a common contributor to dysfunction within access-to-information regimes in Canada.[6]

I don't think striking an appropriate balance should be so complicated, drawn out, or costly for such cases. I see an opportunity for the Government of Newfoundland and Labrador to streamline the province's access-to-information regime by standardizing the collection of the most commonly requested data from government contracts. Much in the same fashion that the finances of charities are required by law to be disclosed in a standard format that highlights how donations are being spent, the government could consider requiring successful bids for contracts to include a similar form. This document would broadly describe what goods or services are being purchased, at what price, and any other important conditions such as guarantees or commitments to maintain equipment. To avoid overburdening small businesses with red tape, such a document would only be required for contracts over a certain dollar amount. This document then could be uploaded automatically to an online government information portal (such as the Open Government website that the Government of Canada operates) or kept on file for expedited disclosure if existing resources could be used to run such a system.

Such a form would not cover all information relating to a contract, nor should it. Within these contracts is both information that would help improve public governance and transparency, and proprietary information that would hurt a vendor's ability to do business if released. By standardizing the release of commonly requested information, resources could be freed up to process more complicated ATIPPA requests, spent elsewhere, or returned to the taxpayer. Through these efficiencies, our province's government and our province as a whole would benefit. ★

About the Author

Stephen Power (Political Science, Memorial University of Newfoundland) is a graduate student completing his Master's thesis in political science. His research focuses on the intersections between Canadians, news organizations, and the government, and how social media alter these relationships. He was born in St. John's and lives in Paradise.

Notes

1. Daniel Berliner, "The Political Origins of Transparency," *Journal of Politics* 76, 2 (2014): 479–91; Ann Florini, "The Battle of Transparency," in Florini, ed., *The Right to Know: Transparency for an Open World* (New York: Columbia University Press, 2007), 9–24.
2. Maria Violeta Cimpoeru and Valentin Cimpoeru, "Budgetary Transparency — An Improving Factor for Corruption Control and Economic Performance," *Procedia Economics and Finance* 27 (2015): 579–86.
3. Berliner, "Political Origins of Transparency."
4. Government of Newfoundland and Labrador, Department of Health and Community Services, "Access to Information and Protection of Privacy Frequently Asked Questions" (2016, last modified 8 Feb. 2017), at: http://www.health.gov.nl.ca/health/faq/atipp.html (accessed 5 Mar. 2017).

5. Rob Antle, "Staples Loses Bill 29 Appeal over MUN Contract," CBC News, 14 Nov. 2015, at: http://www.cbc.ca/news/canada/newfoundland-labrador/staples-atippa-supreme-court-appeal-decision-1.3312914 (accessed 5 Mar. 2017).
6. Mary Francoli, "Open Government at a Crossroad: Canada Needs Better Funding and Access to Information Reform," *The Hill Times*, 8 Feb. 2016, at: https://www.hilltimes.com/2016/02/08/open-government-at-a-crossroad-canada-needs-better-funding-and-access-to-information-reform/49746 (accessed 5 Mar. 2017).

55 Public Policy Think-Tank

Steven Wolinetz

Want more informed debate? Establish a policy think-tank reporting to the @NL_HOA so MHAs have something meaningful to say. #NLpoli #DemocraticReformNL

There are periodic calls to have the House of Assembly open and sitting for longer periods of time. However, this will do little to improve the quality of democracy in Newfoundland and Labrador if members do not have anything to say about the content of government policy and possible alternatives to it. At present, the level of debate is often banal and sometimes vicious, with personal attacks substituting for substantive discussion and analysis.

The presumption behind our Westminster model of parliamentary democracy is that the government's job is to govern and the opposition's job is to oppose. Yet, there is a severe imbalance in information and expertise between the government and ordinary Members of the House Assembly. The government has the civil service at its disposal and is able to commission reports and analyses from outside consultants. In contrast, ordinary members — whether members of opposition parties or, for that matter, the government's backbench — have few, if any, resources of expertise at their disposal. Most are forced to fall back on personal knowledge (which is normally limited) and comments and complaints from constituents and affected interests. Although this may make it possible to critique policies once they have been implemented and their consequences are known, it means that ordinary members and opposition parties can critique proposed policies only in the most general terms when they are proposed and debated. Members of the public are at an even greater disadvantage.

One way to rectify this is to create a research bureau or think-tank attached to the House of Assembly. Think-tanks and research bureaus contribute to public dialogue in most Western democracies.[1] Reporting to opposition parties and backbench members and supervised by an independent board, the research bureau would be mandated to produce analyses of the government budget and selected policies and alternatives to them. Analyses of the budget should examine the consequences of alternate patterns of government spending — for example, the impacts of spending more or less on infrastructure or education and training on rates of economic growth, employment, and the provincial deficit. Reports on proposed policies should explore relevant research and investigate what has been done in other jurisdictions. Reports should be written in ways that not only Members of the House but also ordinary citizens are able to understand them. To foster informed debate, reports should be available to the media and the general public. If done well, reports might provide a basis for better informed debate in the House of Assembly or, should the House choose to do so, investigation by smaller committees.

It may be useful to consider an example of how such a research bureau might operate. In the next year or two, the province is likely to find itself choosing methods to reduce carbon emissions. The principal alternatives are a carbon tax or signing on to an existing cap-and-trade system as Ontario and Quebec are doing. Aware of this, the research bureau could examine existing research, distilling key points into a report on the impacts on different sectors of the economy and groups within the population. With such a report in hand, Members of the House and the public would be in a better position to participate in an informed debate on the topic.

Several cautions are in order: establishing a think-tank will improve the quality of debate only if it has time to conduct high-quality research and analysis. That means that it has to have sufficient notice of proposed initiatives. Nor will it be possible in any year to investigate more than a few policy areas. Expertise and reports will accumulate over time, but not immediately. Second, if the research bureau is to function as a source of independent analysis, then it must not be controlled either by the government or by any one opposition party; rather, oversight must be directed from an independent board that is accountable to the House of Assembly. Government and opposition parties should have input into the policy areas investigated but not a veto over any of them. Third, a research bureau will have limited resources at its disposal, but can counterbalance this limitation by drawing on existing research and analyses. This can be facilitated if it has access to internal government reports and data as well as outside analyses that it can use to bolster its own work. Fourth, a think-tank or research bureau will succeed only if Members of the House of Assembly and the government pay attention to its analyses, take them seriously, and use them as a basis for questions and debate in the House. ★

About the Author

Steven Wolinetz (Political Science, Memorial University of Newfoundland) is professor emeritus. His research and teaching have focused on political parties and democracy in Europe and Canada. He is a long-time observer of Newfoundland politics.

Note

1. Donald E. Abelson, *Do Think Tanks Matter? Assessing the Impact of Public Policy Institutes* (Montreal and Kingston: McGill-Queen's University Press, 2002); Andrew Denham, Diane Stone, and Evert A. Lindquist, *Think Tank Traditions: Policy Analysis across Nations* (Manchester: Manchester University Press, 2004); Diane Stone, *Capturing the Political Imagination: Think Tanks and the Policy Process* (London: Frank Cass, 1996).

56 Taking Politics Out of Governance

Alison Coffin

Tying outcomes to budgets can produce better government. We need less politics, more transparency! #cdnpoli #DemocraticReformNL

The opportunity exists to fundamentally change how we govern this province. To change how we make decisions. How we develop public policy. How we grow as a society.

Provincial public policy can become clearer, more forward-looking, broader in scope, and have greater accountability to, and involvement of, the people. Radical restructuring is not required. Many of the resources already exist. They can be put to better use.

Democracy in Newfoundland and Labrador will improve with the creation of a more rigorous framework for public policy. This is tangible, low-cost, and easy to implement. It requires clear communications, long-term planning, and a focus on outcomes.

The public accounts, the auditor general's reports on the audited financial statements, *The Economy*, and *The Economic Review* combine to give the most comprehensive, unbiased, non-partisan, and factual representation of the provincial economy and fiscal circumstances. The province's financial statements include a summary of the financial health of Newfoundland and Labrador. The auditor general provides comment on the financial statements and the risks and challenges facing the province. Global economic conditions, a provincial economic overview, detailed sector-specific activity, and the most up-to-date economic indicators are presented in *The Economy* and *The Economic Review*. For a complete understanding of the direction and health of the provincial economy and potential effects of public policy, these documents should be read together and in conjunction with other government directives.[1]

The reports are technical in nature, released independently of one another, from different agencies and divisions, at different times, and often buried deep in departmental news releases. The prominence and promotion of more partisan publications such as budget speeches, news releases, and visioning documents further obscure perspectives.

Public input into the political process will improve when citizens have a better understanding of the social, economic, and fiscal circumstances of the province. Clarity will come with co-ordination and simplification. The collective findings of these reports can be summarized in plain language, made easily accessible in video and print, and incorporated into government's overall communications strategy in a manner that reflects the importance of the information.

Realistic budgets span more than one year. Spending on hospitals, schools, roads, police, and most government activities does not stop every 31 March and then resume on 1 April. Continuous or multi-year expenditures are affected by core services, collective agreements, contractual arrangements, and infrastructure investments. These expenditures can be predicted years in advance with reasonable certainty.

Multi-year budgets decrease the variability and uncertainty associated with an annual budgeting process and improve fiscal health, operational efficiency, prioritization, and transparency.[2] They distinguish between necessary and discretionary spending and track changes in both over time. Boards, agencies, and advocacy groups under multi-year funding models have greater freedom to comment on policy and politics without fear of funding cuts.

Government produces strategic plans, activity plans, business plans, and annual activity reports. All describe outcomes of their programs and services. Outcomes include measures of a smarter, safer, healthier, better employed, more democratic society. They represent the desired results of public policy. The community accounts are a database of provincial and community-level information on health, employment, community safety, and quality of school life, as well as an interactive measure of well-being called the Better Life Index.[3]

These plans and data are separate and distinct from the annual budgeting process. At no point are the desired outcomes of government activities linked to government spending. Budgets do not include outcomes and plans do not include budgets. We know how much we spent on health care and education but do not know if it made us healthier or better educated. Outcomes can take years and have long-lasting effects, whereas budgets are annual.

The auditor general does identify potential outcomes of policy action or inaction that could impact provincial revenue and expenditure plans and the province's fiscal circumstances. Our aging population, the volatility of oil and our dependence on it, unfunded pension liabilities, and the potential negative impacts of the Lower Churchill development on taxpayers and ratepayers are consistently identified as long-term risks to the province.[4]

Consider an outcome of low-cost, reliable, green energy for rural areas and an outcome of continued development of energy resources to generate revenue for the province. These outcomes require different, and sometimes competing, policy and budget decisions. Implications of these decisions affect the environment, public health, employment, business activity, and long-term fiscal risk.

Public policy becomes broader in scope and more representative of the people when expenditure and revenue plans include measures of policy outcomes. Multi-year budgets can be linked to the desired results of programs and services. Progress can be measured through the community accounts and the Better Living Index.[5]

Democratic reform happens as political influence on provincial governance is reduced. Minimizing partisan messaging, tracking discretionary spending, and tying outcomes to budgets are improvements. Better-informed citizens, elected officials, and bureaucrats provide more meaningful input. Multi-year budgets improve clarity and continuity and reduce economic uncertainty. Tracking outcomes makes public policy accountable. This framework enables democratic reform. ★

About the Author

Alison Coffin (Economics, Memorial University of Newfoundland) is an economist. She has taught at Memorial University, developed policy and strategic plans for the provincial government, and consulted on public policy, pension plans, and the provincial budget. Her submission reflects of a lifetime of work dedicated to the development of responsible public policy and excellence in governance.

Notes

1. Office of the Auditor General, *Report to the House of Assembly on the Audit of the Financial Statements of the Province of Newfoundland and Labrador for the Year Ended March 31, 2016*. (St. John's: Office of the

Auditor General, 2016).

2. H. Sun, "Improving the Effectiveness of Multi-Year Fiscal Planning," *Government Finance Review* (2014): 44–50.
3. Collaborative Applied Research in Economics, "NL Well-being," 23 Nov. 2016, at: https://www.mun.ca/care/commentaries/progress/wellbeing.php.
4. Office of the Auditor General, *Report to the House of Assembly*.
5. P. Hoskins and D. May, "The Determinants of Life Satisfaction in Newfoundland and Labrador," paper prepared for the 34th IARIW General Conference, Dresden, Germany, 21–27 Aug. 2016, at: http://www.iariw.org/dresden/may.pdf.

57 The House of Assembly Needs a Legislative Budget Officer

Jeffrey Collins

Legislatures should have a budget officer. Retweet if you agree. #cdnpoli #DemocraticReformNL

Newfoundland and Labrador's finances exist in a fog. Our 40 Members of the House of Assembly are constitutionally required to deliberate and vote on billions of dollars' worth of spending contained in budgets, supplementary estimates, and program proposals annually. And yet outside of those select few MHAs who bear the title of finance minister or premier, our elected representatives lack full access to the finance department's technical expertise. In short, MHAs, and indeed the public, operate in the dark when it comes to weighing the financial implications in their decision-making. One way to rectify this is to establish an independent, non-partisan source of budgetary analysis: a Legislative Budget Officer (LBO).

Recent events have illustrated the acute need for an LBO-like function. In 2016 alone, MHAs had to contend with $8.5 billion in expenditures, a $1.8 billion deficit, collapsing oil prices, skyrocketing costs on the Muskrat Falls hydroelectric project, and nearly $15 billion in debt.[1] Amid such overwhelming numbers, MHAs were tasked with having to make sweeping decisions that would affect the province's residents by raising taxes, cutting services, and avoiding a path that would see the provincial economy going over the proverbial cliff.

Getting a grip on the complexities of government revenues,

expenditures, assets, and liabilities is no easy task, but an LBO could go a long way in both directly advancing the financial policy knowledge of MHAs and in countering the governing party's political spin on financial information presented to the public. Advancing the idea of an LBO, Newfoundland and Labrador would be following in the footsteps of the federal Parliamentary Budget Officer (PBO).

A Newfoundland and Labrador LBO would take the PBO as its template. Established in 2008 and focusing exclusively on federal government spending, the PBO traces its origins to a 2006 Conservative Party of Canada election promise.[2] As an independent officer of Parliament, the purpose of the PBO is simple: to provide independent analysis to MPs and senators on a wide range of fiscal concerns in order for them to improve their ability in "scrutinizing the raising and spending of public monies."[3]

In contrast to the federal Office of the Auditor General, which focuses on retrospective analyses of federal government programs, the PBO takes a *prospective* approach. With a mandate to conduct analyses on any matter under federal jurisdiction, the PBO produces semi-annual reports on government's current and projected estimates; quarterly reviews on all federal program spending; reports detailing national economic and labour trends, and on the long-term sustainability of public pension plans; and examines federal–provincial/territorial concerns (e.g., federal spending on post-secondary education). The PBO is also tasked with analyzing demographic trends and new economic developments, as exemplified in the 2015 study measuring the impact of lower oil prices on Ottawa's finances.[4]

Additional ideas for research topics can be requested by any MP or senator and can be submitted to the PBO by e-mail or telephone. MPs and senators also have the option of being anonymous even though the requested study will be made public.

Overall, the PBO experiment is seen as a success by its office-holders and users. However, challenges persist. Despite having statutory authority to access government data, the PBO has had trouble with producing timely reports because of "informational asymmetry with other branches of government."[5] The length of time a department or agency takes in providing information to the PBO has contributed to delays in producing reports, which have ranged from a few months to up to a year. The governing party has also at times not taken kindly to the PBO when its assessments openly question the validity of government policy stances; during the Stephen Harper era, this situation led to very public tensions with the PBO.

Still, in light of such constraints, PBO staff have established themselves as a valued resource for MPs and senators alike in their deliberations. The PBO has also solidified its reputation by presenting information that runs counter to the political spin of the governing party. In fact, the Trudeau government is pushing for empowering the PBO to cost party platforms during elections.[6] This success has been attributed to the mix of informal and formal methods used to obtain information: the non-partisan, independent reputation of the office among civil servants; strong working relationships with government actors; the ability to call on global, subject matter experts for advice; occasional court action; and a philosophical view best espoused by former Assistant PBO Sahir Khan: "For each issue the PBO deals with, half of parliament will like what the PBO produces, and half won't; the problem is that it's always a different half."[7]

While no single solution will completely resolve Newfoundland and Labrador's current economic and fiscal crisis, a Legislative Budget Officer would, at least, ensure that elected officials are informed in their deliberations. In the end, the initial cost to set up and maintain an LBO would be offset by the improved financial literacy of MHAs. Ignorance could no longer be an excuse for costly oversights. In buttressing MHAs' decision-making capacity (hopefully with better knowledge) comes a better exercise of power. ★

About the Author

Jeffrey Collins (Political Science, Carleton) is a Ph.D. candidate at Carleton University and a research associate with both the Macdonald-Laurier Institute and the Atlantic Institute for Market Studies (AIMS). A former Conservative staffer at the provincial and federal levels, Jeff was a policy advisor to Canada's minister of veteran affairs in 2013–14.

Notes

1. Terry Roberts, "N.L. Budget: $1.83B Deficit, Across-the-Board Tax Hikes and Layoffs," CBC News, 14 Apr. 2016, at: http://www.cbc.ca/news/canada/newfoundland-labrador/nl-budget-bad-news-1.3535718 (accessed 11 Nov. 2016).
2. Conservative Party of Canada, *Stand up for Canada* (Ottawa: Conservative Party of Canada, 2006), 11.
3. Office of the Parliamentary Budget Officer, "The Office of the Parliamentary Budget Officer" (2015), at: http://www.pbo-dpb.gc.ca/en/about#WHATWEDO (accessed 11 Nov. 2016).

4. Ibid.
5. Usman W. Chohan, "Canada and the Global Network of Parliamentary Budget Officers," *Canadian Parliamentary Review* (Autumn 2013): 17–20.
6. Liberal Party of Canada, "Parliamentary Budget Officer" (2016), at: https://www.liberal.ca/realchange/parliamentary-budget-officer/ (accessed 19 Nov. 2016).
7. Cited in Chohan, "Canada and the Global Network."

58 Auditing Equity and the Environment

Robert Sweeny

Sweeping commitments on climate change and eliminating poverty require a new type of oversight by legislatures. #cdnpoli #DemocraticReformNL

In December 2015, at the summit on climate change in Paris known as COP 21, Newfoundland and Labrador joined with the other provinces and the federal government in committing to "domestic mitigation measures" in order to limit global warming this century to 1.5° Celsius. By 5 October 2016, with a historic vote in the Canadian House of Commons, sufficient countries had ratified the agreement for it to come into force 30 days later.[1] This ambitious goal will require a sustained and government-wide effort for decades.

Our existing democratic customs and practices of regular elections, ministerial responsibility, and Question Period when the House is in session are not well suited to monitoring this type of long-range, sweeping commitment. Nor would the oft-mooted idea of having sitting committees of the House, an admittedly excellent suggestion, be well suited to monitor government actions across a wide range of departments. Over the past decade, we have experimented with a multi-departmental provincial strategy to reduce poverty, and its limited success suggests we would be better served by a more structured and independent approach.

Successive provincial governments have understandably committed themselves to reducing poverty, as Newfoundland for almost 60 years was the poorest province in Canada. In 2005, the government set a goal to achieve the lowest provincial poverty rates by 2015. A poverty-reduction strategy was developed to co-ordinate actions across differing departments.[2]

Since then, poverty rates have declined. We are by most measures now in the middle of the pack. How much this limited improvement is the result of the extraordinary economic boom of 2005–12, which saw median incomes rise by 43 per cent,[3] and how much is due to the provincial strategy remains an open question.

What is not open to question is that we failed to meet our target and, with the lowest minimum wage in the country, that is unlikely to change. Furthermore, the most recent provincial economic indicators suggest that even this relative improvement might be temporary at best. The current government is planning for unemployment to skyrocket to one in five members of a significantly reduced active workforce by 2019.[4]

In 2002, our neighbours in Quebec adopted a "Law to struggle against poverty and social exclusion," which established an "observatory" to monitor government actions and a special consultative committee of the National Assembly. This was a first in North America, and it came about as result of an exceptional mobilization of civil society led largely by feminist and faith communities.[5] This law has solved neither poverty nor social exclusion in Quebec. Government policies, however, are routinely scrutinized for their impact on these important problems. The result has been a much more informed and sustained public debate.[6]

Quebec's law draws on democratic traditions and customs, most notably the extra-parliamentary consultative processes known as *les États généraux*, which do not exist in English Canada.[7] We do, however, have a respected and well-functioning institution that could serve as a model in monitoring our commitments to the environment and to equity.

Twice a year, the provincial and federal auditors general make headlines. Their reports are produced by officers of Parliament, rather than creatures of particular departments. Auditors general have historically limited their work to what might be described as cost/benefit analysis. Is the government spending our money efficiently? Sometimes, auditors general have even ventured to ask if governments are spending it wisely. These reports do not by themselves change government policy, for that is not their purpose. They do, however, draw our attention to problems that would otherwise go unacknowledged. In so doing, they enrich our democracy.

Why not create similar officers of the House of Assembly with specific mandates to report annually on our progress in meeting our environmental and equity commitments? The experience in Quebec shows that simply establishing good baseline data is difficult and yet so vital for healthy discussions of our progress in addressing ongoing problems: all the more so when we are dealing with an issue as complex as climate change. In order to ensure that these reports do not become a form of public relations, an arm's-length relationship to government would clearly be desirable. Hence, the importance of them being officers of the House rather than serving at the whim of the premier. Over time, as we become more familiar with the nature of these complex problems we, as a democratic society, will be better able to refine these officers' mandates. Keeping track of what our government is doing will not in itself resolve these issues. That will require, as it always has, political action. But surely action based on shared knowledge is better than acting out of ignorance. ★

About the Author

Robert Sweeny (History, Memorial University of Newfoundland) has taught at Memorial University since 1989, where he works on the history of capitalism. He has published extensively both in Canada and abroad. In 2016 he won the Sir John A. Macdonald Prize for the most significant contribution to understanding our past from the Canadian Historical Association and the Governor General's History Award for Scholarly Research.

Notes

1. United Nations Framework Convention on Climate Change, "Paris Agreement — Status of Ratification" (2016), at: http://unfccc.int/paris_agreement/items /9444.php.
2. Poverty Reduction Strategy, *Reducing Poverty in Newfoundland and Labrador: Working Towards a Solution* (St John's: Department of Human Resources, Labour and Employment, 2005).
3. Robert C.H. Sweeny, "Newfoundland's Boom: A Study in the Political Culture of Neo-liberalism," in Bryan Evans and Carlo Fanelli, eds., *Canadian Provincial and Territorial Paradoxes: Public Finances, Services and Employment in an Era of Austerity* (Montreal and Kingston: McGill-Queen's University Press, 2017).
4. Economic Research and Analysis Division, "Provincial Economic Indicators," *The Economy of 2016* (St John's: Department of Finance, 2016).
5. Yves Vaillancourt and François Aubry, *Rapport de recherche sur la Loi visant à lutter contre la pauvreté et l'exclusion sociale: un exemple de co-construction démocratique de politique publique* (Montréal: ARUC Pauvreté invalidante et citoyen neté habilitante, 2014).
6. Collectif pour un Québec sans pauvreté, *Histoire critique et bilan dans le*

cadre du dixième anniversaire de la Loi visant à lutter contre la pauvreté et l'exclusion sociale (Québec, 2013).

7. Charles Bellerose and Jacques Beauchemin, "Communauté national et definition du sujet politique: analyse de deux grandes consultations populaires au Québec, 1967–1995," *Quebec Studies* 28 (1999): 27–55.

59 Efficiency Committees

Jill Power

The key to government efficiency? Unbiased committees of experts providing advice. #DemocraticReformNL

If our government wanted to truly strive for efficiency, it would invest resources into creating an unbiased, non-government committees of experts across a wide spectrum of services. These committees could begin by looking at and re-evaluating how we currently approach services like health care and education. The terms of reference for these committees must be clear and the committee membership must be non-partisan. The experts would look to other countries for proven strategies and processes that display forward thinking and success. Based on their findings, the committees would then make recommendations for change, and, most importantly, the government would then implement their recommendations.

In a Provincial Home Support Program Review for the Department of Health and Community Services, released on 12 July 2016, one can see an example of how *not* to engage committees. In this review, the Government of Newfoundland and Labrador states "Deloitte Inc. (Deloitte) was engaged by the Department of Health and Community Services (HCS) to complete a comprehensive review of the PHSP to determine whether it is operating as efficiently and effectively as possible, to identify opportunities to improve the Program, and to inform changes required to help ensure its future sustainability. . . . The review consisted of four phases of work over a 16-week period and was guided by a Steering Committee comprised of program leadership from HCS and the four Regional Health Authorities (RHAs)."[1]

At a glance, the concept of engaging Deloitte appears worthwhile. However, as noted, Deloitte was directed by a steering committee of Regional Health Authorities, as well as staff members at Eastern Health. It could be assumed that these staff might bring significant biases to the table and truly progressive approaches would rely on objective sources to recommend efficiencies. If open-minded experts are given the freedom to conduct a proper review, research-informed recommendations for improved efficiencies would be the end result.

Let's consider one basic service that could benefit from this approach. In our province today, an expectant mother has seven prenatal class types from which to choose. It could be argued that prenatal programming could be offered more efficiently without Eastern Health nurses providing direct delivery.[2] In Australia, Childbirth and Parenting Educators of Australia, Inc., a "not-for-profit, voluntary, professional association provides high quality, accessible and responsive education to women and their families during pregnancy and early parenthood."[3] Instead of eliminating the jobs of these Eastern Health nurses, they could be reassigned to nursing duties needed by our aging communities.

As for education, it is a well-known fact that Scandinavian countries have progressive and highly successful education systems.[4] According to the Conference Board of Canada June 2014 Provincial and Territorial Ranking of High School Attainment, Newfoundland and Labrador scored below average when compared with other provinces in Canada. What might a committee of independent, non-partisan experts recommend to our government leaders on how to improve our education system for our children?

In our province, government provides direct delivery of specialized health equipment. This service is another example of a disturbing trend of inefficiency within government. Committees of unbiased experts would soon discover that in other provinces in Canada (Nova Scotia and New Brunswick, for example) specialized health equipment is provided by non-profit organizations such as the Canadian Red Cross. With highly acclaimed recycling programs in place, these non-profit organizations provide services in a cost-effective and efficient manner. The result is patients are released from hospital sooner and public servants can focus on tasks other than direct delivery.

"Invading" government departments with efficiency committees would inevitably upset many apple carts. Unions would focus on how their employees would lose jobs when committee recommendations were implemented. Governments would argue studies and committees cost taxpayers money, and that during a deficit they could not "waste" money on studies and steering committees. The reality is, current government practices are costing us money in inefficiencies. These include both fiscal inefficiencies and quality of service.

Independent filmmaker Michael Moore's recent documentary, *Where to Invade Next*, closes with an interview of three Scandinavian women politicians. They state, "every kid should have the same opportunity; the basic opportunity to get education and health care . . . it's just a good society."[5] They describe their government as being structured with a "we" state of mind, rather than a "me" state of mind, as we see in the Western world today. Implementing a practice of establishing non-partisan expert committees to study, review, and recommend changes is the step needed for the Government of Newfoundland and Labrador to have a "we" state of mind — the opportunities are limitless. ★

About the Author

Jill Power (Music, Memorial University of Newfoundland) is an undergraduate student at Memorial University, studying voice with Dr. Jane Leibel in the School of Music. Outside of her academics, you'll find Jill at CMHR, the campus radio station, where she hosts her weekly Morning Show. Jill is an avid volunteer in her community and takes great pride in the culture and heritage of Newfoundland and Labrador.

Notes

1. Government of Newfoundland and Labrador, Department of Health and Community Services, "Provincial Home Support Program Review," 12 July 2016, at: www.health.gov.nl.ca (accessed 26 Oct. 2016).
2. Eastern Health, "Prenatal Classes — Patient Information" (May 2016) (accessed online 27 Oct. 2016).
3. Childbirth and Parenting Educators of Australia, Inc., "About CAPEA" (n.d.) (accessed online 28 Oct. 2016).
4. Central Connecticut State University, "World's Most Literate Nations" (2016) (accessed online 29 Oct. 2016).
5. *Where to Invade Next* (2016), dir. Michael Moore. Dog Eat Dog Films.

60 Governance and Appointments

Lynn Moore

Government appointments: more merit, less banana republic. #NLpoli #DemocraticReformNL

The civil service and the provincial court bench would be well served by appointments made exclusively on merit (insofar as it is possible for decision-makers to put aside bias and prejudice). The civil service is the branch of government that delivers government programs and services. The work is wide-ranging and includes almost every facet of our lives, from education and health to policing. Likewise, the reach and the power of the judiciary is of critical importance. The importance of the work cannot be overstated. Citizens have a legitimate interest in having all positions filled by persons competent to do the work.

While the Public Service Commission Act [1]emphasizes and requires the application of the merit principle for many government jobs, large swaths of positions are exempt from that legislation. Positions not covered under the Act include: the Clerk of the House of Assembly; the Citizens' Representative, the Child and Youth Advocate; the Commissioner for Legislative Standards; the Chief Electoral Officer; deputy ministers and assistant deputy ministers; barristers or solicitors; medical doctors and dental surgeons; and contractual employees. The Act should be amended to require merit-based appointments. Notably, many of the positions exempt from the requirement for merit-based appointments are leadership positions or positions that play a watchdog role.

Occasionally, persons who are handpicked without competition are exceptional individuals who excel. Sometimes, the disregard for merit, the lack of competition, and the lack of oversight in the selection process result in incompetent persons appointed to important positions. Always, the handpicking of employees without competition or regard for merit is a serious blow to the morale of talented, industrious, and hardworking civil servants. This is especially so when the appointee's arrival is preceded by the unlawful dismissal of a competent worker. Additionally, unlawful dismissals are costly because those dismissed are owed pay in lieu of notice and severance, and often they successfully sue.

Further, under the current and previous administrations, the growing practice of hiring private individuals or companies on a contract or piecework basis is not fiscally prudent. An example of this imprudence is the decision by the Department of Justice to hire two private lawyers to prosecute a murder.[2] They were paid hourly. At last tally, the cost was $700,000. The work involved a lone case that took about eight weeks in court. Even assuming equal preparation time (a luxury unknown to any staff Crown attorney), the government paid for 32 weeks of work — two lawyers at eight weeks of trial and eight weeks of preparation. Top-earning trial lawyers with government cost $127,000 a year in salary (plus mandatory employment-related costs) and generally work 48 weeks a year. Instead of 32 weeks of work, the government could have hired staff lawyers and netted 224 weeks of work.

Another branch of the government that plays a fundamental role in maintaining democracy is the judiciary. The federal government has recently revamped its process for the selection of judges to heighten the emphasis on the merit principle. The recent appointment of Malcom Rowe to the Supreme Court of Canada involved a level of openness and transparency befitting a democracy. The provincial government appoints Provincial Court judges. Yet, the provincial selection process is completely secretive. An application and a secret list of lawyers' names are sent by the Chief Judge to the Minister of Justice. Applicants are not told if their names are on the secret list. Consequently, they are also not told why they have been deemed to be incompetent or what they might do to rectify their candidacy.

The Provincial Court deals with 95 per cent of all criminal cases. Reason dictates that those entrusted with implementing the criminal law have experience in criminal law or at least current knowledge of it. Like the senior bureaucrats who are handpicked without any merit assessment, some of the judicial appointees lacking current knowledge of criminal law become respected jurists, but others struggle.

The constitutionally enshrined principle of judicial independence prohibits dismissing judges for the decisions they make. Judges have to act without fear of reprisal for making the very decisions they were appointed to make. Mistakes are fixed on appeal. Judges without any current knowledge of the criminal law are more apt to make mistakes. The fact that these mistakes may be fixed on appeal is both costly and cold comfort to victims and accused persons who must live with the decisions in the meantime. It also places the safety of the rest of us at unnecessary risk.

The Independent Appointments Commission (IAC)[3] is a step in the right direction. However, the vast majority of the IAC's appointments involve volunteer positions. If the idea of the IAC is to prevent political patronage, its scope should be expanded. Checks and balances in the form of openness and transparency in the selection process for the hiring and promotion of civil servants and judges will ensure that the work is completed by competent individuals. The rigorous application of the merit principle is fiscally responsible, ensures the most competent people are doing the work, and promotes democracy. ★

About the Author

Lynn Moore (Morris Martin Moore law firm) is a lawyer who represents survivors of sexual abuse. Before entering private practice in 2013, she spent 20 years working with the province's Department of Justice as a Crown prosecutor and civil solicitor. Lynn completed her studies in Political Science and French at Memorial University in 1989. She lives in St. John's.

Notes

1. Government of Newfoundland Labrador, Public Service Commission Act (2016) (St. John's: Queen's Printer, 2016), at: http://www.assembly.nl.ca/legislation/sr/statutes/p43.htm.
2. Ariana Kelland, "How Much Did It Cost for Philip Pynn's Manslaughter Conviction?" CBC News, 9 Jan. 2015, at: http://www.cbc.ca/news/canada/newfoundland-labrador/how-much-did-it-cost-for-philip-pynn-s-manslaughter-conviction-1.2892723.
3. Government of Newfoundland and Labrador, "Appointments to Agencies, Boards and Commissions: Frequently Asked Questions" (2016), at: http://www.psc.gov.nl.ca/psc/abc/faqs.html.

61 Appointments to the Boards of State-Owned Companies

Jeffrey Pittman

We need to stop appointing directors of provincially-owned companies from the government's social and political networks in #NLpoli. #DemocraticReformNL

The role that sound corporate governance structures play in protecting the financial interests of Newfoundland and Labrador's residents has largely flown under the radar in public policy circles. For example, extensive theory and evidence imply that monitoring by boards of directors of companies, including state-run enterprises like Nalcor, suffers when persons with social or political links to the government are appointed to the board.[1] In one of their main responsibilities, boards of directors are supposed to actively monitor management to ensure that its decisions reflect the best interests of the company's shareholders.[2] In the case of Nalcor, for instance, its shareholders are essentially the province's residents. However, recent research suggests that directors with social or political connections to the government are reluctant to impose strict monitoring or challenge the company's current strategic direction because they want to avoid damaging the relationship with the governing party that led to their appointment in the first place. It is important to appoint directors without social or political ties to the government because tough external monitoring requires both competence (e.g., the ability to identify issues that threaten to undermine the company's long-term goals) and independence (e.g., the willingness to raise these sensitive issues in the boardroom).

Regrettably, board appointments that reflect the government's social and partisan political networks are likely to suffer on both fronts. First, rather than the government casting a wider net in recruiting for director positions, they tend to focus on a shallower pool of connected persons: in turn, appointees may lack the necessary expertise to serve on the board. Second, directors coming from social and political networks will have strong incentives to remain loyal to the government that appointed them rather than focusing intently on protecting the interests of the company's shareholders (i.e., the residents of the province). To use Nalcor as an example, rather than serving as a watchdog for the province's residents, the captured board — in the sense that its independence is highly questionable — may become a lapdog for the government.

Another downside to allowing appointments to stem from durable social and political networks is that it lowers the likelihood that women will be invited to join the board, as recent research suggests. Even setting aside the clear social justice implications, extensive evidence implies that corporate governance improves when boards are more gender diverse.[3] In fact, companies benefit when women join the director ranks. This situation routinely results in boards performing better in both monitoring and strategy formulation: its two core responsibilities. The presence of women on boards tends to translate into better information-sharing and collaboration among directors as well as less groupthink. Gender-diverse boards are more likely to confront difficult and delicate issues. Similarly, boards with women are more likely to adopt a co-operative decision-making framework that improves decision quality when there are competing interests at stake. Regrettably, boards are likely to remain dominated by men when existing social and political networks shape the recruitment of new directors.

From a public policy standpoint, a natural reform would be to rely on an independent body to handle all board-level appointments to state-owned companies like Nalcor. Indeed, the provincial government has taken steps to move in this direction by launching Newfoundland and Labrador's Independent Appointments Commission in May 2016. However, recent research suggests that they should resist the temptation to allow exceptions that would enable the government, at its discretion, to bypass the Commission's vetting process: these very situations are apt to lead to the appointment of board members without the required competence and independence. In other words, the Commission should be responsible for all board-level appointments without any interference from the government, that is, the government should not have the flexibility to circumvent the recommendations of its own Independent Appointments Commission. Finally, the Independent Appointments Commission Act could be amended to include a provision requiring government boards to meet quotas for gender diversity. ★

About the Author

Jeffrey Pittman (Business Administration, Memorial University of Newfoundland) primarily analyzes the role that firm- and country-level governance structures play in shaping economic outcomes in private and public companies. He was appointed Memorial's Chair in Corporate Governance and Transparency in 2011.

Notes

1. See, for example, M. Faccio, "Politically Connected Firms," *American Economic Review* 96 (2006): 369–86; L. Bruynseels and E. Cardinaels, "The Audit Committee: Management Watchdog or Personal Friend of the CEO," *Accounting Review* 89 (2014): 113–45.
2. M. Mace, *Directors, Myth, and Reality* (Boston: Harvard Business School Press, 1971); R.B. Adams, B.E. Hermalin, M.S. Weisbach, "The Role of Boards of Directors in Corporate Governance: A Conceptual Framework and Survey," *Journal of Economic Literature* 48 (2010): 58–107.
3. R. Adams and D. Ferreira, "Women in the Boardroom and Their Impact on Governance and Performance," *Journal of Financial Economics* 94 (2009): 291–309; D. Carter, B. Simkins, and W. Simpson, "Corporate Governance, Board Diversity, and Firm Value," *Financial Review* 38 (2003): 33–53.

62 Re-Democratizing School Governance in Newfoundland and Labrador

Gerald Galway

School boards play an important part in teaching and learning. So why is local democratic authority for education at risk? #DemocraticReformNL

Haven't school boards outlived their usefulness? That's a question I am frequently asked by reporters who write about education in Canada. As an education researcher I've been studying the ways school boards and education departments interact with each other in making decisions that influence schools and communities. Those interactions have been changing. Reporters, or anyone else who has been observing a growing centralization of authority over education, may well wonder about how school boards will function in the new order.

In the recent past, school boards have been charged with a long list of sins including underfunding schools, setting restrictive rules for bussing eligibility, and unnecessarily closing or consolidating schools (or, in some cases, failing to do so). They have been accused of acceding too quickly to the will of government, and also, paradoxically, criticized for contesting government policy. Although school boards bear the brunt of public dissatisfaction, many, if not most education policies originate within education ministries and are enacted — sometimes reluctantly — by the formal decisions of school district trustees. The relationships among school boards and governments, therefore, are complex and sometimes acrimonious. Provincial governments typically take the position that school boards are quasi-autonomous agencies and make their own decisions within their legislated mandate. Yet, from time to time, legislators will overturn their decisions if they run counter to ministry directives or are otherwise politically problematic. For example, during a 2005 by-election in the District of Exploits, Premier Williams reversed a controversial school board decision to close a school, justifying the interference as an example of government's obligation to overturn wrong decisions in favour of the "right ones."[1] Some provincial governments have even taken to dismissing entire school boards, such as in the recent case of the dismissal of the Vancouver School Board over delays in bringing in a balanced budget and resistance to the closure of several city schools.[2]

Some critics might well argue that parents and the public do not care that much about school boards. They are relatively invisible to the average taxpayer, voter turnout is quite low, and, unlike municipal council meetings, school board business is typically not covered by the news media. In the normal course of operations, therefore, most people are not well informed about the work of school boards. In fact, it is this very feature of school boards — that they are fundamentally invisible agencies — that has enabled the Government of Newfoundland and Labrador to twice restructure the provincial school system from 10 English school districts to four regional districts (2004) and then to a single district (2013) in less than 10 years (while maintaining the Conseil scolaire francophone provincial). This occurred without any public consultation or debate. Still, there is good evidence to show that school boards play an important role in advancing teaching and learning. In one recent Canadian study, the researchers concluded that although the provincial ministry of education had a large indirect influence on student learning, the effect was almost entirely dependent on school district leadership.[3] This is consistent with evidence from several other studies,[4] where the researchers concluded that school boards are an important systems-levels link between government and school communities and that they have a positive impact on system-wide learning.

The assault on public school districts/boards in Newfoundland and Labrador has been framed as a means to eliminate duplication and reduce administrative costs. However, as has been demonstrated elsewhere, such efficiencies are often short-lived.[5] Moreover, they leave unanswered questions about whether efficiency — or perhaps the perception of efficiency — should supersede the principle of local democratic authority for education. The government's All Party Committee on Democratic Reform has a mandate to consult with the public in Newfoundland and Labrador, and to find ways to improve democratic processes. One place they could start is to recommend a review of the current school governance structure in this province, including the electoral process, which should rightly fall under the auspices of Elections NL. The ideals of the shared decision-making model involve local responsibility for most decisions about teaching and learning in schools, coupled with centralized provincial government authority for such things as curriculum and assessment standards and school construction. However, the drift towards a single English educational authority, situated in St. John's, has disrupted the governance balance and placed almost all substantial power over educational policy in the hands of the provincial government. This is troublesome for a number of important reasons but the crux of the problem is this: narrowing the sphere of influence in deciding how education should be governed is a de-democratizing process. It moves education from a regionalized stewardship model with many locally elected decision-makers to a centralized model where local influence is marginalized and where decisions may be more susceptible to political influence.

School boards have historically existed as a reflection of society's deep-rooted belief that educational governance should reflect community and regional values and priorities. They serve to protect the diversity of community and regional interests characteristic of the Canadian mosaic. School trustees, therefore, should begin a constructive dialogue with the All Party Committee to both educate them and help enlist the views of the public about the importance of sustaining a local voice in educational governance. If we are to continue to enjoy good schools that produce well-educated and informed citizens, authentic local authority over education should be preserved. ★

About the Author

Gerald Galway (Education, Memorial University of Newfoundland) is an Associate Professor and Associate Dean of Education at Memorial University. In his career he has undertaken extensive policy research at both the provincial and national levels on topics including teacher resourcing, student financial assistance, e-learning, research-informed policy, and educational governance. His most recent co-edited book is *Inspiration and Innovation in Teacher Education* (Lexington Books, 2013).

Notes

1. Alex Marland, "Executive Authority and Public Policy in Newfoundland and Labrador," in A. Marland and M. Kerby, eds., *First Among Unequals: The Premier, Politics, and Policy in Newfoundland and Labrador* (Montreal and

Kingston: McGill-Queen's University Press, 2014), 3–31.

2. Lisa Johnson, "Vancouver School Board Fired by B.C. Education Minister," CBC News, 17 Oct. 2016, at: http://www.cbc.ca/news/canada/british-columbia/vancouver-school-board-fired-1.3808674 (accessed 29 June 2017).
3. Bruce Sheppard and David Dibbon, "Improving the Capacity of School System Leaders and Teachers to Design Productive Learning Environments," *Leadership and Policy in Schools* 10 (2011): 1–21.
4. Michael Fullan, *Leadership and Sustainability* (Thousand Oaks, Calif.: Corwin Press, 2005); Ken Leithwood, "Introduction to New Evidence on District Effects," *Leadership and Policy in Schools* 9 (2010): 243–44.
5. Gerald Galway, "Educational Governance and Policy," in A. Marland and M. Kerby, eds., *First Among Unequals: The Premier, Politics, and Policy in Newfoundland and Labrador* (Montreal and Kingston: McGill-Queen's University Press, 2014), 178–93.

PART 9: SPEND AND SPEND AND SPEND AND NEVER GET BACK CHANGE

Sir M.P. Cashin turning first sod of Southern Shore Railway, 1911. On 11 May 1911, Sir Michael Patrick Cashin, Minister of Finance and Customs and MHA for the District of Ferryland, turned the first sod to mark the opening of the Southern Shore rail line. A notation points out "P.K.D. [Patrick K. Devine] on right." He was then Clerk of the House of Assembly. The ceremonial shovel bore a silver plate and was decorated with native ribbons. Also in attendance: Minister of Justice and Acting Prime Minister Donald Morison, H.D. Reid (for contractors), members of the Cabinet, City Council, Board of Trade and the press. For additional detail, see *Newfoundland Quarterly*, Oct. 1911. (Source: Provincial Archives)

It is a tad unfair to blame politicians for the current financial crisis in Newfoundland and Labrador. Few consider that elected officials are prone to overspend because they are reflecting the demands and pressures of society. For instance, the media are lured by the drama of demonstrators calling for more spending and voicing outrage against cutbacks, but there are never protests demanding that government spend within its means or raise taxes. To address this conspicuous silence, institutional mechanisms must be installed to ensure that politicians listen to all voices, not just the squeaky wheels, and to help counterbalance the considerable political pressure they face from organized interests and constituents adept at demanding a share of finite resources.

Essays in this section discuss the politics of public money and the economy. Andreae Callanan starts off with a poem reminding us that there is good reason why demands for government spending are made — and that good public policy need not always be dominated by financial considerations. Journalists Peter Cowan and Ashley Fitzpatrick sound the ethical alarm on the flow of donations to political parties from corporations, unions, and the wealthy. In doing so, they demonstrate the importance of a flourishing fourth estate to monitor the executive, legislative, and judicial branches of government. Gordon Cooke considers the flow of public resources to pensions, while Jennifer Dyer looks at the funds from philanthropists to the arts. Natalie Slawinski rings off by pointing to the economic promise of social enterprise, an approach to revitalizing rural communities by recognizing the unique characteristics of each community and responding with the collaboration of entrepreneurship, local firms, institutions of learning, and local leadership. Ka-ching!

63 The Debt

Andreae Callanan

Andreae Callanan's latest poem: The government has a debt to pay, and it's not what you think. #NLpoli #DemocraticReformNL

I have said no to unlit city streets, I have said
no to highways splitting parkland, no
to cuts that make one person do the work
of three. I have said no to shutting schools
and clinics, no to warplanes tracing
ancient paths of caribou, to sea-bed
bombs that box the ears of whales. I have said
no to filth in rivers.

And, too, I have said yes, I live at this address,
yes, you've spelled my name correctly
on the card, that's it, that's me, yes. Yes
in cabbage-scented parish halls, church
basements, yes in gymnasiums
and auditoriums, yes in libraries, yes
under cold tube lights, over carpeted floors.

We are all debtors here, beholden
to this jagged place for every lungful
of spruce-laced salted air, each slap
of ocean blasting rock and boat, dock

and ankle. Each berry-bucket filled
begs something in return. I pay
my dues with words: a *no* to harm, a *yes*
to harder work. I pay my dues in placards,
ballots, chants, in reckoning. ★

About the Author

Andreae Callanan (English, Memorial University of Newfoundland) is a poet and essayist from St. John's. Her work has appeared in *The Walrus* and on CBC Radio, and in numerous journals, including *Riddle Fence*, *The New Quarterly*, and *CV2*. She is currently pursuing her Master's degree in English literature at Memorial University.

64 Taking Corporate and Union Influence Out of Politics

Peter Cowan

Why are other provinces banning donations from corporations and unions, but not in NL? @CBCNL's Peter Cowan comments. #NLpoli #DemocraticReformNL

Political parties are central to a functioning democracy in Newfoundland and Labrador and while their role is clear, the best way for them to pay their bills and fund election campaigns is not. Right now, political parties rely heavily on corporate money. Many companies and a few unions make big donations (more than $5,000 in a year) and there are very few controls to limit corporate and union influence on the democratic system. Technically a company could write a cheque to pay for an entire party's operations.

Unlike many other provinces, there are no limits to individual, corporate, or union donations, and parties rely heavily on those big donations. For the provincial Progressive Conservatives and Liberals their two big fundraisers every year are a golf tournament and a $500-a-plate leaders' dinner. Very few people pay for the tickets themselves. The tables are generally bought by corporations (and a scattered union), many of which have direct business dealings with the government. For example, at the Liberal's fall 2016 fundraiser, the accounting firm EY bought a table. Since the Liberals took power, the company has been awarded several untendered contracts to produce reports on the provincial library system and the Muskrat Falls hydroelectric project. This situation is just one example of something that happens under governments of all stripes. When the Progressive

Conservative Party was in power, companies that did business with government were also filling the party's coffers. In 2013, Hearn Fougere Architects gave more than $6,500 to the PCs[1] and received more than $1.7 million in untendered contracts in 2013–14.[2] The New Democratic Party has never held power and its balance sheet reflects this fact, with some union donations but substantially fewer corporate donations. Under current rules neither the parties nor the companies are doing anything wrong, and the parties that benefit have shown little interest in cutting off the flow of corporate money.

It undermines public confidence in the system when doubt is cast about whether government contracts are being awarded in the best interests of the public or the best interests of the party. Even if buying a table doesn't give you a contract, it is clear that it gives you access. These fundraisers are filled with MHAs and cabinet ministers, and part of the value some companies feel they get out of these events is the face time with those in power.

Other jurisdictions have recognized this conflict and modernized their election financing rules. As the former head of Elections Canada, Jean Pierre Kingsley, told the CBC: "People don't put money into something unless they expect that it will have a return."[3] The rules in Newfoundland and Labrador desperately need to catch up. The solution implemented by other provinces and the federal government is to ban corporate and union donations and to put a cap on individual donations. It has worked at the federal level since a ban was implemented in 2007.

If companies aren't paying to keep parties running, then who does? Parties will be able to make up some of the losses by expanding their fundraising efforts to more individual donors, an area parties don't target heavily when they can rely on deeper corporate pockets. However, that may not be enough; in many provinces, taxpayers help fund party operations. Per-vote subsidies of between $1 and $2.50 exist in six provinces and were used at the national level to wean parties off corporate money. Federally, the parties have millions of individuals to ask for support, but in a small province it's much harder to make up that loss of funds with individual donations.

The idea of taxpayers putting their money into the partisan work of parties is a tough sell. In some provinces parties refuse their subsidies because of the optics. Based on similar-sized subsidies the cost to the taxpayer would be $200,000 to $500,000 a year. It's not just who is donating that needs to change but the transparency around how those donations are reported. Right now district associations and leadership races are not obliged to report who supports them. Rules need to be brought in to change that.

Elections Newfoundland and Labrador reports party and candidate donations but is often very slow at providing that information. It often doesn't post donation or expense information until 12–14 months after an election or the end of a year. That means a government can be one-quarter of the way through its mandate before the public gets to see who helped it get there. That's unacceptable. Federally, the information is posted within two to three months after an election, and there's no reason Elections Newfoundland and Labrador can't follow similar timelines, but these timelines need to be enshrined in legislation to guarantee proper transparency.

These measures amount to a substantial change in how political activity is funded, but they are changes that are badly needed to restore public confidence in our political system and to ensure that politicians are motivated to work in the interests of those who elected them instead of those who financed them. ★

About the Author

Peter Cowan (CBC NL) has covered Newfoundland and Labrador for a decade with the CBC, first in Happy Valley-Goose Bay and now St. John's. His investigation into illegal corporate campaign contributions received by Conservative cabinet minister Peter Penashue forced Penashue's resignation and led to convictions against his campaign manager. Peter has also been recognized for uncovering the Humber Valley paving scandal.

Notes

1. Elections Newfoundland and Labrador, "2013 Calendar Year: Contributions to Political Parties" (2013), at: http://www.elections.gov.nl.ca/elections/PoliticalFinanceReports/PDF/finance.2013/Annual/2013Contributions.pdf (accessed 2 Dec. 2016).
2. Government of Newfoundland and Labrador, Department of Finance, "Consulting/Professional Service Fees 2013–2014" (2014), information released under the Access to Information and Protection of Privacy Act, 20 Oct., at: http://atipp-search.gov.nl.ca/public/atipp/requestdownload?id=325& (accessed 2 Dec. 2016).
3. R. Jones, "Corporate Political Donations in N.B. Prove Need for Ban, Says Ex-Elections Head," CBC News, 19 July 2016, at: http://www.cbc.ca/news/canada/new-brunswick/corporate-political-donations-new-brunswick-ban-1.3685673 (accessed 2 Dec. 2016).

65 A Start for Tackling Pay to Play

Ashley Fitzpatrick

$ needed to access politicians in #NLpoli? Well, that's the perception writes @TeleFitz. #DemocraticReformNL

You can argue money does not buy influence in Newfoundland and Labrador politics, but it's hard to say it doesn't buy access. And voters have long since taken notice. The perception is absolutely of a pay-to-play political system.

It applies across all parties, where corporations or unions — as opposed to individuals — have become a target and basis for party fundraising. And when you look beyond the annual $500-ticket premiers' dinners with 500 or 600 people in attendance to golf tournaments and boat tours, there's no denying these events offer face time with political decision-makers. Dealing with the pay-for-play impression first and foremost requires greater transparency. It means providing information about donors and fundraisers faster, with easy access, so individuals can answer their own questions as they arise and investigations are less onerous.

In Newfoundland and Labrador, a legislated 1 April deadline for annual filings by political parties to Elections NL (Elections Act, 1991, s. 303)[1] has been regularly surpassed, with Elections NL allowing extensions well into the summer. Elections NL then requires its own private review of the data before release. While quarterly listings of major donations are available in some provinces, Newfoundland and Labrador struggles to provide public information even before the end of the calendar year following the year a donation was made.

Sticking to the stipulated deadline would be beneficial, as would posting information "as submitted," with official confirmation to follow. That approach could apply even to specific events. Imagine posts immediately (within a week) following a fundraiser! Although few people know it, event information is already issued to Elections NL in "supporting schedules" with annual party financial filings. It is a basic form sheet, but these forms are sometimes handwritten and difficult to read. They are available in a binder kept at the Elections NL office in St. John's, or, should they choose to disclose them, through the parties.

The legislation specifies you can only donate as "a corporation, individual or trade union," leaving unincorporated firms — legal, architectural, financial — unaddressed (Elections Act, 1991, s. 282). But these firms are large business entities with political interests. The argument is you can identify individuals associated with a firm and determine a firm's contribution, but that is easier said than done — and quite a burden to place on the average person looking for basic information on how much a partnership has provided to a given party. Omitting firms also creates a situation where an individual (a lawyer, for example), who is without any desire to contribute to a particular political party, is recorded as a donor simply because his or her firm has decided to secure a table at a fundraising dinner and the bill is split evenly between partners. At least with a corporation, the interest is clearly identified.

This province maintains the mindset that allowing corporations and unions to contribute allows for greater transparency with fewer attempts at illegal workarounds. With a flat ban, corporations might attempt to make political contributions through individual employees and family members, with the promise of reimbursement later by the company. Essentially, it can be difficult to enforce. But at the same time, Newfoundland and Labrador already has large business entities with no clear record of contributions.

Potential limitations on donations are worth debating, if for no other reason than publicly visible awareness of the rules. There is no restriction right now, for example, on amounts contributed provincially or on contributions coming from outside the province. Political contributions in Newfoundland and Labrador can be made by corporations whether or not they carry on business here, and trade unions can contribute even if they have no bargaining rights in the province.

Wrenching the tap and shutting the flow of donations would spark pushback in the form of attempts by parties and potential donors at working around the restrictions and would add pressure on remaining donors, and in both instances this could be no more than fertilizer for growing scandal.

But placing at least some restrictions could force increased outreach and more creative fundraising that, by its very nature, would have to target individuals currently feeling alienated, ostracized, unneeded, and unwanted by the system. And while it is not required, there is precedence for review, as demonstrated by Ontario's election finance reform legislation passed in late 2016, which bans corporate and union donations and the attendance of politicians at political fundraising events, among other measures.[2]

Memorial University of Newfoundland's Department of Political Science can be a trusted source for the community in improving the understanding of campaign finance and related issues to support debate. To the 2015 election, professors had not made a point to dig into provincial campaign financing, and I suggest a research grant or other incentive might encourage this work. Given the many corporate donors stating a deep desire only to support our democratic system, there should be no shortage of financial contributions to help with that. ★

About the Author

Ashley Fitzpatrick (*The Telegram*) began as a journalist in Newfoundland and Labrador with *The Western Star* in Corner Brook and is now in her eighth year with *The Telegram* in St. John's. She produced a series of stories on provincial party fundraising in 2015.

Notes

1. The Elections Act, 1991, "An Act Respecting Elections Controverted Elections and Election Financing," can be accessed at: http://www.assembly.nl.ca/legislation/sr/statutes/e03-1.htm.
2. Government House Leader's Office, "Ontario Reintroduces Election Finance Reform Bill," Ontario Newsroom, 13 Oct. 2016, at: https://news.ontario.ca/ghl/en/2016/09/ontario-reintroduces-election-finance-reform-bill.html.

66 We Need to Discuss the Fairness of Public-Sector Pensions

Gordon Cooke

To be more financially prudent and democratic, defined-benefit public-sector pensions need to be replaced. #NLpoli #DemocraticReformNL

Good governance involves putting in place inclusive, fair, and transparent laws, systems, and procedures, but that is not enough. The need to discuss problems that are complicated and sensitive is sometimes overlooked. In Newfoundland and Labrador, a much more vigorous and open discussion is needed about the financial and demographic challenges facing the province now and in the future.[1] While it would be nice to be able to afford everything that we want, or everything that we have become used to having, we have a fiscal problem that requires attention. It's a question of choosing what we want, what we can afford, and what we have to give up, even if we don't want to. We are also overdue to discuss the affordability of the defined benefit pension plan that public-sector workers, and essentially only these workers, receive.

Members of political parties within this province have a bad habit of avoiding difficult conversations. One party line is to insist that they didn't overspend. Just because their budgets included spending at twice the rate of inflation for a decade didn't mean overspending. Another party line is that they thought cuts could be avoided and that they didn't know the situation was serious until they had a chance "to look at the books." Another party line is to insist that the other two parties have a lack of vision. I would argue that the problem is the math, not the vision (perhaps a shortage of $1 billion per year). But good governance means having a role for the general public, too. I argue that, collectively, the general public has punished politicians — or others — who have tried to initiate a frank discussion of our fiscal situation.

Many of us grumble about employment insurance when we have to pay into it but do not receive benefits. What many of us fail to understand is that the ones who receive it are the ones who need it: paying in and not ever receiving it is a good thing. Unfortunately, defined benefit public-sector pensions are the opposite. Taxpayers — many of whom do not have a defined benefit pension or any retirement benefit from their employer — have to pay for a pension that that they *do* need but will never get. That is undemocratic.

In short, the current system could be seen as unfair because very few besides full-time, permanent members of the public sector receive defined benefit pensions, while the rest of the population (and that's roughly 75 per cent of society) have a riskier/smaller defined contribution pension or nothing at all. This pension gap has serious financial implications for the province, but its effects are much more than financial. This unfair polarization of working conditions, in which a privileged few receive benefits that others cannot access, was predicted two decades ago by Betcherman and Lowe[2] and unfortunately has come to fruition. Of course, it would be nice if more members of society could receive an employer-provided defined benefit pension to augment CPP payouts. But, in practice, the model is for employers to provide either no (company) pension or a modest defined contribution pension. That battle has been fought and lost.

Yes, oil revenues are way down. But this problem does not go away when oil revenues improve. When governments finally decide to balance the books, and hopefully more ratings downgrades are not required to overcome inertia, public-sector workers are going to be affected. The "do nothing" option does not mean the problem is solved. It means the problem will grow. A substantial pension liability (i.e., debt) needs to be addressed.[3] A substantial annual deficit needs to be addressed. Good governance means that our political parties must present a plan that shows a realistic path to balanced budgets going forward, even if it creates discomfort. Similarly, members of the public have an obligation to focus on the idea, rather than questioning the motives behind the message.

As discussed by Hebdon and Brown,[4] public-sector bargaining is a different beast because management negotiators must keep an eye on public opinion rather than fiscal discipline. But the time has come for public policy-makers and the general public in Newfoundland to face our fiscal deficit now; we can no longer wait for it to reach crisis levels. Suppose that government negotiators push hard — with the expressed consent of the public — to negotiate collective agreements that wind up defined benefit pensions going forward, to be replaced with defined contribution pensions on a 50–50 cost-sharing basis. This would lessen future (and current) spending obligations. It would also give us breathing room as we wade through the much more unpalatable choices of reducing more rural services or schools, or public-sector wage cuts and layoffs. It would also show the public that we are all in this fiscal situation together. That discussion, while uncomfortable, is long overdue and part of the price of good governance. ★

About the Author

Gordon Cooke (Business Administration, Memorial University of Newfoundland) studies the changing nature of work, that is, non-standard work arrangements like fluctuating work schedules, long or short workweeks, casual/on-call/non-permanent employment, and non-traditional work locations (e.g., telework). He also studies the impacts of these labour market changes on subgroups of the population, such as younger vs. middle vs. older workers, and those in rural vs. urban communities.

Notes

1. Conference Board of Canada, *Provincial Outlook 2013: Long-term Economic Forecast* (2013).
2. G. Betcherman, G.S. Lowe, and Canadian Policy Research Networks, *The Future of Work in Canada: A Synthesis Report* (Ottawa: Canadian Policy Research Networks, 1997).
3. CBC, "N.L. Credit Rating Downgraded to Lowest in Canada by Bond Rating Agency Moody's," 22 July 2016, at: http://www.cbc.ca/news/canada/newfoundland-labrador/moodys-nl-credit-ratings-downgraded-1.3690848.
4. R. Hebdon and T. Brown, *Industrial Relations in Canada*, 3rd ed. (Toronto: Nelson Education, 2016).

67 Strategic Philanthropy

Jennifer Dyer

Here's what business gets back when donating to the arts. #DemocraticReformNL

Newfoundland and Labrador is renowned for its vibrant and dynamic culture that celebrates the arts in all its forms, including music, theatre, visual art, humour, literature, textiles, dance, and traditional arts. Indeed, the burgeoning tourism industry capitalizes on this reputation. It is well established that support for the arts both raises the quality of life for inhabitants and makes the province more attractive for investors, business, and newcomers.[1] The need to develop the arts in Newfoundland and Labrador is a key factor in business assessments of the province, and it is key to developments in educational curricula, quality of life, interaction among diverse peoples, and the maintenance of our arts industries.[2] Its corporate benefits include strongly impacting regional development, corporate responsibility, employee attraction and retention, and marketing. Social benefits include education, community engagement, multiculturalism, and regional identity.[3] And publicly accessible art and cultural development promote primary values of our society: freedom, experimentation, diversity, and concern.

Given all this, what might our government do to develop productively that support base? How might we leverage the role of arts to encourage community interaction and citizen engagement in the continued well-being of the province?

One way to support the arts is historical: by reminding ourselves that society has always supported the arts precisely for their social benefits.[4] This should not be something for which we are obliged to argue. Rather, we must outline an extremely compelling case not to support the social value of the arts when we decide not to fund them.

Another way is to dynamically foster activities that democratize the arts by actively maintaining a well-developed, interactive provincial online platform. A dedicated online space that connects arts practitioners, users, and supporters could link to pre-existing online organizational spaces, but would remain a strong connector mobilizing interaction for potential arts users and for visitors. Specifically, the creation of a Newfoundland and Labrador arts and culture online platform would open web-accessible space to hold virtual workshops, online magazines, virtual "jam sessions," critical and explanatory blogs, and ongoing province-wide calendars of events that identify cultural happenings. The rich talent in tacit local knowledges, such as carving, storytelling, knitting, and singing, and more organized forms of arts knowledge, such as theatrical productions, publishing houses, galleries, and art educators, would have a real forum to publicize the province's arts and culture as a whole and to promote engagement with the arts more broadly and clearly. We must develop public appreciation for what the arts can offer Newfoundlanders and Labradorians, because without it the province loses its lively identity. Promoting culture attracts newcomers and investors. A dedicated curated web-space will help to overcome the vast geographical distances separating regions of artists and audiences, and thereby will help to facilitate planning, interaction, and mutual support.

A manageable way of developing support for the arts also requires new models of two fundamental practices: giving and asking. Models of giving are encouraged by promoting initiatives that connect funders with practitioners. For instance, championing more strongly meaningful "Patron of the Arts" awards for individuals and especially for businesses and organizations at regional and provincial levels would encourage novel modes of connecting arts practitioners with new communities. Similarly, creating public art projects for public spaces — from town centres to walkways to parks — brings art into the spaces people move through daily.

New modes of asking include developing community–business initiatives that encourage the participation of artists in public celebrations, such as outdoor light projections or temporary sculpture parks. Here, artists could educate and publicize their practices while businesses could promote themselves; asking is made specific and mutually beneficial to everyone, and the arts are made democratically public to everyone's benefit. For example, the House of Assembly could lead this process by reconsidering the legislative chamber's adornment with large-scale oil paintings of past speakers that memorialize a past that is no longer representative of the voices or interests of the province. The House could initiate public consultations with our arts communities to rehouse these portraits in a suitable explanatory environment, and to revitalize the chamber with a political neutrality and inclusivity.

Ultimately, involving artists in public representations, developing new models of arts patronage, and developing a province-wide calendar of events would help to democratize the arts for maximal impact and accessibility across the province. New initiatives for interaction would boost the changing identity of the province, sustain regional points of identity, encourage accessibility into remote and specialized cultural forms, develop job opportunities, and integrate public and private industries into our cultural life. ★

About the Author

Jennifer Dyer (Gender Studies/Humanities, Memorial University of Newfoundland) is a frequent commenter at the institutional, civic, and provincial levels in Newfoundland and Labrador on arts funding, corporate cultural engagement, and the social value of art.

Notes

1. Nanos, "Comparison of Skilled Workers and Businesses," Business for the Arts (Ontario), Apr. 2016, at: http://www.businessforthearts.org/wp-content/uploads/2011/01/2016-733-Business-for-the-Arts-Comparison-of-Workers-and-Businesses.pdf; see also Bruno Frey, *Arts & Economics: Analysis & Cultural Policy*, 2nd ed. (New York: Springer Science & Business Media, 2013); David Throsby, *Economics and Culture* (Cambridge: Cambridge University Press, 2001), 63.
2. Lars K. Hallstrom et al., *Sustainability Planning and Collaboration in Rural Canada* (Edmonton: University of Alberta Press, 2016), especially chs. 6 and 14.
3. An excellent example of these social benefits can be found in E. Strom and R. Kerstein, "Mountains and Muses: Tourism Development in Asheville, North Carolina," *Annals of Tourism Research* 52 (May 2015): 134–47.
4. Arnaldo Barone, *A New Economic Theory of Public Support for the Arts: Evolution, Veblen, and the Predatory Arts* (London: Routledge, 2016).

68 Helping Rural Newfoundland and Labrador Flourish through Social Enterprise

Natalie Slawinski

Social enterprise holds promise for tackling challenges faced by rural places. #DemocraticReformNL

Finding a viable future for rural Newfoundland and Labrador presents a number of challenges to policy-makers, not the least of which are the province's geography and demography. Newfoundland and Labrador has hundreds of geographically dispersed and remote communities, many with small and declining populations. Finding a way forward requires community leadership, creativity, and courage, and requires community members to work together to find specific solutions to the issues they face. One way to enable such leadership is for government to effectively support social enterprises in rural communities. These enterprises have the potential to empower community members and to help build sustainable local capacity.

Social enterprises are not new to Newfoundland and Labrador. Co-operatives, for example, are a form of social enterprise and have existed in the province for over a century. The term "social enterprise," however, has gained popularity over the last decade. Signalling the importance of these enterprises for Canada, the federal government recently defined them as organizations that seek "to achieve social, cultural or environmental aims through the sale of goods and services."[1] Whether non-profit or for-profit, the majority of surpluses or profits must flow to the social goals of the organization rather than to its shareholders and owners. When done well, these organizations can bring employment, resources, and an enhanced sense of pride to rural communities.

A growing number of social enterprises in Newfoundland and Labrador are helping to bring hope and opportunity to rural areas. For example, Rising Tide Theatre Company has helped to revitalize Trinity and surrounding communities; the Shorefast Foundation is working to bring new opportunities to Fogo Island and unique ways of thinking about rural economic development that is respectful of nature and culture; the Battle Harbour Historic Trust has preserved the resettled fishing village of Battle Harbour, Labrador, by creating a tourism venture; and a group of students at Memorial University, Enactus Memorial, have been working on numerous social enterprise projects across the province and beyond. The group's latest venture is bringing hydroponics to remote locations in Labrador and across Canada, enabling communities to grow their own food.

These Newfoundland and Labrador enterprises share a number of characteristics. First, each was started by individuals who were not from the community or who returned to the community after time spent away. Second, these social enterprises have helped build capacity and leadership in their communities. Finally, all of these organizations have been recognized locally and in some cases globally for their positive impact on people and/or the natural environment.

Despite the potential for social enterprises to help revitalize communities, rural Newfoundland and Labrador presents several obstacles. For instance, rural communities struggle to access key resources often taken for granted in urban areas. Such resources include a skilled and educated workforce, training opportunities, and standard business infrastructure and ecosystems such as transportation networks, telecommunications, the Internet, banks, professional advisers, and social networks.[2] Perhaps the most challenging obstacles are the feelings of hopelessness and fear that accompany population decline and such cultural barriers as a negative perception of business.

Despite the challenges, rural Newfoundland and Labrador communities also possess assets that larger centres often lack, including less congestion, unspoiled nature, and unique traditions. Perhaps the most valuable asset is local knowledge — knowledge that can only be obtained by living and working within the community. Communities that leverage their unique place-based assets and knowledge to create new opportunities can benefit greatly from social enterprise. The challenge is bringing communities together in a way that encourages collaboration. The key is to empower communities to discover their internal leadership potential and to find their own path forward. Social enterprises are ideally suited to rural places because they are attentive to local needs and assets.[3]

Proponents of social enterprise could learn from the experiences of Memorial University's Extension Service between 1959 and 1991. Extension fieldworkers lived in rural communities and helped residents develop skills, talent, and leadership.[4] They were encouraged to experiment with creative approaches to community development. A well-known example was the Fogo Process, a partnership between MUN's Extension Service and the National Film Board of Canada, which helped Fogo Islanders find a way forward in the face of pressures to resettle. The Fogo Process helped spawn the Fogo Island Co-op, which continues to contribute to the local economy to this day.

Past regional development initiatives in this province have had mixed success.[5] While not a silver-bullet solution, social enterprise represents a promising approach to tackling some of the challenges faced by rural places, helping to bring enhanced resources, leadership, and pride to communities. The Department of Tourism, Culture, Industry and Innovation has recognized the importance of these enterprises for the province's rural economic development. For social enterprise to be effective in rural communities, the government needs to act as a facilitator, break down barriers to success, and ultimately provide communities with the support needed to enable them to forge their own destiny. If supported in this way, social enterprise can take hold and be a catalyst for rural renewal throughout Newfoundland and Labrador. ★

About the Author

Natalie Slawinski (Business Administration, Memorial University of Newfoundland) received her Ph.D. from the Ivey Business School at the University of Western Ontario. Her research lies at the intersection of business and sustainable development, and has been published in journals such as *Organization Science*, *Journal of Business Ethics*, and *Organization Studies*.

Notes

1. Government of Canada, Innovation, Science and Economic Development Canada, "Directory of Canadian Social Enterprises" (2016), at: http://www.ic.gc.ca/eic/site/ccc_bt-rec_ec.nsf/eng/h_00016.html (accessed Oct. 2016).
2. L. Siemens, "Embedding Small Business and Entrepreneurship Training within the Rural Context," *Entrepreneurship and Innovation* 13, 2 (2012): 165–78.

3. Senate of Canada, *Beyond Freefall: Halting Rural Poverty*, Final Report of the Standing Senate Committee on Agriculture and Forestry (Ottawa, 2008).
4. J.A. Webb, "The Rise and Fall of Memorial University's Extension Service, 1959–91," *Newfoundland and Labrador Studies* 29, 1 (2014): 84–116.
5. R. Gibson, "Life beyond the Zone Boards: Understanding the New Reality of Regional Development in Newfoundland and Labrador," *Newfoundland Quarterly* 105, 4 (2013): 39–42.

PART 10: ORDERS OF THE DAY

Muskrat Falls on Grand River, Labrador, 1930s postcard. (Source: Provincial Archives)

In a legislature, "orders of the day" refers to the list of business to be attended to that day, similar to a meeting agenda. Here we use it to refer to topical issues, specifically, the importance of oil in Newfoundland and Labrador society, and the considerable controversy surrounding the Muskrat Falls hydroelectric megaproject that has dominated public discourse. Contributors do not tackle the alarming financial costs of that project or express joy that it will provide a much-needed stable supply of clean energy. Rather, they express consternation about the social implications of the development and about the government barrelling forward against the objections of some.

Fiona Polack begins by questioning society's materialism and its "petroculture" of dependency on oil. There is an increased need for the public's voice in making the most of this oil dependence, argues Angela Carter. Turning to Muskrat Falls, contributors Vick Allen, Erin Aylward, Elizabeth Zarpa, Scott Neilsen, and Stephen Tomblin argue for a greater say by Indigenous citizens specifically, for Labradorians generally, and in turn, less exclusivity for government executives. The section ends with Mark Stoddart's call for greater public concern for environmental protections in the face of economic development.

69 The Politics of Energy Sources

Fiona Polack

Energy sources and political cultures are closely intertwined. We need a new language of power in #NLpoli. #DemocraticReformNL

How a society chooses to produce, distribute, and consume energy profoundly affects its political culture. This connection is blatant but unacknowledged in Newfoundland and Labrador.

Historian Timothy Mitchell[1] explains how the industries that evolved around coal in the nineteenth century and then oil in the twentieth century shaped modern democracy. Coal brought large numbers of workers together to form collective social movements, and, because of the centralized nature of its distribution, allowed them to exercise power by disrupting its transport. Oil, by contrast, inhibited communal action because it required a smaller, peripatetic workforce to produce and could be shipped via pipeline and sea, which are harder to intercept.

Mitchell speaks of global phenomena, and it is impossible to contemplate the relationship between energy and society in Newfoundland and Labrador in isolation from the wider world. We are all, to varying degrees, unavoidably immersed in "petroculture." It is a globalized, post-industrial culture shaped by fossil fuels in material senses — our ubiquitous cars and trucks, planes, and plastics — as well as immaterial ones. Petroculture reflects our oil-facilitated consumerism and commitment to economic growth.[2]

But it is also true that in an era of escalating climate change, the Western world urgently needs innovative models for imagining societies that produce and consume energy in new ways. Indeed, some of the most promising of these are actually emerging in places that, like Newfoundland and Labrador, have long been perceived as marginal.[3] At issue here is not just leaving behind fossil fuels, although that must happen too, but rather devising ways to seize the opening energy transition offers not just for recasting our technologies but also our social and political relationships.

That Newfoundland and Labrador is ignoring this opportunity is exemplified in the entrenched language its politicians use to describe its energy potential. It is tempting to speculate these attitudes might be traceable to the heyday of the misguided exploitation of another kind of energy resource: the Atlantic codfish. Over the last decade, both Progressive Conservative and Liberal governments have repeatedly dubbed the province an "energy warehouse."[4] The metaphor conjures images of the island's natural resources — its water, wind, oil, and gas — as commodities conveniently stockpiled in extensive quantities and available at cut-price to the canny purchaser. It also casts the provincial government in the role of merchant and implicitly suggests that the relationship of most importance is not that which exists between the government and the people but between the government and those who wish to purchase the energy products it markets.

Democracy can mean different things. As Mitchell notes, in the era of oil, governments have tended to deploy the popular consent bestowed at the ballot box as a means of actually limiting claims for greater equality and justice and for meaningful public participation in decision-making. Important arenas, the economy chief among them, have been established as areas in which only those in power need have a say. Energy policy, despite its crucial influence on the kind of society we become, has emerged, under successive governments of differing political orientation, as another such terrain in Newfoundland and Labrador. This tendency has been compounded by the fact that the major projects developed in the province since the second half of the twentieth century have been located offshore (Hibernia, Terra Nova, White Rose, and, most recently, Hebron) or in areas with small, dispersed populations whose voices have long not been adequately heard (the Churchill Falls and Muskrat Falls hydroelectric developments in Labrador). By illustrative contrast, long-standing initiatives to introduce net metering in Newfoundland and Labrador, which would allow residents to generate their own power and supply it to the grid, proceeded at a glacial pace.[5] While Mitchell is preoccupied with what he calls "carbon democracy," it seems that "hydro democracy" closely resembles it in very significant ways in Newfoundland and Labrador.

There is another kind of democracy, though, one founded on the principle of creating more equitable and just forms of communal life. It is exactly this form that we need to have firmly in mind as we go about the task of crafting our energy future, a task with the very potential to help us get there. Language is crucial to this endeavour. It sets the tone and subtly establishes the directions we take. Now is the moment to depart permanently from the discourse of "energy warehousing" and the deeply entrenched and problematic mentality it reflects, and prioritize instead principles of "energy and equity." Power, quite literally, needs to be put in the hands of the people. ★

About the Author

Fiona Polack (English, Memorial University of Newfoundland) works in the field of energy humanities. She is a member of the Petrocultures Research Group and recently co-chaired the international conference "Petrocultures 2016: The Offshore." Fiona contributed to the writing of *After Oil* (University of West Virginia Press, 2016), and is co-author with Danine Farquharson of an essay on cultural representations of offshore oil rigs in *Fueling Culture: 101 Words for Energy and Environment* (Fordham University Press, 2017).

Notes

1. Timothy Mitchell, *Carbon Democracy: Political Power in the Age of Oil* (London: Verso, 2011).
2. Petrocultures Research Group, *After Oil* (Morgantown: West Virginia University Press, 2016).
3. Jarra Hicks and Nicky Ison, "Community-Owned Renewable Energy: Opportunities for Rural Australia," *Rural Society* 20, 3 (2011): 244–55.
4. Government of Newfoundland and Labrador, Department of Natural Resources, "Energy" (2016), at: http://www.nr.gov.nl.ca/nr/energy/ (accessed 14 Oct. 2016). See also links on the same page to the former Williams government's "Energy Plan."
5. Ashley Fitzpatrick, "Net Metering Ready to Roll in N.L.," *The Telegram*, 19 May 2017, at: http://www.thetelegram.com/business/2017/5/19/net-metering-ready-to-roll--in-newfoundland.html (accessed 19 June 2017).

70 Engaging the Public to Avert the Risks of Oil Dependency

Angela Carter

Here's how we can plan for the last chapter of NL's oil sector, one that is fair and environmentally sound. #DemocraticReformNL

Oil wealth is a mixed blessing. While oil represents an incredible economic opportunity, it also comes with multiple risks. The Cougar helicopter crash in 2009 and the sinking of the *Ocean Ranger* in 1982 emphasized the tragic price sometimes paid by workers and their families for oil. Newfoundlanders and Labradorians are also now experiencing first-hand the boom-and-bust volatility of economic dependence on oil. Further, oil development poses environmental threats to human health, climate stability, and ecosystems. Underlying all these risks are political challenges faced by oil-rich governments, even in affluent democracies like Canada.[1] Oil wealth is associated with less competitive elections: thanks to oil revenue, political leaders can increase public spending while reducing taxes, appealing to voters' short-term interests and securing more time in office. Meanwhile, to keep oil revenues flowing, oil-rich governments tend to prioritize the oil industry ahead of protecting communities and the environment. Oil development can also heighten regional, class, ethnic, and gender inequality — this is never good for democracy. How should Newfoundland and Labrador avert the multi-faceted risks of oil dependence? Given the mounting evidence on how oil wealth hollows out democratic governance,[2] reviving democratic practices should be an essential part of answering this question.

Oil is an extraordinarily valuable asset that belongs to the public but is predominantly developed by private corporations. Is the province getting a fair share? Public engagement on this fundamental question depends on the public having access to comprehensible information about how much revenue the Government of Newfoundland and Labrador retains of the total value of oil extracted, cutting through the baffling complexity of royalty regimes, corporate taxation, equity stakes, and revenue-sharing arrangements with the federal government. Similarly, accessible information on the number, quality, and location of jobs created by the sector would be insightful as well. Moreover, how does the share of oil's value captured by the province compare to corporate profits and to revenues collected by other governments? And what of provincial and federal government subsidies offered to Newfoundland and Labrador's oil industry?[3] How much is the public paying to support this sector?

With this information in hand, Newfoundland and Labrador could follow Alberta's lead in fostering comprehensive panel reviews and citizens' assemblies to debate what counts as a fair share. This could become a regular public conversation supported by yearly audits by the auditor general. Collectively deciding how to capture value from oil is a first step to averting the economic risks of oil dependence. The next is to determine how to spend oil revenue fairly.

Extracting oil is likened to selling the "family silver."[4] It is a valuable asset that can be sold just once. But selling oil does not guarantee long-term economic security; rather, oil revenue must be transformed to generate sustainable income. What is more, the family silver belongs to the entire family, present and future. The pressing question, then, is how can extracting oil promote equity across Newfoundland and Labrador's communities today and into the future?

The province could benefit from a collectively developed plan for generating province-wide benefits from remaining oil revenues and for sharing those benefits with future generations. Norway has set the global example by establishing a sovereign wealth fund. Likewise, citizens of Newfoundland and Labrador could debate the merits of safeguarding oil wealth and diversifying the economy away from oil while also addressing the province's high levels of inequality.

These discussions should also include consideration of a central problem posed by oil: its extensive environmental risks and costs to human health, ecosystems, and other economic sectors. The offshore oil projects are among the largest greenhouse gas emitters in Canada and life-cycle assessments of the industry anticipate stunning cumulative emissions.[5]

These emissions contribute to global temperature increases resulting in climate instability and ocean acidification. Recent scientific studies advise keeping at least 74 per cent of Canada's oil reserves in the ground to avoid catastrophic climate instability.[6] Not only does Newfoundland and Labrador's expanding oil sector run contrary to this global responsibility, but it contributes to undermining the stability of renewable sectors in the province, such as the fisheries.

These environmental risks raise significant democratic questions, for while the immediate benefits of oil may not be widely shared, oil development degrades commonly shared ecosystems that sustain our economies and communities. What, then, must Newfoundland and Labrador do? The public discourse needed to answer this question first requires public access to very basic information about the current and anticipated cumulative environmental impacts of this sector, across the marine ecosystem. To date, these impacts are not measured. Once available, this information could form the basis for democratic debate on environmental regulations surrounding the oil industry. Ideally, an independent advisory board, comprised of scientific specialists and members of the broader public, would guide this research and lead these deliberations.

The recent debate around fracking in western Newfoundland showed citizens' hunger for renewed democratic participation in decisions about the province's oil economy. It demonstrated that citizens are deeply concerned about the economic, health, and environmental consequences of intensifying oil activity — and they want to participate in decisions on this sector. But public involvement is premised on accessible, comprehensible information about what exactly is gained from oil and at what cost. In the wake of the recent oil price dive, this is an opportune moment to re-engage the public and plan collectively for the last chapter of the province's oil sector. ★

About the Author

Angela Carter (Political Science, University of Waterloo) is originally from Newfoundland. She researches comparative environmental policy regimes surrounding oil developments, primarily in Alberta, Newfoundland and Labrador, and Saskatchewan. Angela is a co-investigator on the Social Sciences and Humanities Research Council Partnership Grant "Mapping the power of the carbon-extractive corporate resource sector."

Notes

1. Laurie Adkin, ed., *First World Petro-Politics: The Political Ecology and Governance of Alberta* (Toronto: University of Toronto Press, 2016).
2. Michael Ross, *The Oil Curse: How Petroleum Wealth Shapes the Development of Nations* (Princeton, N.J.: Princeton University Press, 2012).
3. EnviroEconomics Inc., Dave Sawyer, and Seton Stiebert, "Fossil Fuels — At What Cost? Government Support for Upstream Oil Activities in Three Canadian Provinces: Alberta, Saskatchewan, and Newfoundland and Labrador," International Institute for Sustainable Development (2010), at: https://www.iisd.org/gsi/sites/default/files/ffs_awc_3canprovinces.pdf.
4. John Warnock, "Selling the Family Silver: Oil and Gas Royalties, Corporate Profits, and the Disregarded Public," Parkland Institute and Canadian Centre for Policy Alternatives (2006), at: https://www.policyalternatives.ca/sites/default/files/uploads/publications/Saskatchewan_Pubs/2006/Selling_the_Family_Silver.pdf.
5. Office of the Auditor General of Canada, "Response to Petition, 'Cost-Benefit Analysis of Offshore Oil and Gas Development in Newfoundland and Labrador'" (2014), at: http://www.oag-bvg.gc.ca/internet/English/pet_356_e_39406.html.
6. Christophe McGlade and Paul Ekins, "The Geographical Distribution of Fossil Fuels Unused When Limiting Global Warming to 2 °C," *Nature* 517 (2015): 187–202, at: http://www.nature.com/nature/journal/v517/n7533/full/nature14016.html.

71 Muskrat Falls

Vick Allen

Why Muskrat Falls needed more consultation and more consideration for Indigenous voices. #Aboriginal #NLpoli #DemocraticReformNL

During the occupation of the Muskrat Falls Lower Churchill project site, I took part in a sit-in at Confederation Building. As I sat there, I began to wonder about Truth and Reconciliation. I began questioning what we, the people, were doing to facilitate reconciliation within the province. I then thought about what they, Nalcor Energy, were doing.

I've read portions of the Labrador Inuit Land Claims Agreement (LILCA) but none pertaining to water and land rights, so I brushed up. I also read all 94 Calls to Action put forward by the Truth and Reconciliation Commission of Canada. I focused on Business and Reconciliation. When it comes to a business that wishes to develop Indigenous resources and lands, Call to Action 92 calls on businesses to: "Commit to meaningful consultation, building respectful relationships, and obtaining the free, prior, and informed consent of Indigenous peoples before proceeding with economic development projects."[1]

Consultations occurred. Relationships were respectful. Informed consent was given by one of three Indigenous groups in the region. Each aspect, with respect to this Call, was met. I then wondered what our Indigenous legal rights were. Specifically, the rights afforded to the Nunatsiavut Government after the LILCA was signed and ratified. I took a look at the water rights. In LILCA under Chapter 5, section 5.3.2 states: "Subject to this chapter, Inuit have the right to enjoy Water[2] that is on, in, under, flowing through or adjacent to the Labrador Inuit Lands substantially unaltered as to quantity, quality and rate of flow." While Lake Melville is not Labrador Inuit lands, it is adjacent to Labrador Inuit lands and is part of the Labrador Inuit settlement area. LILCA section 5.2.6 states: "Nothing in this chapter permits a Person[3] to discharge Waste into Water without a Water Use Permit from the Minister."

If you read a little further, section 5.4.14 states:

> Notwithstanding that the definition of Water does not include Tidal Waters, if a power Development is proposed within the area set out in the Map Atlas . . . that substantially alters the quantity, quality or rate of flow of Tidal Waters adjacent to Labrador Inuit Lands within the area shown in schedule 5-A, the Development shall not be permitted to proceed until the Nunatsiavut Government and the Developer have concluded a Compensation Agreement, Inuit shall be entitled to claim for losses likely to result from the substantial alteration to the quantity, quality or rate of flow of the Tidal Waters adjacent to Labrador Inuit Lands within the area shown in schedule 5-A.[4]

Here's where it gets complicated. The water from the Muskrat Falls Lower Churchill project will flow into the land claim area. However, because neither Lake Melville nor Muskrat Falls is on Labrador Inuit lands, they technically do not have to negotiate with the Nunatsiavut Government. They do not have to obtain a permit to discharge waste into water and they are not required to develop a compensation agreement.

Interestingly, compensation was suggested. It has been rejected by the Nunatsiavut Government, which took its response directly from the Inuit in the Lake Melville region. The response from the people was: "You cannot put a price on our way of life." Both parties seem to be at a standstill. Nalcor Energy stands to lose months of preparation and possibly suffer damage to the dam if the project is not permitted to proceed. On the other hand, the Inuit of Lake Melville (myself included) are terrified that their main food source will be poisoned after the floodwaters are released.

What can we take from this situation? How can we avoid this in the future? How can we promote reconciliation in this province? In order to facilitate true reconciliation with regard to business, it must be taken further than what the Call to Action recommends.

Don't simply consult. Listen. Listen to the concerns of the people whose lives you will be impacting. Build respectful relationships. Visit the place that you are developing. Speak to the people. Build a connection to them and to the land before you break ground. When I spoke about respect earlier, it is more akin to being cordial than respect. True respect comes when you get to know people, understand their lives, and appreciate the daily struggles they face.

When obtaining consent from the Indigenous people, ensure that *all* Indigenous groups are consulted. Above all, before developing lands that we, as Indigenous people, have occupied for thousands of years, ensure that we are able to continue to survive. Because we live in the Arctic, it is imperative that we adapt to survive. We are good at it. But we cannot adapt to poison. ★

About the Author

Vick Allen (St. John's Native Friendship Centre) is an Inuk from Rigolet, Nunatsiavut. She holds a Bachelor of Arts in Archaeology from Memorial University of Newfoundland. After finishing as the conference co-ordinator for the Inuit Studies Conference, she became the catering co-ordinator at the St. John's Native Friendship Centre. Her passions include cooking and advocating.

Notes

1. Truth and Reconciliation Commission of Canada, *Calls to Action* (2015), at: http://www.trc.ca/websites/trcinstitution/File/2015/Findings/Calls_to_Action_English2.pdf.
2. Land Claims Agreement between the Inuit of Labrador and Her Majesty the Queen in Right of Newfoundland and Labrador and Her Majesty the Queen in Right of Canada (2005) (Labrador Inuit Land Claims Agreement, LILCA), at: https://www.aadnc-aandc.gc.ca/DAM/DAM-INTER-HQ/STAGING/texte-text/al_ldc_ccl_fagr_labi_labi_1307037470583_eng.pdf, p. 79. "Water" means surface and subterranean water in liquid or frozen state located in or derived from a natural channel, a lake or other body of inland water but does not include "Tidal Waters."
3. Ibid., p. 78. "Person" includes an individual, a partnership, a corporation, a trust, a joint venture, an unincorporated association, a government or any agency or subdivision of a government, and their respective heirs, executors, administrators, and other legal representatives.
4. Ibid., p. 81.

72 Creating Spaces for Indigenous Labradorians in Provincial Governance

Erin Aylward and Elizabeth Zarpa

Challenges in Labrador's Indigenous communities require action. #Aboriginal #NLpoli #DemocraticReformNL

With a population of just over 15,000,[1] Labrador's Indigenous groups[2] exist in an uneasy, and at times reluctant, relationship with the Government of Newfoundland and Labrador. Frequently, provincial decision-makers are unfamiliar with these communities' cultures and fraught historic relationships with provincial/ Crown institutions. Perhaps not surprisingly, many Indigenous Labradorians feel misrepresented and neglected by provincial democratic institutions. Here, we argue that reconciliation and trust-building are essential preconditions to fostering meaningful democratic engagement with Labrador's Indigenous groups; we also suggest that greater work is needed to ensure that Indigenous Labradorians are included in public office.

Efforts to alter the Muskrat Falls flooding process in October 2016 point to the complexity of renewing democracy in Labrador. In addition to reflecting this region's history of Indigenous-led non-violent protests, the mobilization of civil society and Indigenous governments in response to concerns about methyl-mercury poisoning demonstrates a deep-seated sentiment of mistrust towards provincial authorities that has been fostered over decades. For example, one young Nainimiuk[3] at a Muskrat Falls protest explained:

> I'm here for a lot of reasons, but the main reason is history. For many years in our history, Inuit and many other Aboriginal groups were afraid to speak up against governments, churches and other leaders. . . . My family was told they were being relocated. They were told they were being sent to residential school. Our communities were ripped apart. Today these people are trying to tell us that we have no choice — just like they did for the last 400 years. No. We're not scared to speak up anymore. We're not gonna be forced to put our lives and families on the line anymore. We are fighting for our rights and we're gonna keep fighting like I bet my family then wish they could have.[4]

As this young woman's remarks suggest, recent provincial history is rife with examples of government interventions that have further fomented historical mistrust. From the 1970s to the 1990s, the provincial government engaged in commercial logging, mining, fishing, and developing the Churchill Falls hydroelectric project without consulting Indigenous groups,[5] and the federal government used its Goose Bay base for low-level flight training by Canada and four NATO allies. Residential schools, where children were taken from their homes, families, communities, and culture, and put into Anglo-Saxon missionary schools, operated in Labrador until as late as 1980. For decades and ongoing today, social workers and law enforcement officials put many Indigenous children into care without their family's consent or — in some cases — without even their families' knowledge, which has caused significant detriment to children and their families for generations.[6]

While Labrador's Indigenous communities are often associated with high levels of poverty and substance abuse, most public servants and members of the general public have embarrassingly little awareness of how colonialism and intergenerational trauma have contributed to such conditions.

If we want to advance the quality of democracy in our province, it is vital that individuals serving in public office develop greater cultural competence and a deeper awareness of the complex history that connects Labrador with the provincial and federal governments. This need is echoed in the Truth and Reconciliation Commission's recommendation that public servants receive education and training on past and present Aboriginal–Crown relations and Indigenous rights.[7]

However, although strengthening public servants' awareness of the diversity and complex histories that exist within our province is important, it alone is insufficient: the concerns and knowledge of Indigenous Labradorians, as well as their trust in democratic institutions, should also be advanced through greater participation of Indigenous Labradorians in our province's democratic institutions. The past two decades have seen some encouraging momentum in this direction; for example, the Labrador Inuit Land Claims Agreement was ratified in 2005, which led to the autonomous Inuit region and government, Nunatsiavut; the Southern Inuit/Metis' community association has successfully developed into NunatuKavut; and Labrador's four seats were maintained during the remapping of electoral boundaries in 2015. However, more work is needed to ensure Indigenous Labradorians are well represented at the provincial level and that the next generation of Labradorian decision-makers has access to the resources, programs, and the respect required for deeper democratic engagement.

The ongoing challenges facing Labrador's Indigenous communities demand action. Such action, however, must be informed by an understanding of how colonial/neo-colonial relations have actively contributed to these challenges. Moreover, such action must recognize Indigenous Labradorians' efforts and abilities to engage with local, municipal, provincial, and federal governance structures. One concrete action that can be taken in this direction is for the Truth and Reconciliation Commission's recommendation on professional development and training for public servants to be formally integrated into the Public Service Commission Act, and for affirmative action measures to be explicitly outlined in the Public Service Collective Bargaining Act. Relatedly, we urge that protocol be established to ensure strong Indigenous Labradorian representation on advisory councils, commissions, and other bodies established to advance the interests of the province. ★

About the Authors

Erin Aylward (Political Science and Gender & Women's Studies, University of Toronto) is a Ph.D. student and a 2015 Pierre Elliott Trudeau Foundation Scholar. Erin is an international development researcher/practitioner whose research focuses on human rights, social movements, gender, and sexuality.

Elizabeth Zarpa (Inuit Tapiriit Kanatami) is a student at heart and has experience living across Canada, but home is Labrador. She enjoys hiking, and an intellectual conversation every once in a while.

Notes

1. This number is based on the following estimates: Nunatsiavut officials confirmed via e-mail that the number of Nunatsiavut beneficiaries as of 14 November 2016 was 7,164; Labrador's two Innu communities, according to an Aboriginal Peoples Television Network report, are estimated to have a population around 2,100, (Michelin 2014), and the NunatuKavut website suggests that there are at least 6,000 Southern Inuit/Métis. See Ossie Michelin, "Nearly a Third of Kids in Protective Custody in Newfoundland and Labrador Are Aboriginal," Aboriginal Peoples Television Network, 29 Oct. 2014, at: http://aptn.ca/news/2014/10/29/nearly-third-kids-protective-custody-newfoundland-labrador-come-aboriginal-communities/ (accessed 16 Nov. 2016); NunatuKavut, "Who We Are" (n.d.), at: http://www.nunatukavut.ca/home/home.htm (accessed 16 Nov. 2016).
2. Indigenous groups from Labrador include the Inuit predominantly from the northern regions, Innu predominantly from the interior, and the Metis (or southern Inuit of Labrador) mostly from southern Labrador.
3. An Inuttitut word meaning "someone from Nain." Nain is the most northerly community in Labrador, and is part of Nunatsiavut, the autonomous Inuit region of Newfoundland and Labrador.
4. Christina Isabelle Tellez, in Facebook (Muskrat Falls Land Protectors), at: https://www.facebook.com/photo.php?fbid=10153819818521993&set=gm.315720345466177&type=3&theater (accessed 1 Nov. 2016).
5. C. Alcantara, "Explaining Aboriginal Treaty Negotiation Outcomes in Canada: The Cases of the Inuit and the Innu in Labrador," *Canadian Journal of Political Science* 40, 1 (2007): 185–207.
6. Michelin, "Nearly a Third of Kids in Protective Custody."
7. Truth and Reconciliation Commission of Canada, *Truth and Reconciliation Commission of Canada: Calls to Action* (Winnipeg, 2015), at: http://www.trc.ca/websites/trcinstitution/File/2015/Findings/Calls_to_Action_English2.pdf (accessed 1 Nov. 2016).

73 An Increased Role for Indigenous Citizens in Decisions Affecting Labrador

Scott Neilsen

Muskrat Falls boondoggle stresses need for increased role for #Aboriginal citizens in decisions affecting Labrador. #NLpoli #DemocraticReformNL

I am not a Labradorian, although I do live in Labrador. In late 2010 and early 2011 I was one of a number of self-selected respondents who took part in a survey (n = 285) and virtual town hall (n = 111–306 touchtone votes) commissioned by Todd Russell, the MP for Labrador at that time. The themes of the survey and town hall focused on environmental impacts, local benefits, and Indigenous rights. The questions were designed to "canvass the diversity of views in Labrador."[1]

In response to each of the questions asked, a majority of respondents indicated that they had significant concerns with the Muskrat Falls project. In relation to Indigenous rights specifically, approximately two-thirds of the respondents indicated that the project agreement did not respect Innu, Inuit, and Metis rights. Among respondents from Upper Lake Melville and the Labrador coast — the regions with the highest proportion of Indigenous population in Labrador[2] — only 7 per cent of respondents indicated that the project respected Innu, Inuit, and Metis rights.[3]

The resulting report by Russell, *Where We Stand: Labradorians' Views of the Muskrat Falls Proposal*, while not without its methodological issues, is the only attempt I know of to quantify Labrador citizens' views of Muskrat Falls prior to construction. In contrast to Russell's report, a Corporate Research Associates poll published in *The Atlantic Quarterly*[4] and reported in *The Telegram* states that a majority of the 400 Newfoundland and Labrador residents surveyed "completely/mostly support" the Muskrat Falls project. Within this overall sample, however, only about 6 per cent of the respondents, or 24 people, are from Labrador; and they are not distinguished from Newfoundlanders living on the western portion of the island.[5] So, while the headline that a majority of the province's residents support the project may be true within a national context, in the provincial context it is just as likely, if not more so, that a majority of Labradorians do not support the project, while a majority of Newfoundlanders do.

Discords between the two geographic regions of the province, such as that above, are not new. Newfoundland and Labrador is not a single terrestrial, social, or cultural unit. Within the population of the province, residents of Labrador are outnumbered about 18 to 1, and the 2006 Canadian census shows that the Innu and Inuit make up 37 per cent of the overall Labrador population.[6] Within the provincial union, Labrador cannot muster a majority, and, within Labrador, the Indigenous population cannot muster a majority. This is in spite of the fact that the largest portion of the Quebec–Labrador Peninsula — Nitassinan and Ungava — is indisputably Indigenous territory. It is where they live, and where they became the societies they are today. The Innu and Inuit, respectively, have been here for millennia and centuries longer than settlers.

This is colonialism through demographic incursion. As the Muskrat Falls project and the 2016 protests in Upper Lake Melville have shown, resource management within Labrador is not undertaken at the will of local citizens, whether settler or Indigenous. Labrador independence has often been suggested as one solution to this imbalance of power, and perhaps it would help. As the population numbers show, however, Innu and Inuit would remain outnumbered, and they would still not have an equitable say in the management of the territory.

One mechanism that may help to remedy this imbalance of power has come to light through another tragedy of resources in Nitassinan and Ungava. The Ungava Peninsula Caribou Aboriginal Roundtable has formed in response to the mismanagement and drastic decline of the George River caribou herd. This group includes representatives of all the Indigenous communities in Labrador and eastern Quebec, and does not include any members of the provincial or federal governments.[7] The community representatives ask the questions and pursue the answers, and in the process draw on experts from the Eeyou (Cree), Innu, Inuit, and scientific communities.

Through legislation the Government of Newfoundland and Labrador could create an Indigenous resource management table in Labrador, with a mandate to pose questions and compel answers from proponents of development and regulators and to reach consensus around management parameters and mitigation prior to the issuing of development and other permits (assuming that development is wanted at all).

Those around the table would come from the Indigenous communities. They would represent various segments of Indigenous society, and they would not be sitting members of government. The conflict-of-interest guidelines would be strict, and the table's directives to proponents and regulators would be binding.

This table is conceived as a step beyond the co-management that comes with a land claim or the social licence to operate that some resource developers seek today.[8] The goal would be to decolonize the process of resource management in Labrador and to ensure that Innu and Inuit ways of knowing and being are maintained, fostered, and fortified through the process of resource management, and not on an ad hoc basis. ★

About the Author

Scott Neilsen (Archaeology, Labrador Institute, and Grenfell Campus of Memorial University of Newfoundland) lives and works in Labrador, and has a keen interest in the long-term history of Indigenous peoples in the region and their relations with one another, settlers, visitors, government, and the environment. He is co-ordinator of the Certificate in Aboriginal and Indigenous Studies at Memorial University, and sits on the President's Advisory Committee on Aboriginal Affairs.

Notes

1. Todd Russell, MP, *Where We Stand: Labradorians' Views of the Muskrat Falls Proposal* (2014), at: http://www.ceaa.gc.ca/050/documents/48961/48961F.pdf, p. 3 (accessed 4 Nov. 2016).
2. Nathaniel Pollock, Shree Murray, James Valcour, and Michael Jong, "Suicide Rates in Aboriginal Communities in Labrador, Canada," *Applied Journal of Public Health* 106, 7 (2016).
3. Russell, *Where We Stand*, 11.
4. Corporate Research Associates Inc., "Muskrat Falls Hydroelectric Project," *The Atlantic Quarterly* (Winter 2013): 43–44. Also see "Majority of N.L. Residents Support Muskrat Falls Development, CRA Poll Says," *The Telegram*, 2 Apr. 2013, at: http://www.thetelegram.com/News/Local/2013-04-02/article-3211673/Majority-of-N.L.-residents-support-Muskrat-Falls-development,-CRA-poll-says/1 (accessed 4 Nov. 2016).

5. Personal communication with Corporate Research Associates, Mar. 2017.
6. Pollock et al., "Suicide Rates in Aboriginal Communities."
7. Adamie Delisle Alaku, "Other Models — Ungava Peninsula Caribou Aboriginal Roundtable: Responding to Declines and Mitigating Pressures on Ungava Migratory Caribou," 22 Oct. 2014, at: http://www.srrb.nt.ca/index.php?option=com_docman&view=document&slug=9-1-other-models-ungava-peninsula-upcart-pdf-1&layout=default&alias=972-9-1-other-models-ungava-peninsula-upcart-pdf-1&category_slug=barren-ground-caribou&Itemid=697 (accessed 17 June 2017).
8. Marc G. Stevenson, "Decolonizing Co-Management in Northern Canada," *Cultural Survival Quarterly* 28, 1 (2004), at: https://www.culturalsurvival.org/publications/cultural-survival-quarterly/canada/decolonizing-co-management-northern-canada (accessed 4 Nov. 2016).

74 Defensive Expansionism in Newfoundland and Labrador

Stephen Tomblin

Muskrat Falls is latest example of too much power concentrated in the Premier's Office, says @TomblinStephen #NLpoli #DemocraticReformNL

Border defence guided by populist rhetoric, more a product of executive capacity and autonomy than of good policy practice, has become a salient issue with Brexit and recent calls for building walls in North America, but it can also be connected to the Muskrat Falls "boondoggle."[1] In Canada, building energy walls has a long history and is closely connected to province-building. Yet, as discussed recently by Wilder and Howlett, despite earlier scholarly enthusiasm for understanding the pros and cons of province-building border defensive actions, such initiatives have for the most part fallen off the radar.[2] It is time to refocus on the concept of province-building in Newfoundland and Labrador in light of the Muskrat Falls controversy. It matters that the executive branch was able to push such a controversial, risky project while constraining public debate.[3]

Province-building, with the decision to build hydro energy infrastructure for purposes of defending/promoting the territorial-jursidictional interests of premiers despite high costs and policy risks, remains a common practice, even a core value in Canadian federalism. Yet, it has not received sufficient attention in the Newfoundland and Labrador energy discourse.[4] The primary objective here is to focus more on the challenges of executive power and how this has undermined effective energy governance and public policy. It seems Premier Danny Williams and multiple premiers who inherited the Muskrat Falls hydro project were more concerned with territorial-jurisdictional battles than developing the most efficient, cost-effective form of energy production.

The combination of a cabinet-parliamentary and federal system, where provincial governments own energy as well as natural resources and enjoy much autonomy and capacity, has reinforced a pattern of decision-making that is, by design, outside the reach of the public. Goals of territorial boundary defence have remained key priorities as opposed to facilitating policy discussions focused on the functional needs of citizens. The territorial brand of pluralism that exists in Canada (inherited by Danny Williams) is designed to manufacture well-crafted products (whether societies, patterns of communication, or physical infrastructure) critical to the survival of province-building. The literature is full of examples of provincial governments working in isolation and constraining knowledge with the clear goal of defending and promoting their territorial-jurisdictional interests first and foremost. Citizens in such a system are, by design, merely spectators.

Problems created for democracy, governance, and public policy are connected to the autonomy and capacity enjoyed by the executive branch. In this light the Muskrat Falls debacle can be viewed as a product of executive domination. Lack of policy debate and oversight is common since the executive controls information flow, the role of the legislature, and oversight agencies, such as public utility boards. At first, Muskrat Falls proved popular under the leadership of Premier Danny Williams. But popularity did not make for good policy.

There has been a history of these kinds of concerted efforts to control information flow when it comes to building physical infrastructure and promoting the territorial-jurisdictional goals of provincial community building.[5] What are the solutions? To a great extent these are well known, but the strength and control of the executive branch make reform difficult.[6] Even faced with policy failure and political crisis, it has been difficult to reform powerful executive-dominated systems designed to sidestep goals of democracy, governance, and evidence-informed public policy.

What can be done? First, Newfoundland and Labrador needs to find ways to be better plugged in south of the border. Quebec, Ontario, Alberta, Manitoba, and other jurisdictions have invested in infrastructure (e.g., office space) in key U.S. locations. Knowledge is power, and our province has been too isolated when it comes to identifying and filling critical knowledge gaps on U.S. market conditions and policy regulatory traditions. As a result, there was and is little understanding of the shale gas revolution, infrastructural challenges, and U.S. policy trends. Second, executive decision-makers need to question the merits of risky sabre-rattling behaviour that compromises democracy, national unity, governance, and evidence-informed policy choices that the public pays for. The building of the Muskrat Falls hydroelectric project based on territorial-jurisdictional objectives was not a wise policy choice, but it was popular within a competitive province-centred federal system. In response, more attention should be placed on adopting a more citizen-centred approach to improving federal governance and working together more collaboratively across systems.[7] We also need to embrace recent efforts of the prime minister to strengthen pan-Canadian intrastate mechanisms and processes. Finally, within the province, new forms of communication and evidence-gathering are required. Ending the executive domination and manipulation of knowledge construction requires opening up democracy, strengthening the role of the House of Assembly and its committees, and increasing oversight of the public utilities and other agencies. Finding ways to reconnect with communities and to engage community knowledge should also be more of a priority. Finally, as in Europe, there must be a focus on facilitating dialogue across systems, so, for example, regional communities in our province could share information and create a dialogue with other regional communities in other provinces and states. ★

About the Author

Stephen Tomblin (Political Science, Memorial University of Newfoundland) has published widely in various areas of public policy and governance. This includes research on regionalization dealing with economic development, continentalism, and other cross-border issues, and research about health restructuring developments, including efforts to devolve power on a regional basis.

Notes

1. Stan Marshall, who was appointed CEO of Nalcor Energy in April 2016, characterized Muskrat Falls as a boondoggle. See http:www.cbc.ca/news/Canada/Newfoundland-labrador/stan-marshal-muskrat-falls-update-1.3649540.
2. See Matt Wilder and Michael Howlett, "Province-Building and Political Science," in Christopher Dunn, ed., *Provinces*, 3rd ed. (Toronto: University of Toronto Press, 2016), 89–108.
3. See James P. Feehan, "Connecting to the North American Grid: Time for Newfoundland to Discontinue Inefficient Price Regulation," *Canadian Public Policy* (Dec. 2016): 482–95.

4. For further discussion, see, for example, Stephen Tomblin, *Ottawa and the Outer Provinces* (Toronto: Lorimer Press, 1995); Pierre Olivier Pineau, "Fragmented Markets: Canadian Electricity's Underperformance," in F.P. Sioshansi, ed., *Evolution of Global Electricity Markets: New Paradigms, New Challenges, New Approaches* (London: Academic Press, 2013).
5. For more details, see Tomblin, *Ottawa and the Outer Provinces*.
6. See Donald Savoie, *What Ever Happened To the Music Teacher?* (Montreal and Kingston: McGill-Queen's University Press, 2013).
7. For discussion on intrastate federalism, see Roger Gibbins, *Regionalism* (Toronto: Butterworth, 1982).

75 Democratizing Environmental Governance

Mark Stoddart

We need more engagement with different dimensions of environmental governance in #NLpoli. #DemocraticReformNL

Economic development often overshadows the environment in the Newfoundland and Labrador political sphere. Similarly, public opinion research indicates that provincial residents are more concerned with health care and unemployment than with natural resource management or climate change.[1] However, recent controversies over the environmental and social risks of the Muskrat Falls hydroelectric project, where community members are worried about increased methyl-mercury in downstream fish populations, and over potential hydraulic fracturing in western Newfoundland demonstrate that many people are concerned about environmental governance in this province.

The environmental impacts of economic development — including issues such as fisheries and ocean health, forestry management, and climate change — are complex and can rarely be addressed within the scope of a single political jurisdiction. A significant body of research describes how environmental governance is evolving to better deal with this complexity, while pointing to ways in which governance can be made more democratic. I will introduce two key elements from this literature and then suggest an additional element from my own research, which bridges natural resource conflicts, climate change, and nature-based tourism.

The first element involves the "vertical" dimension of governance.[2] Environmental issues have causes and consequences that cross local, regional, national, and international geographical and political scales. Previous research highlights the need for increasing connectivity and collaboration across political spheres, including municipalities, provinces, federal governments, and multilateral agencies.[3] There are challenges to accomplishing this, due to differences of power and resources among various political actors, as well as jurisdictional struggles. However, successfully addressing complex problems like climate change or ocean health requires communication and collaboration across these different political spheres.

The second element involves the "horizontal" dimension of governance.[4] This refers to the range of actors engaged in political debate about environmental issues. In many democratic societies, there is a move away from government as the only institution involved in policy discussion.[5] More democratic systems incorporate participation from diverse sectors, including the general public, non-governmental organizations, Indigenous governments and organizations, scientists, and the private sector. Environmental governance outcomes appear to be better when they are crafted through input from diverse actors.[6] However, government needs to be receptive to meaningful input into political decision-making. The boundaries of public engagement cannot be set too narrowly or the process may be seen as illegitimate.[7] Rather, strengthening the horizontal dimension demands that governments recognize and support the political efficacy of non-governmental actors.

The third key element, which derives from my research, is to build greater connectivity across different domains of environmental policy-making. This element is not as developed in the environmental governance literature, but similar ideas about assessing cumulative impacts of different types of activity for regional landscapes are emerging elsewhere in environmental sciences. In this province, economic relationships with our environment include offshore oil, fisheries, nature-based tourism, mining, and forestry. These industries represent different pathways for how we live with, and make a living from, our landscapes and coastal areas. However, planning and policy-making for these sectors often occur in silos rather than through engagement across sectors. Most often, these sectors only come into contact when specific conflicts emerge, such as controversy over the potential Old Harry oil development in the Gulf of St. Lawrence or regarding hydraulic fracturing near Gros Morne National Park. Furthermore, all of these sectors are impacted by, and often contribute to, climate change, which is also treated as a separate sphere of planning and policy-making.

A concrete step that would help democratize environmental governance is to create regular "contact points" for communication and collaboration across sectors that share environmental space, so that divergent interests are not only visible during times of conflict. In the summer of 2016, the provincial government announced the creation of an Oil and Gas Industry Development Council, which is designed to improve communication between government and the oil industry. A similar approach — councils oriented around landscape-level dialogue and planning — could be used to build connections across various economic sectors, provincial and local governmental and non-governmental organizations, and interested members of the public. Take Muskrat Falls as an example: if such a council had provided space for meaningful discussion among Nunatsiavut, NunatuKavut,[8] the Innu Nation, the provincial government, affected municipalities, Nalcor, and labour unions throughout the development of the project, then many of the environmental and social issues that are now the focus of contention could have been identified and resolved much earlier.

Environmental issues have causes and consequences that spill over any single political jurisdiction and cut across multiple spheres of economic activity. Social science research identifies several elements for democratizing environmental governance. The three elements identified here are to build governance systems that: (1) work across local, regional, national, and international political spheres; (2) facilitate meaningful input from a wide range of governmental and non-governmental participants; and (3) create connectivity across sectors that share ecological space, but are currently treated as political silos. Councils for landscape-level dialogue and planning, which embrace these elements, would help Newfoundland and Labrador better address environmental issues and move towards greater social, economic, and ecological sustainability. ★

About the Author

Mark Stoddart (Sociology, Memorial University of Newfoundland) publishes on nature-based tourism, offshore oil, environmental movements, climate change, and mass media. He is the author of *Making Meaning out of Mountains: The Political Ecology of Skiing* (University of British Columbia Press, 2012). His work has recently appeared in *Global Environmental Change*, *Environmental Politics*, *Society & Natural Resources*, *Sociological Quarterly*, and the *Canadian Review of Sociology*.

Notes

1. Ipsos, "The Majority of Newfoundlanders Support the Seal Hunt but Show an Openness to a Buy-Out Plan: Newfoundlanders' Views on the Canadian Seal Hunt" (2011), at: http://ipsos-na.com/tools/link.aspx.
2. M. Francesch-Huidobro, "Institutional Deficit and Lack of Legitimacy: The Challenges of Climate Change Governance in Hong Kong," *Environmental Politics* 21, 5 (2012): 791–810.
3. P.J. Stoett, *Global Ecopolitics* (Toronto: University of Toronto Press, 2012).
4. Francesch-Huidobro, "Institutional Deficit and Lack of Legitimacy."
5. F. Berkes, *Coasts for People: Interdisciplinary Approaches to Coastal and Marine Resource Management* (New York: Routledge, 2015).
6. E. Montpetit, *Misplaced Distrust: Policy Networks and the Environment in France, the United States, and Canada* (Vancouver: University of British Columbia Press, 2003).
7. J. Parkins, and D. Davidson, "Constructing the Public Sphere in Compromised Settings: Environmental Governance in the Alberta Forest Sector," *Canadian Review of Sociology* 45, 2 (2008): 177–96.
8. NunatuKavut is a Southern Inuit territory in Labrador, formerly referred to as the Labrador Metis Nation (http://www.nunatukavut.ca/home/who_we_are.htm).

PART 11: CONCLUSION

Newfoundland Coat of Arms, 1920s postcard. (Source: Provincial Archives)

Now what?

This concluding piece identifies a suggested process for the All-Party Committee on Democratic Reform to follow. It takes no position on the more than 70 contributions up to this point: it is up to readers to arrive at their own opinions about whether or not they agree with the arguments. These should be understood to constitute only a sample of the many ways that academics, journalists, students, and others might suggest to reform democratic governance.

Before any changes are introduced, it is incumbent on the All-Party Committee to agree on an inclusive process that will result in tangible, pragmatic recommendations for reform. As this project has shown, the Committee should not shy away from approaching members of the Memorial University of Newfoundland community and beyond to offer assistance with this important work.

76 What the All-Party Committee on Democratic Reform Should Do

Alex Marland

Here it is: The Democracy Cookbook's conclusion. What the All-Party Committee on Democratic Reform should do now. #cdnpoli #NLpoli #DemocraticReformNL

Newfoundland and Labrador Needs a Democratic Audit

We can learn from other jurisdictions — Canadian federal, provincial, and territorial governments in particular. A bold "made right here" approach is required to resolve many of the embedded problems in Newfoundland and Labrador politics and governance. The political will must exist to address the chronic underlying issues that cross party lines, some of which have lingered for generations.

It is up to others to establish the terms of reference for the All-Party Committee on Democratic Reform and how it should proceed. We can, however, draw on past practices as well as contributors' submissions to this volume to suggest a possible pathway. In doing so we must be sensitive to local social circumstances and realistic about economic constraints.

Democratic Reform is More Than Electoral Reform

There are different ways to reform a democratic government. *Electoral* reform looks at methods of electing representatives. *Parliamentary* and *legislative* reform identify ways to change the operations of the three branches of government, principally the legislative branch. *Democratic* reform is much broader. It encompasses those and just about any other manner of improving governance, such as changing the operations of the public service itself. This is what is needed in Newfoundland and Labrador.

Recent experiences in other parts of Canada are instructive. A wave of democratic reform began in the early 2000s. Quebec's minister for the reform of democratic institutions issued a position paper to spur public debate. His cover letter describes a situation that has wide-ranging relevance:

> we note a growing divide between representatives and their constituents, and between elected officials and citizens. The mistrust directed at political leaders and the reduced sense of responsibility are becoming a real source of concern, along with the unfair, but oft shared belief that politicians do not really care about the population, but are primarily motivated by their own self-interest. This sense of frustration and disillusionment felt by a large sector of the population is accompanied by an increasingly worrisome lessening of civic responsibility. The crisis in citizenship leads individuals and special interest groups to overload the system with requests, with little regard for its capacity to handle them, nor concern for how their own requests impact on the needs of others. The dilemma posed by the gulf separating the people from those who represent them, and by their general apathy towards the governance of their communities is not solely explained by the nature of democratic institutions, although they do share some responsibility for current difficulties.[1]

The Quebec cabinet subsequently created a nine-member Organizing Committee on the Reform of Democratic Institutions. It was comprised of a mix of scholars, public servants, and activists. The Committee was supported by 17 regional representatives from across Quebec. All of these individuals then came together to form the Estates General on the Reform of Democratic Institutions. Extensive public consultations informed a final report that presented a portrait of citizen opinions, prioritized types of democratic reform, offered a list of recommendations, and suggested next steps.[2] The government's interest fizzled in the face of diverging opinions about the Estates General's recommendations, though some strides were made. In 2007, Quebec unveiled the country's first gender-balanced cabinet.

In New Brunswick, a Commission on Legislative Democracy was created in 2003 to look into democratic reform, electoral reform, and legislative reform. The Commission spent a year on research, public consultation, and deliberation. Its recommendations mirror many of the same democratic values that contributors express in *The Democracy Cookbook*. This is encapsulated in the Commission's search for "fairer, more equitable and effective representation in the Legislative Assembly; greater public involvement in decisions affecting people and their communities; more open, responsive, and accountable democratic institutions and practices; and, higher civic engagement and participation."[3] The New Brunswick government responded by releasing two successive reports outlining commitments to improve democracy in the province.[4] When there was a change of government, the new administration did not follow through on its predecessor's pledge to hold a referendum on electoral reform, although an electoral commission recently recommended a preferential ballot system.[5]

Unfortunately, democratic reform is often hijacked by demands to change the first-past-the-post electoral system. Under this system of electing representatives, so-called "false majorities" often occur whereby the governing party wins a majority of seats without winning a majority of votes.[6] This is unfair to smaller parties and is most acute at the provincial level where lopsided majorities and minuscule oppositions can be found. Such circumstances result in a breakdown of responsible government because the legislative branch is effectively fused with the executive branch and there is insufficient monitoring of government behaviour. Fairness issues aside, in small jurisdictions the opposition parties are barely able to hold the government in check, which is fundamental to guarding against an authoritarian style of governance. Conversely, at other times the party that obtains the most votes does not form the government. The 1989 election in Newfoundland and Labrador is one such example, where the PC Party received the highest share of the popular vote but the Liberals won the most seats. Opposition parties are also subject to such treatment, as with the province's New Democratic Party obtaining more votes than the Liberals in the 2011 election, and yet the Liberals formed the official opposition on the basis of vote concentration in western Newfoundland that resulted in that party winning the second-most seats. In such situations it is easy to overlook the benefits of the simplicity of the first-past-the-post system and its ability to produce stable majority governance.

In an attempt to reconcile such concern, British Columbia created a Citizens' Assembly on Electoral Reform, involving the random selection of citizens to sit on the Assembly.[7] Proposals to change the electoral system were defeated in referendums in 2005 and 2009 — yet the issue continues to be pushed by small parties. In Prince Edward Island the topic of a different electoral system has been discussed for years. In 2003, a retired chief justice was appointed to look at options, and in 2015 the government released a white paper on electoral reform.[8] In a 2016 plebiscite voters picked a new electoral system, but this decision by the electorate was nevertheless rejected by the premier on the basis of low turnout. In Ontario, a Democratic Renewal Secretariat was created within the government in 2003, leading to a Citizens' Assembly on Electoral Reform.[9] The Assembly's recommendation for a new electoral system was defeated in a 2007 referendum. Democratic reform initiated by Justin Trudeau's government likewise turned on the electoral system. An all-party committee was formed, the minister of democratic reform held consultation sessions across the country, expert witnesses testified to a parliamentary committee, and public debate occurred about the government's mandate to proceed without a referendum. Postcards were mailed to residences across Canada inviting citizens to participate in a non-statistical online survey. By early 2017, Prime Minister Trudeau issued a new mandate letter to a new minister, stating that "a clear preference for a new electoral system, let alone a consensus, has not emerged" and that "changing the electoral system" would not be in the minister's mandate.[10] It is unclear whether an electoral system debate would produce a different outcome in Newfoundland and Labrador. In any event, the question is not whether the province needs a new electoral system, but what mechanisms will ensure that there is always competent government with credible oversight.

Greater success with democratic reform has been achieved on other matters. Many jurisdictions have set up quasi-independent advisory boards to recommend government appointments and have been revising their political financing regulations. New Brunswick committed to changes that are by now common across Canada, such as fixed-date elections. Other New Brunswick commitments include a compulsory civics education program for youth,[11] offering additional campaign spending rebates for women candidates,[12] exploring lowering the age of voting to 16 years,[13] and banning donations from corporations and unions.[14] Newfoundland and Labrador has been a leader with respect to reforms of the management of legislature finances[15] and access to information.[16]

Each attempt at reform seems to build on the other, which is to say that efforts in one jurisdiction have some direct or indirect benefit to efforts in other areas of Canada. Newfoundland and Labrador must learn from others' experiences in developing a homegrown process that will result in meaningful change in how the province is governed.

Topics That Should Be Prioritized in a Democratic Audit

The rules governing political parties, campaigning, and political finance need to be refreshed, and these issues should be among the first orders of business. Only after that should ways to improve how MHAs are elected be researched. Efforts ought to concentrate on identifying a system that will result in a House of Assembly more proportionate to citizens' choice of political party, that better reflects the representative nature of the demographic characteristics of the population (particularly women), and that reasonably ensures that the province's Indigenous peoples always have a voice. As well, the viability of citizen-initiated plebiscites and referendums should be examined, as should related matters that have been contemplated in other jurisdictions. Above all, the Elections Act needs to be updated for immediate application within the existing electoral system.

What needs to be examined? The policies and practices of the House of Assembly need further updating. Ways to strengthen scrutiny of government decision-making need to be identified, particularly with respect to the role of opposition parties and the media. If resources allow, offices of the legislature should be created with responsibility for arm's-length oversight of the government's finances, and perhaps its environmental policies. The appointment of individuals to positions ranging from judges to boards needs to be even more transparent and to better reflect the socio-economic diversity of the population. Key statutes and rules to be updated include the House of Assembly Act, the House of Assembly Accountability, Integrity and Administration Act, the legislature's standing orders, and the recently introduced Independent Appointments Commission Act.

A list of other possible areas for improvement needs to be compiled. Some are identified in this compilation and many others would surely be uncovered through broad scholarly research and public consultation. Beyond the confines of academia, suggestions are needed from people who have specialized knowledge about systemic shortcomings, notably former and current public servants, political party executives, former premiers and members of cabinet, MHAs, election candidates, leaders of business and labour organizations, lobbyists, officers of the legislature, and others. A sample of issues to be considered includes the following:

- Civic education: Institutional mechanisms are needed to build and sustain public awareness and knowledge about the varied aspects of democratic governance in Newfoundland and Labrador, for citizens and legislators alike.
- Diversity of opinion: Forums are needed to encourage viewpoints

and expertise that challenge conventional wisdom without fear of repercussion. In particular, vulnerable populations need to be able to safely express their perspectives.

- Diversity of population: Ways to foster an even more inclusive society that welcomes input and participation from those on the periphery of power need to be explored.
- Local decision-making: Opportunities to improve the capacity of regional, community, and localized decision-making should be identified, possibly resulting in amendments to the Municipal Affairs Act and the Municipal Elections Act.
- Community engagement: New ways to encourage and recognize public engagement need to be identified, such as by expanding the Volunteer Service Medal Act.
- Public consultations: The government needs to be formally required to conduct and integrate public consultation on policy decision-making, including different categories of normal processes of consultation that are both transparent and followed.
- Communications technology: Government must have a clearer understanding of how digital communications technology can be used to improve democratic engagement and information exchange. This may entail updating the Transparency and Accountability Act, while simultaneously figuring out ways to create more opportunities for in-person relationships to develop between citizens and ministers/MHAs.
- Memorial University of Newfoundland: The Government of Newfoundland and Labrador can do more to tap into the expertise of scholars at Memorial University, possibly by identifying this in the Memorial University Act, while respecting the important principle of academic freedom.
- Public administration: Information about how to improve all aspects of government must include the public service itself. This needs to move beyond business plans and annual reports. A comparative search for ideas to improve ways of conducting government business within existing resources is warranted.
- Recurring reviews: Democratic reform should be constant. Mechanisms are needed to ensure that renewal occurs automatically over time.

This is by no means an exhaustive list and is highly reflective of current dynamics. For instance, a compilation organized at many other junctures would undoubtedly include multiple submissions urging caution about the amount of power concentrated in the Premier's Office and a review of the

Executive Council Act.[17] That, of course, assumes authors would not worry about the repercussions of doing so.

Suggested Process for the All-Party Committee

Research is required to lay the foundation for a meaningful public discussion. It would not be enough for the All-Party Committee on Democratic Reform to commit to the default approach of a travelling road show, whereby members tour the province to demonstrate they are listening but then, possibly, are faced with empty rooms or a small number of vested interests.[18] Reports must not be generated to sit on shelves or exist in cyberspace. As much as possible, work must not be tinged with the suspicion of partisanship or a sales operation. Equally, forums must not be commandeered by special interests to push an agenda, or cannot diverge into opportunities for critics to disparage the government on unrelated matters.

In Newfoundland and Labrador the most successful process of reform tends to be led by current or former judges who conduct a fact-finding venture. The Commission of Inquiry on Hormone Receptor Testing (Cameron Inquiry),[19] the Review Commission on Constituency Allowances and Related Matters (Green Commission),[20] and the Access to Information and Protection of Privacy Act Independent Statutory Review Committee[21] are examples of thoughtful change being implemented and of this province becoming a role model for others. A less tangible approach is a political exercise that places demands on outsiders, as with the Royal Commission on Renewing and Strengthening Our Place in Canada. On that, it is noteworthy that the 2003 Throne Speech committed to creating a "people's congress" to "bring together elected federal and provincial officials from all parties, municipal leaders, Aboriginal leaders, representatives of the social, business and labour sectors, with representation from women, youth and seniors" in order to develop "an action plan."[22]

A suggested three-step pathway is presented below and summarized here. First, the minister responsible for the Office of Public Engagement (currently the premier) would be well advised to work with the All-Party Committee and others to identify the guiding principles that will steer any proposed changes to democratic governance in Newfoundland and Labrador. This should culminate in the creation of a Public Consultation Act that clarifies the relative duty to consult externally during most, if not all, forms of government decision-making. Second, while that bill is being crafted, a small group should be appointed by the Independent Appointments Commission to perform an audit of democratic reform processes in other provinces vis-à-vis government operations in this province. The group's terms of reference must be wide-ranging so that democratic reform clearly is understood to be much broader than electoral reform or parliamentary reform. The group's preliminary findings should be publicly available and subject to public input. Third, after considering those findings, the All-Party Committee should develop guiding principles for examining democratic reform. A free vote on these principles should be held in the House of Assembly. Ideally, unanimity would be achieved; otherwise, a minimum threshold might be a majority of MHAs in each political party voting to support the proposed process. Only then should work begin to enumerate democratic reforms. Following this or any other pathway will require political will to confront those who are anxious for a specific type of change and who see debate about process as stonewalling. While it is important to work within clearly identified timelines, it must be understood that democratic reform is a unique undertaking, and that in other jurisdictions considerable effort has been exerted only to end up with the status quo.

Step 1: Introduce a Bill to Create a Public Consultation Act

Upon forming government, Premier Dwight Ball issued a mandate letter to his then-minister responsible for the Office of Public Engagement. The letter includes the following passage:

> Every citizen deserves to have their voice heard. Residents of the province can provide valuable insight into issues that matter to their lives. To engage the public, I expect you to host regular engagement activities including town hall meetings in communities throughout the province and use technology to expand the options to participate. Through these engagement activities government policy will better reflect the needs of Newfoundlanders and Labradorians.[23]

This reflects a new reality that public expectations of consultation are intensifying in the digital age. In the past, it was accepted that the premier and the governing party decided how to distribute public goods. As government grew, it was an innovation to require that ministers and departmental personnel consult with each other, and it was also good enough to designate ministers with special responsibility to look out for the interests of certain industries, regions, citizens, and so on. Later it was novel to require that public servants apply policy lenses to recommendations in cabinet submissions. Letters exchanged with citizens by post that once involved a month or longer have given way to messages sent from smart phones that people expect to be resolved immediately. Hours of talk radio programming are now supplemented with a litany of unfiltered social media chatter occurring in real time. Above all, internal and one-way consultation processes must give way to external two-way communication. Citizens want to know that their input matters and is being listened to. They may not like some decisions, but they are more likely to respect them if they have been offered meaningful opportunities to participate in decision-making along the way. Problems arise when this does not happen. Among the reasons is the absence of a statutory requirement to do so.

The first order of business ought to be researching and preparing a bill to create what might be styled as a Public Consultation Act. This would enshrine in legislation a duty to meaningfully consult with citizens. It would outline some basic parameters as well as establish when consultation is not required and the relative importance of cabinet confidences. Such an Act should legislate a requirement to educate citizens about government processes at every point of consultation so that there is a constant effort to improve civic knowledge. Once broad principles are outlined in a short piece of legislation, guidelines and best practices can be identified on a government website, which can evolve over time. There needs to be a public understanding of the normal criteria for what types of government action require different levels of consultation, who should be consulted and when, and what modes of communication should be used. As well, it should be understood that there is a duty to provide information updates about the process of decision-making.

Extensive public consultation comes with trade-offs.[24] Some of these might be welcomed by people outside of government, such as cabinet relinquishing some of its autonomy. Other trade-offs are frustrating to all, including lengthening the timelines and reducing the number of files that can be advanced due to added workloads. While there may be fewer protests in some instances, in others a minority of citizens and/or special interest groups will have more opportunity to mobilize to block change they do not want. As well, some politicians and vulnerable populations are subject to personal disparagement, and people with different points of view need to be encouraged to safely share their perspectives. This is why formalized processes of consultation and constant civic education are important: it must be understood that if meaningful consultation has occurred this does not mean that everyone gets their own way.

Step 2: Appoint a Small Group to Review Democratic Reform Processes in Other Provinces and Agree on a Process for Exploring Democratic Reform in Newfoundland and Labrador

In his 2015 mandate letter to the government House Leader, Premier Ball wrote:

> As government House Leader, one of your primary goals will be to respect the House of Assembly and encourage cooperation among all parties. In particular, I will expect you to work with your colleagues and through legislative, regulatory and Cabinet processes to deliver on the following priorities: modernize the province's legislative process and engage elected representatives from all political parties; make better use of existing committees and seek opportunities for further nonpartisan cooperation, including establishing legislative review committees to review proposed legislation; and, bring a resolution to the House of Assembly to establish an All Party Committee on Democratic Reform.[25]

A democratic reform exercise should not proceed in the absence of agreement on the process. Otherwise, policy proposals will be prone to criticism about legitimacy rather than about the substance of what is being proposed. Recent experiences with democratic reform elsewhere in Canada should be examined to identify a suitable process for Newfoundland and Labrador. Identifying a process should be led by a judge and a small research team. The team should include some former government insiders (e.g., a past Speaker, Chief Electoral Officer, a high-ranking public servant in Executive Council) and government outsiders (e.g., a retired member of the press gallery, an academic, a former interest group or business leader). They should be recruited and appointed in a transparent manner organized by the Independent Appointments Commission, taking great care to consider the socio-demographic composition of membership. The group should recommend a process for examining democratic reform, compile a draft list of topics to be examined, and clearly justify the rationale for its recommendations. This should be made available for public comment on the day it is submitted to the All-Party Committee, ideally in line with the principles of consultation outlined in the Public Consultation Act and on an accompanying government consultation website.

Step 3: Hold a Free Vote in the House of Assembly to Sanction the Process of Exploring Democratic Reform

The All-Party Committee should agree on a public engagement process to be followed and outline the principles of this process. These, too, should be made available for public comment. The proposed process should be put to free vote in the House of Assembly. Work on democratic reform should only proceed if a majority of MHAs in each party votes in favour (or, ideally, if the proposed process passes unanimously). Only once there is agreement about the process to be followed should work on examining democratic reform proceed. Done right, this should be fair-minded and multi-partisan, with an express understanding that it simply constitutes agreement to explore various types of democratic reform. Ideally, the mandate should include exploring the introduction of legislation that each decade will automatically install a multi-partisan process for examining democratic renewal. This would build on the experiences of processes used to establish arm's-length reviews of related matters, such as electoral district boundary commissions or independent statutory review committees for access to information. A legislated requirement that every 10 years a group must be formed to identify ways to update the system of democratic government would position Newfoundland and Labrador as a model for the rest of Canada. The process should be designed to withstand a change in government, as this has derailed democratic reform in other provinces.

All of this will take time to get things right. Whatever route is followed, Newfoundlanders and Labradorians must not be satisfied with Churchill's belief that democracy is inherently the best form of governance.[26] For that to hold true, democratic governance must evolve over time, reflect the public interest, and uphold the highest standards of professionalism. ★

Notes

1. Jean-Pierre Charbonneau, *Citizen Empowerment: A Paper to Open Public Debate* (Quebec: Minister for the Reform of Democratic Institutions, 2002), 2, at: https://www.institutions-democratiques.gouv.qc.ca/publications/pouvoirauxcitoyens_en.pdf.
2. Government of Quebec, *Take Your Rightful Place!* Report of the Organizing Committee of the Estates General on the Reform of Democratic Institutions (2003).
3. Commission on Legislative Democracy, *Final Report and Recommendations* (Fredericton: Government of New Brunswick, 2004), 4, at: http://www.electionsnb.ca/content/dam/enb/pdf/cld/CLDFinalReport-e.pdf.
4. Andre Barnes and James R. Robertson, "Electoral Reform Initiatives in

Canadian Provinces," Library of Parliament, 18 Aug. 2009, 5, at: http://www.lop.parl.gc.ca/content/lop/researchpublications/prb0417-e.pdf.

5. Jacques Poitras, "N.B.'s Electoral Reform Commission Proposes Preferential Ballot," CBC News, 3 Mar. 2017, at: http://www.cbc.ca/news/canada/new-brunswick/electoral-reform-provincial-election-1.4008021.
6. Peter H. Russell, *Two Cheers for Minority Government: The Evolution of Canadian Parliamentary Democracy* (Toronto: Emond Montgomery, 2008).
7. Mark E. Warren and Hilary Pearse, eds., *Designing Deliberative Democracy: The British Columbia Citizens' Assembly* (New York: Cambridge University Press, 2008).
8. Government of Prince Edward Island, *White Paper on Democratic Renewal*, July 2015, at: http://www.gov.pe.ca/photos/original/democraticrenew.pdf.
9. Citizens' Assembly on Electoral Reform, "One Ballot, Two Votes: A New Way to Vote in Ontario," Recommendation of the Ontario Citizens' Assembly on Electoral Reform, 15 May 2007, at: http://www.citizensassembly.gov.on.ca/assets/One%20Ballot,%20Two%20Votes.pdf.
10. Justin Trudeau, "Minister of Democratic Institutions Mandate Letter" (2017), at: http://pm.gc.ca/eng/minister-democratic-institutions-mandate-letter.
11. Office of the Premier of New Brunswick, "Province Releases Response to Commission on Legislative Democracy Report," news release, 20 June 2006, at: http://www.gnb.ca/cnb/news/ex/2006e0794ex.htm.
12. Jacques Poitras, "Political Parties to Get Financial Incentive to Run Female Candidates," CBC News, 22 Mar. 2017, at: http://www.cbc.ca/news/canada/new-brunswick/financial-incentive-women-candidates-1.4036359.
13. Kevin Bissett, "New Brunswick Electoral Commission Recommends Lowering Voting Age to 16," Canadian Press, 3 Mar. 2017, at: http://globalnews.ca/news/3285491/new-brunswick-electoral-commission-recommends-lowering-voting-age-to-16/.
14. Kevin Bissett, "N.B. Government to Ban Corporate and Union Political Donations," Canadian Press, 30 Mar. 2017, at: http://atlantic.ctvnews.ca/n-b-government-to-ban-corporate-and-union-political-donations-1.3348216.
15. C.E.S. Franks, "Quis Custodiet Ipsos Custodes? The Contribution of Newfoundland and Labrador to the Reform of Management of Canadian Legislatures," *Canadian Public Administration* 51, 1 (2008): 155–69.
16. "New Access to Information Changes to Make N.L. a World Leader: Advocate," CBC News, 27 Apr. 2015, at: http://www.cbc.ca/news/canada/newfoundland-labrador/new-access-to-information-changes-to-make-n-l-a-world-leader-advocate-1.3049934.
17. See, for example, Christopher Dunn, "The Persistence of the Institutionalized Cabinet: The Centralized Executive in Newfoundland

and Labrador," in Luc Bernier, Keith Brownsey, and Michael Howlett, eds., *Executive Styles in Canada: Cabinet Structures and Leadership Practices in Canadian Government* (Toronto: University of Toronto Press, 2005), 47–74.

18. See, for example, Nicholas Croucher, "Provincial Health Consultation Finds Empty Room," *The Gulf News* (Port aux Basques), 9 Aug. 2010, at: http://www.pressreader.com/canada/the-gulf-news-port-aux-basques/20100809/281556582122195; Transcontinental Media, "Low Turnout for Pre-budget Consultation in Grand Falls–Windsor," *The Advertiser* (Grand Falls–Windsor), 2 Mar. 2015, at: http://www.gfwadvertiser.ca/news/local/2015/3/2/low-turnout-for-pre-budget-consultation-4062456.html; Rachel Zelnicker, "Little Notice, No Translation Lead to 'Very Disappointing' Election Reform Consultation in Iqaluit," CBC News, 29 Aug. 2016, at: http://www.cbc.ca/news/canada/north/electoral-reform-meeting-maryam-monsef-1.3740475.
19. Margaret A. Cameron, *Commission of Inquiry on Hormone Receptor Testing*, vol. 1 (St. John's: Government of Newfoundland and Labrador, 2009), at: http://www.releases.gov.nl.ca/releases/2009/health/Volume1_Investigation_and_Findings.pdf.
20. Derek J. Green, *Rebuilding Confidence: Report of the Review Commission on Constituency Allowances and Related Matters* (St. John's: Government of Newfoundland and Labrador, 2007), at: http://www.gov.nl.ca/publicat/greenreport/mainreport/mainreport.pdf.
21. Clyde K. Wells, *Report of the 2014 Statutory Review of the Access to Information and Protection of Privacy Act*. Full report (St. John's: Government of Newfoundland and Labrador, 2015), at: http://www.ope.gov.nl.ca/publications/pdf/ATIPPA_Report_Vol2.pdf.
22. Government of Newfoundland and Labrador, Speech from the Throne, 19 Mar. 2003, at: http://www.exec.gov.nl.ca/thronespeech/2003/thronespeech_2003.htm.
23. Dwight Ball, "Ministerial Mandate Letter to Siobhan Coady," 14 Dec. 2015, at: http://www.exec.gov.nl.ca/exec/cabinet/ministers/pdf/Minister_Coady_Mandate.pdf.
24. See, for example, pages 20-22 in Michael Barber, *How to Run a Government So That Citizens Benefit and Taxpayers Don't Go Crazy* (Milton Keynes: Penguin Books, 2016).
25. Dwight Ball, "Ministerial Mandate Letter to Andrew Parsons," 14 Dec. 2015, at: http://www.exec.gov.nl.ca/exec/cabinet/ministers/pdf/Minister_Parsons_Mandate.pdf.
26. Hansard, *Debates*, 11 Nov. 1947, vol. 444, cc. 203–321, at: http://hansard.millbanksystems.com/commons/1947/nov/11/parliament-bill.

FOOD FOR THOUGHT: RECIPES

Right: *Innu woman cooking meal over campfire, 1929*. Innu woman kneeling at campfire cooking, child standing nearby. (Source: Provincial Archives)

Left: *"The Gospel of hard bread."* Young boy in long woollen stockings, sailor suit, and leather boots, eating bread, possibly aboard a vessel (c. 1906–08). The photograph was later published in *Among the Deep Sea Fishers* and the boy is identified as one of the first orphans at St. Anthony. (Source: Provincial Archives)

What's a cookbook without some recipes for some meals and desserts? The following pages feature contributions from former ministers and MHAs affiliated with all three of the province's main political parties. This is rounded out by recipes submitted from restaurant operators and chefs from across the province. All recipes have a Newfoundland and Labrador theme. We hope these sumptuous feasts and snacks will whet readers' political appetite!

77 Transparent Snow Crab Rice Paper Rolls

Andrea Maunder

Ingredients

Rice Paper Rolls with NL Snow Crab

Around 300 g rice vermicelli noodles (packages range from 250-500 g)
12 large rice paper wrappers
12 oz Newfoundland Snow Crab leg meat
1 large carrot, shredded into ribbons using a vegetable peeler, or coarsely shredded
1 cucumber, shredded into ribbons, or cut into matchsticks
12 leaves of tender lettuce (leaf or butter/Boston; if romaine, remove ribs)
1 bunch fresh mint, leaves pulled from stems
½ cup roasted salted cashews

Spicy Peanut Dipping Sauce

1 tbsp soy sauce
2 tbsp water
1 tbsp rice wine vinegar (or lemon or lime juice)
1 tsp honey (or sugar)
1 inch piece of fresh ginger, grated finely
1 garlic clove, finely minced
½ cup peanut butter (your choice — smooth or crunchy)
1 tsp Sriracha or other hot sauce (or to taste)

Directions

Sauce: Mix soy sauce, water, vinegar, honey, ginger and garlic. Warm in microwave for 30 seconds. Whisk in peanut butter until smooth. Add hot sauce. Sauce should be thick for dipping but not solid. Taste. If too thick, add water, soy, honey or vinegar.

Rice noodles: Soak rice noodles in very hot tap water (about five minutes). Taste. Will be firm but tender enough to bite through. If they resist a bite, drain, refresh hot water, and soak a few minutes longer. Drain and set aside.

Rice paper: Fill a large bowl with very hot tap water. Discard any cracked rice paper wrappers. Working with one wrapper at a time, dip rice paper in hot water, rotating to ensure all parts are hydrated. Wrappers will soften and become pliable. Remove from water before completely soft. Place on work area and smooth out.

Filling ingredients: Laterally, in bottom third of rice paper sheet nearest you, leaving an inch clearance at bottom and right and left sides, lay down a half-palm sized, log-shaped bundle of rice noodles, one crab leg, a handful of cashews, 4–5 each of carrot and cucumber ribbons, 4–5 mint leaves and a leaf of soft lettuce. Pile ingredients to form log-shaped stack. Pick up bottom curve and fold it over the filling. Holding in place, pick up left side curve and fold it in to enclose left side. Rice paper will stick to itself. Do same with right side. Roll up from bottom, tucking and using moderate pressure to form a neat, fairly tight roll. Top curve will stick to the roll, sealing itself. Repeat until all filling is used. Don't let completed rolls touch, or they will stick to each other, tearing the rice paper. After the first couple, you will get to know how long to soak the rice paper to make it easiest to roll — not long enough and it's too stiff to roll, too long and it disintegrates.

Makes 12 rolls, enough to serve four people. Feel free to customize to your tastes. Poached shrimp or scallops, cooked chicken or beef would be delicious. Cilantro, basil, or chives are great substitutions. Almost any thinly julienned vegetables would work. Avoid anything too stiff, such as celery or broccoli, as it will tear the rice paper. And choose a soft lettuce. Mixed baby greens or arugula are also nice. ★

About the contributor

Andrea Maunder is Owner, Wine Expert, and Pastry Chef of Bacalao (http://bacalaocuisine.ca), a St. John's restaurant specializing in bold flavours with local flare.

78 Baked Cod Worth Crossing the Floor For

Margaret Burden

Ingredients

6 small cod fillets
1 tbsp olive oil
2 medium carrots, sliced
¾ cup turnip, chopped
1 medium potato, chopped
1 small onion, chopped
1 cup green/red/yellow peppers, chopped
Salt and pepper to taste
1 tsp garlic, minced

Directions

Cut fillets in half and lay flat in a heated pot with olive oil. Let cod simmer for 15 minutes. Add all other ingredients and one cup of hot water. Add salt, pepper and garlic. Cook at 275F for 20 minutes. This dish is served best as a midday meal. It is very tasty and healthy. Serves six. ★

About the Contributor

Margaret Burden owns the Alexis Hotel (www.alexishotel.ca) in Port Hope Simpson, Labrador.

79 Filibuster Fried Cod

Caroline (Kay) Young

Ingredients

¼ lb salt pork
4 cod fillets
½ cup flour
1 egg
½ cup milk
2 cups cracker crumbs
Salt

Directions

Cut salt pork into small cubes and fry in a cast iron skillet until the pork cubes are crisp and fat is rendered. Set aside the pork cubes, which are now considered scrunchions. Beat the milk and egg together. Cut the fillets in serving portions. Cover the cod pieces with flour and dip in the milk and egg mixture. Coat cod pieces with cracker crumbs to which salt has been added. Using medium heat and the fat rendered from the pork cubes, fry the cod until golden brown. Reheat the scrunchions and serve with the cod. My mother (Nellie Diamond) would serve the cod with lemon wedges, mashed potatoes, and either coleslaw or canned green peas. ★

About the Contributor

Caroline (Kay) Young is a former Member of the House of Assembly for Terra Nova.

80 Multiparty Moose Stew

Timothy Charles

Ingredients

1 big moose heart, cleaned and diced large
2 lb moose, diced large
7 large onions, sliced thick
12 cloves garlic, sliced
2 cups fatback, diced small
1 cup flour
4 bottles of beer (full)
2 cups partridgeberries
Salt

Directions

Clean and dice the heart and moose meat. Render back fat and then brown the moose in a large pot. If you do not have enough space be sure to brown the diced meat in small batches. Once the meat is all browned add your onions and garlic and cook until soft. Add the flour and beer to the moose meat, onions, and garlic, and stir. Bring the pot to a boil and then reduce the heat until it reaches a gentle simmer, then cover with a lid. Check every 15 minutes and stir so as to be sure it does not burn. After about three hours the stew should be ready. Reduce the heat and add the partridgeberries. Season with salt. ★

About the Contributor

Timothy Charles is Chef at the Kitchen Collective of Fogo Island Inn (www.fogoislandinn.ca) located on Fogo Island, off the northeast coast of Newfoundland.

81 Red-Hot Lobsters – In Hot Water Again

Rex Gibbons

Ingredients

9–10 lobsters
Salt water, right from the ocean (not salted fresh water)

Directions

Put salt water in a big pot over an outdoor propane burner. Bring the water to a boil. Drop the lobsters into the pot (remove the rubber bands from the claws). Boil for 15–20 minutes. Use a sharp square-top knife to chop each claw. Split the bodies from the top of head through the tail. Serve on paper plates if available. Provide diners with appropriate utensils and bibs. Have bowls or plates available for garbage. Pair with salad and finish with an appetizing dessert. A visit to the nearest deli for a ready-made coleslaw and a green salad will do — anything more formal would be superfluous. Makes one or two one-pounders per person, depending on their appetite. It is always a gluttonous meal, served with a choice of cool refreshments. A perfect summer treat at the cabin. ★

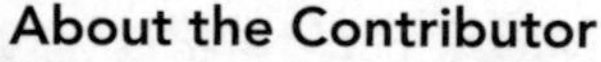

About the Contributor

Rex Gibbons served as Member of the House of Assembly for St. John's West. He is a former Minister of Mines and Energy and Minister of Natural Resources.

82 Right Honourable Rabbit Stew

Christopher Welsh

Ingredients

½ cup butter
¼ cup onions, diced
½ cup flour
2 tsp garlic, minced
3½ cups vegetable stock
2 cups beef stock
1 lb cooked pulled rabbit
2 cups carrots, diced
2 cups potatoes, diced
3 tbsp fresh parsley, finely chopped
1 tsp fresh thyme
¾ tsp onion powder
¾ tsp garlic powder
½ tsp Mt. Scio Savoury
Salt and pepper

Directions

Pulled Rabbit Preparation

Place rabbit into large pot with water just covering the top of the rabbit. Add ½ cup (25%) of beef stock to the water for flavour. Bring to boil for 1½–2 hours. Strain and pull meat off the bones

Stew Preparation

Melt butter into large pot. Add garlic and onions and sauté them until onions are soft. Allow the onions to caramelize and turn brown. Add flour and stir constantly as it cooks and creates a roux. Approximately two minutes.

Add remaining beef stock slowly while whisking to ensure there are no lumps. Add all the vegetable stock and then the carrots and potatoes. Bring the mixture to a rolling boil and then simmer on medium low for approximately 30 minutes until the carrots and potatoes are cooked. Add the pulled rabbit, then herbs and spices. Stir to mix thoroughly. Add salt and pepper to taste. Serve hot. Makes about 8–10 portions. ★

About the Contributor

Christopher Welsh is the Sous Chef and Chef Apprentice at Java Jack's Restaurant & Gallery (http://javajacks.ca) in Rocky Harbour, western Newfoundland.

83 Seafood Chowder that Will Leave the House Speaker Speechless

Colleen Hiscock

Ingredients

Vegetables

1 cup carrots, diced
1 cup turnip, diced
1 cup celery, diced

Seafood

1 lb cod fillets, skinned, boneless, cut in 1½″ cubes; fresh or frozen and thawed. Can use any white groundfish fillets or trimmings
½ lb lobster meat and scallops; cut small approximately ½″ x ½″
½ lb other combination of any seafood (lobster, mussels, scallops, shrimp) cut into small pieces approximately ½″ x ½″

Chowder Base

½ cup flour
½ cup butter
½ cup onion, finely chopped
3 cups milk (or cream)
2 tbsp dried tarragon
Salt and pepper

Directions

Add three cups of water to a saucepan and add vegetables. Bring to a boil, then reduce heat and cook over medium heat until *al dente* (still firm, not soft), approximately 10–15 minutes. When cooked, strain the vegetables but retain the vegetable water for the cream sauce in another bowl. Set both aside.

Add cubed fish to another saucepan and fill the saucepan with water just to the level of the fish. Do not cover the fish with water as the fish will create its own liquid during cooking. Cook gently so the fish is just cooked but not falling apart, approximately seven minutes. When cooked, strain the fish and retain the fish liquid for the cream sauce in another bowl. Set both aside.

To make the base, start with melting the butter in a large stock pot. Add the onions to sweat in the butter, until the onions are translucent, soft and sweet, approximately three minutes. Add the flour to the onions and butter. Stir consistently and cook on medium heat for three minutes. Whisking constantly, slowly add in the milk and heat thoroughly until a thick consistency is achieved. Then add in the fish stock. Typically, use all of the fish stock. Then add the vegetable water until it is a creamy texture. Add then the vegetables and fish and stir gently. Add the tarragon and some salt and pepper to taste. Simmer for 5–10 minutes before serving. Serves 6–8. ★

About the Contributor

Colleen Hiscock owns Java Jack's Restaurant & Gallery (http://javajacks.ca) in Rocky Harbour, the largest community in Gros Morne National Park.

84 By-Election Bakeapple Dessert

Judy Manning

Ingredients

Graham Crumb Base

- 2 cups graham crumbs
- ½ cup unsalted butter, melted

Bakeapple Topping

- 3 cups (approx.) bakeapples
- 2 tbsp sugar (or to taste)

Cream Cheese Filling

- 1 package Dream Whip™, prepared as directed on package
- ½ lb cream cheese (brick style)
- 1 tbsp lemon juice
- ½ cup granulated white sugar

Directions

Preheat oven to 350F. Grease an 8″ x 10″ pan. Gently boil bakeapples and sugar in small saucepan, until mixture begins to slightly thicken, stirring occasionally. In a bowl, mix together crumbs and melted butter. Press mixture into prepared pan and bake for five minutes. In a separate bowl, whip cream cheese, sugar, and lemon juice together. Fold in prepared Dream Whip™. Spread over graham crumb base. Add bakeapple mixture as topping. Let stand for a few hours in refrigerator. ★

About the Contributor

Judy Manning practices law in St. John's. She is a former provincial Minister of Justice and Public Safety.

85 Patriotic Partridgeberry Cake

Sharlene Hinz

Ingredients

Cake

- 2 cups flour
- 1 cup sugar
- 3 tbsp baking powder
- 1 tsp salt
- 2 eggs
- 1 cup milk
- 1 tsp vanilla extract
- 3 tbsp canola oil
- 2 cups fresh or frozen partridgeberries

Sauce

- 1 cup sugar
- ½ cup hard margarine (not butter)
- ½ cup Carnation evaporated milk (not 2%)

Directions

Cake: Combine dry ingredients together with the wet ingredients gently. Fold in the partridgeberries. Turn into a tube pan. Bake for 40 minutes at 350F. **Sauce:** Combine sugar, margarine, and evaporated milk. Bring to a boil. Boil for one minute only. Serve over warm cake.

Makes a Newfoundland partridgeberry cake with a warm sauce that is to die for. The berries with the sauce create a tart, sweet, creamy dessert that everyone loves. Until now the sauce recipe has been kept a secret. ★

About the Contributor

Sharlene Hinz — also known as Aunt Edna — operates Aunt Edna's Boarding House B&B (www.auntednaslbi.com) in Little Bay Islands, Notre Dame Bay.

86 Poli-tea-cal Tea Buns

George Murphy

Ingredients

2 cups of flour
4 tsp of baking powder
Dash of salt
½ cup of sugar
½ cup of melted butter
1 egg
1 cup of milk
1 cup of raisins (if desired)

Directions

Mix the butter into the flour mixture. Mix an egg and the milk into the flour mixture. Relatively simple (as all things political should be!), bake in the oven at 400F and check for firmness after 12 minutes. I usually leave them in until they are golden brown. If you want, add raisins to the flour mixture and voila! A great addition when you're having a district association meeting, you'll be quick to nominate these for a top patronage position whenever your "tea party" arises! ★

About the Contributor

George Murphy is a researcher for the Consumer Group for Fair Gas Prices (gasandoil.blogspot.com). He is a former Member of the House of Assembly for St. John's East.

87 Strawberry and Rhubarb Political Fool

Jill Curran

Ingredients

1 lb rhubarb
½ lb sugar
¾ lb strawberries
10 oz of whipping cream

Directions

Cut rhubarb into chunks and add to saucepan with sugar. Cook for 15–20 minutes over a gentle heat until soft. Be sure to stir often! Once cooked, stir rhubarb to mash using a wooden spoon. Set aside to cool. Whip cream. Slice strawberries. Once rhubarb is cold, gently fold in the whipped cream and sliced strawberries. Keep dessert chilled until ready to serve. Serve with fresh mint. ★

About the Contributor

Jill Curran is owner of Lighthouse Picnics (www.lighthousepicnics.ca) in Ferryland, on the southeast coast of Newfoundland's Avalon Peninsula.

APPENDIX

Recruitment Document Provided to Contributors

Note: abridged for length

Contribution Parameters

- Contributors will be part of a broad collaborative non-partisan project designed to inform democratic renewal in Newfoundland and Labrador, and possibly other jurisdictions if this model is successful.
- Thinking about the political turmoil of recent years, situated within NL's political history, authors will identify concrete ways that the All-Party Committee on Democratic Reform can draw upon towards improving democratic governance in NL. They will offer fresh approaches to conventional thinking.
- Examples of potential topics are outlined in the appendix.
- This is not about the current government or the recent budget but rather about disturbing patterns that point to chronic underlying issues. It is not a forum to advocate resources for socio-economic issues, to advance pet projects, to lobby for resources, or to bash politicians or parties. Rather, authors should pitch institutional reform that will have enduring relevance for future generations irrespective of which party is in power (i.e., improved democratic processes).
- Submissions will be peer reviewed: initial review by the editors, followed by ISER Books formally providing the draft manuscript to arm's-length external reviewers.
- *The Telegram* is interested in reproducing select contributions.

Word count

- 700 to 850 words (like an op-ed submission or an intellectual blog).
- Stick as close to the word count as possible, rather than expect the editors to cut content.
- Do not use headings/subheadings within your submission.

- Optionally include one table or figure, outside of the word count.

Topic parameters

- Contributions must fit within the umbrella of renewing democracy in Newfoundland and Labrador, with particular emphasis on provincial governance.
- Identify a democratic problem, then present a proposed solution. This will make it easier for the NL House of Assembly's All-Party Committee on Democratic Reform to establish courses of action.
- Offer a holistic perspective that will have pragmatic value to the Committee specifically and NL society generally.
- Solutions must be cost-neutral — this is not about pushing for resources, it is about doing things better within existing resources. They should also be enduring, so that future administrations will be unlikely to revert back. Thus, focus on institutional reform, such as changing the way things operate or revising legislation.
- Consider how things are done in other jurisdictions and/or democracies.

Writing style

- Contributions must be non-partisan, even if the contributor is not.
- Do not mention individuals, such as the names of sitting politicians. However, using the name of a former premier to situate past practices under a previous administration is okay (e.g., "In the Wells government" or "When Dunderdale was premier . . .").
- Authors are encouraged to challenge the status quo and norms, while employing a constructive tone (no polemics). Be provocative and assertive, but do not be quarrelsome, dismissive, ideological, or extremist.
- Ideally, contributions will employ a form of methodological reasoning.
- Communicate in an accessible manner to a wide audience of non-specialists. Generally consider the op-ed tips available at http://newsoffice.duke.edu/duke_resources/oped.html.

References

- Cite obscure information, but avoid unnecessary citations. Generally speaking there is an upper limit of five citations.
- Full citation information should appear in the bibliography.
- References are outside of the 700 to 850 word count.

File format

- Submit as a Word file.
- Remember to submit a photograph if you have not done so (optional but encouraged).

Examples of Topics for Academic Contributors

The following ideas are presented to assist prospective contributors with their brainstorming when identifying a subject area to propose to write about. We are seeking a pluralistic approach and welcome perspectives from across the ideological spectrum with a shared objective of identifying ways to strengthen the nature of democracy and governance in Newfoundland and Labrador. Thus, the following is by no means a definitive list of ways to improve the democratic process, and is not intended to imply normative assumptions. Whatever the agreed topic, contributions will identify ways that ensure appropriate representation of public interests and sound public policy decisions made by government officials, ideally by making better use of existing resources.

1. How Government Works

This section will offer a primer about how government works and is organized, with emphasis on the provincial system within Canada as a whole. It assumes limited familiarity and seeks to demystify decision-making.

2. The Ridiculousness of Newfoundland and Labrador Politics

This tongue-in-cheek section will engage readers by taking a creative approach to the turmoil of NL politics. Can be written humour, poetry, song, editorial cartoons, or other forms of creative expression.

3. The Seriousness of Improving Governance in Newfoundland and Labrador

This section will contain broad submissions about how to improve governance in the province that are written in an all-encompassing manner that serve as an overall introduction.

4. Historical Strengths and Weaknesses with Democracy in Newfoundland and Labrador

This section provides some historical context about democratic practices and ideals in NL. Examples of possible questions:

- What is historically unique about the democratic system in Newfoundland and Labrador?
- What lessons can be drawn from other provinces to inform NL governance?

- How can the political culture of Newfoundland and Labrador be changed to strengthen its democratic system of government?
- What can be done about fiscal budgeting within the government of NL to avoid the province being periodically drawn into crisis situations?
- Are there past forms of governance that were working in NL that should be brought back?

5. Understanding "Patriotic Correctness" in NL (i.e., issues about which solutions are not fully discussed because of social pressure to conform to local ways of thinking)

This section will seek to understand the basis for conventional wisdom, practices, and topics that tend to be immune from criticism and difficult to discuss publicly, particularly those that are not discussed at all. Examples of questions:

- What strengths and weaknesses of democracy are unique to a small polity such as NL?
- How can public policy that evokes strong emotions (e.g., fishery, rural NL, unemployment, public–private partnerships, fracking, and so on) be appropriately discussed so that sound public policy decisions can be made?
- How can public policy that is often deemed a low priority (e.g., environment, natural resource management, avoiding government deficit/ debt, and so on) be appropriately discussed so that sound public policy decisions can be made?
- When should NL nationalism be harnessed — and when should it be resisted?
- What needs to happen to be inclusive of "CFAs" and "mainlanders" and "new Canadians" who make NL their home?
- What are the democratic implications of the proliferation of unofficial flags in Newfoundland and Labrador?

6. Improving Civic Education and Democratic Engagement in NL

This section will discuss political culture and public opinion in Newfoundland and Labrador: what must be done to increase public knowledge of how government works and how it can operate better, and how to improve engagement of everyday citizens in the public policy process. Examples of questions:

- What are some ways to improve public knowledge about how government works?
- What can we learn about democracy from the Government of Nunatsiavut?
- What can be done to encourage more academic study of governance in NL?
- What can we learn from the public opinion research industry?

7. Renewing NL Elections and Political Financing

This section will identify ways to improve the rules governing election campaigning and the role of money in politics. Examples of possible questions:

- What actions can be undertaken to improve voter turnout?
- What can be done to encourage citizens to run for office? What about those who are particularly under-represented in the legislature?
- Other jurisdictions have overhauled their elections legislation — why not NL?
- Does the province's electoral system need reform and if so what process should be used to arrive at a revised system?
- Is there any mechanism to ensure that public policy platforms are released early in a campaign so that they can be properly discussed during the campaign?
- Do appropriate privacy regulations exist for the collection, storage, and sharing of voters' list data by candidates, campaign workers, and political parties?
- How can the rules governing political fundraising and/or spending be improved?
- Are any changes required with respect to the conduct of by-elections in NL?
- Are the rules of party nomination contests appropriate?

8. Democratizing NL's Political Parties (Extra-Parliamentary Wing)

This section will examine ways to strengthen and improve NL's political parties, from grassroots organization to the preparation of policy books for leadership and election campaigns. This section deals with political parties as entities outside of the House of Assembly. Examples of possible questions:

- Do the constitutions of NL's political parties require change?
- How can NL's political parties become more "professionalized"?
- How can opposition parties in NL be strongly organized entities?
- What are the strengths and weaknesses of some non-political parties tending to be the government's most well-organized and best-funded opposition?
- Is it a problem that an interim party leader can participate in seeking the permanent leadership?

9. Democratizing the Executive Branch of the Government of NL

This section will focus on ways that the cabinet (premier and ministers), the Premier's Office, and ministers' offices should change, as well as comment on the nature of the lieutenant governor position. Examples of possible questions:

- How can the Premier's Office demonstrate that the government is listening to the concerns of citizens?

- What special circumstances arise when the premier is a populist and/or nationalist?
- What controls, if any, should be introduced to limit the power and influence of the Premier's Office?
- Is it a problem that an interim premier can participate in seeking the permanent position?
- To what extent should public awareness of unelected public servants who hold senior positions in the government be increased (e.g., should the chief of staff be active on social media or not)?
- How can MHAs keep the power of the executive branch in check?

10. Democratizing the Legislative Branch of the Government of NL

This section will explore ways to improve the House of Assembly as an institution, the function of governing and the official opposition, the role of MHAs, and offices of the legislature. Examples of possible questions:

- How can we promote a culture of respect, co-operation, and creative problem-solving among all parties in the House of Assembly?
- What can be learned from the Muskrat Falls controversy with respect to the role of the legislature in ensuring good government?
- How should the House of Assembly improve its legislative committee system?
- What can be learned from Aboriginal peoples' approaches to governance?
- When are appropriate times to hold a referendum on major policy issues in lieu of the people's elected representatives making decisions?
- How do we reconcile that an elected official is eligible to seek elected office at another level of government while continuing to draw on public resources?
- How can we ensure that statutory offices of the House of Assembly (e.g., Chief Electoral Officer, Child and Youth Advocate, Officer of the Information, and Privacy Commissioner) are arm's-length from government?
- What are the reasons that the House of Assembly sits so rarely — and to what extent is this a problem?
- Should the House of Assembly live-tweet proceedings in lieu of journalists doing so?
- What can the annual NL Youth Parliament teach the House of Assembly?
- Why is private members' business not a significant feature of the House of Assembly?

11. Democratizing the Judicial Branch of Government of NL

This section will describe associated ways that the courts and the legal community can improve. Examples of possible questions:

- Is the process for nominating judges in NL appropriate?
- How do we ensure gender balance for judges assigned to the bench?
- Should court proceedings be audio or video recorded for public and media use?
- Does it matter that a judge from NL has never been appointed to the Supreme Court of Canada?

12. Increasing the Democratic Nature of the NL Public Service

This section will examine related ways that the Government of Newfoundland and Labrador as an entity, and the permanent civil service as its employees, can be improved. Examples of possible questions:

- How should a provincial government department or agency/board/commission consult the public to inform government decisions?
- What needs to happen to ensure that the provincial government makes smart policy decisions?
- What processes can be introduced so that executive positions in government better reflect the diversity of the NL population?
- Is the traditional practice of a travelling "road show" as a means of consultation still relevant?
- How can public servants collect a variety of perspectives from within NL without being afraid of the consequences of compiling views that might embarrass the government or derail its agenda?
- How can the public service ensure a strong and positive relationship with Indigenous groups in the province, such as NunatuKavut, Innu, Qalipu?
- Why does some legislation linger and become outdated when the Government of NL can simply draw upon legislation in other jurisdictions?
- How can we ensure that citizens derive maximum benefit from Crown corporations?
- What can be done to ensure that severance packages are in line with the public interest?

13. Democratizing Municipal Governance in NL

This section will delve into matters of local governance. Examples of possible questions:

- What can be done to increase the number of candidates in municipal elections?

- How can Municipal Affairs encourage increased voter turnout in municipal elections?
- How do we ensure appropriate oversight of municipal council affairs?
- What kinds of training supports can be introduced to encourage strong municipal governance?
- How can municipal politicians be encouraged to mentor young people to get involved?

14. Increasing the Democratic Role of the News Media in NL

This section will consider the role of the news media in Newfoundland and Labrador governance. Examples of possible questions:

- How do we ensure that the NL news media acts as an appropriate watchdog of government?
- Can social media be used to strengthen democracy in Newfoundland and Labrador?
- What can be done about the influence of public opinion polls that focus on the premier's popularity as opposed to deeper measures?
- Are there ways to improve the legitimacy of media straw polls and feedback forums?

15. Democratizing Community Groups and Grassroots Activism in NL

This section will consider the role of third-sector groups and activists. Examples of possible questions:

- How can citizen-based interests groups in Newfoundland and Labrador be more effective in promoting democratic governance?
- How can we resolve problems that groups experience in their encounters with the government?

16. Newfoundland & Labrador's Place within the Canadian Federation

This section will look at how the province is represented in Ottawa and on the national stage. Examples of possible questions:

- What can the province do to strengthen working relationships between all levels of government?
- What can be done to ensure that NL's interests are appropriately represented in the executive, legislative, and judicial branches of the federal government?

INDEX

For more information on the democratic process in Newfoundland and Labrador, the editors recommend visiting the House of Assembly website:

www.assembly.nl.ca

Collection of the House of Assembly. Photo by Erica Yetman.

★

View live and archived webcasts and read official transcripts (Hansard) of the House of Assembly; take a video tour of the chamber; and find ways to connect with your representative in the legislature.

ABOUT THE EDITORS

Alex Marland (Political Science, Memorial University of Newfoundland) was a public servant in the Government of Newfoundland and Labrador from 2003 to 2006. He co-edited *First Among Unequals: The Premier, Politics, and Policy in Newfoundland and Labrador* and co-authored the textbook *Inside Canadian Politics*. His book *Brand Command: Canadian Politics and Democracy in the Age of Message Control* won the Donner Prize for best public policy book by a Canadian and the Atlantic Book Award for scholarly writing.

Lisa Moore (English, Memorial University of Newfoundland) has written two collections of short stories, *Degrees of Nakedness* and *Open*, and three novels, *Alligator*, *February*, and *Caught*, as well as a stage play based on her novel *February*, by the same title. Lisa's most recent work, *Flannery*, is a young adult novel. She is the co-editor of *Great Expectations: 24 True Stories about Birth by Canadian Writers* and the editor of the anthology *The Penguin Book of Contemporary Short Stories by Canadian Women*.

THE DEMOCRACY COOKBOOK PHOTOGRAPHY EXHIBITION

Confederation Building ★ September – November 2017

An exhibit in the foyer of the East Block of the Confederation Building displays information about *The Democracy Cookbook* and its archival photographs (September 2017). Continued on page 392.

Collection of the House of Assembly. All photos by Andrea Hyde.

Collection of the House of Assembly. All photos by Andrea Hyde.